O Little Town

BEATRICE E HAYDEN (BOGNER.
1649 9TH AVE N
SASKATOON   SK
S7K 3A2

1-306-653-4116

you can get it at:
  Mary Scorer Book Store   1750
       234   21 St. S.E.   tax 1.23 tax
       (across from Marvel)

Order   or
       1-800 565 9523

17.50 + Tax $1.23 + .18 on freight $2.53
                                   Shipping
              21.43

O Little Town

Remembering Life in a
Prairie Village

Harlo L. Jones

THE UNIVERSITY OF MANITOBA PRESS

© The University of Manitoba Press 1995
Winnipeg, Manitoba R3T 5V6

Printed in Canada

Printed on recycled, acid-free paper ∞

All photographs courtesy the Jones family unless otherwise credited.

Front cover illustration: Snipe hunting and searching for duck eggs around 1921, near Dinsmore, Saskatchewan. Back cover illustration: Harlo Jones clowning on his bicycle, about age fifteen. Both illustrations courtesy the Jones family.

Design: Eye to Eye Design

Canadian Cataloguing in Publication Data

Jones, Harlo L. (Harlo Lloyd), 1923—

O little town

ISBN 0-88755-633-7

1. Jones, Harlo L. (Harlo Lloyd), 1923—
2. Dinsmore (Sask.) –Biography. 3. Dinsmore (Sask.)
–Social life and customs. I. Title.

FC3549.D55Z49 1995   971.24'2'092   C95-920068-1
F1074.5.D55J6 1995

The publication of this book has been assisted by a grant from the Canada Council.

To my beloved wife, Ethel, who has given me unfailing support
through all the vicissitudes of my life — moral, mental and physical
— for more than forty-eight years. She has lovingly mothered three
wonderful children, now approaching middle age, in whose
accomplishments and successes we take great pride.

Pg.
227 – If wishes were horses - - -
232 – Pregnancies + Betty G.
125   Each institution in our town was
      a part of our home
89   Girls' code of honour, would not let
         her divulge the real culprit
104   Hard hits Dr. Blakeley
107   Mrs Herb Taylor Gates
112   Contents of fire tanks pulled by men
125   What the P.O. meant to us + how we knew
         everyone's spouses inside-out
124   Chicago Tribune comics
143   Tractor adventure on Outlook Bridge

O little town of Bethlehem
how still we see thee lie!
Above thy deep and dreamless sleep
the silent stars go by;
yet in thy dark streets shineth
the everlasting light;
the hopes and fears of all the years
are met in thee tonight.

(Traditional Hymn)

Contents

Preface

CHILDREN HAVE A MOST DISCONCERTING WAY of shattering our adult complacency and making us think differently about things. To me, one of their most thought-provoking and ego-shattering questions is, "What were things like in the olden times when you were a little boy?" It is thought provoking because, before being asked that question, few of us probably don't see our own pasts from the point of view of today's child. It is ego shattering because it makes us realize that, no matter how young we may feel, too much time has passed since we were children.

To children, the life of an adult goes back into the dim reaches of a past long, long ago. Adults may be only amused by this relegation into antiquity but a little reflection discloses that we really are ancient from the perspective of today's child – probably more so than at any other time in history. When one looks at the changes in the world in the past fifty years, roughly since the end of our own childhood, we recognize that those really were "olden times."

When we were youngsters, the olden times about which we asked our parents covered a much greater span of history – back, actually, to the Industrial Revolution, because life in a rural community didn't change very rapidly before our time. Our fathers drove horses, ploughed with walking plows, hoed crops and lived, in great measure, in the same way their fathers had lived and in which we began our lives. The events and objects of the past were not strange to us because a good part of that past was still with us. The great changes in the life of the rural community began in our time, and our generation, more than any other, witnessed and grew up with the true revolution in the rural world. It was in our time that the Industrial Revolution ceased to be a matter of steam engines and English textile factories that we read about in books; it was translated into the facts of our everyday lives. We saw the oil lamp replaced by electricity, the horse by the tractor, the buggy by the automobile, the water pail by running water, the outhouse by modern plumbing, the washboard by the powered washing machine, the coal bucket by the oil or propane tank, and the hosts of farm hands by multi-"man"-power machines. So it is no wonder that the olden times of fifty years ago are more strange to our children than were centuries of olden times to us. We lived still on the edge of an old world; they live in a completely new one.

In the sweep of western Canada toward this new world, however, there was a period of hesitation when time stood still or even, in some respects, backed up. This was the period of the Great Depression. On the prairies, the Depression drew the country up short like a wild horse is wrenched about in its tracks by a lariat snubbed to a post. The country halted, frightened and trembling, shied, and even drew back a few paces. But eventually the fear died and the country paced forward again. It was a soul-searing period in the history of the West and will be remembered with bitterness by many.

In this book I describe my childhood in a small prairie village during the years immediately preceding, and of, the Great Depression. It is not a bitter social document, as are many stories that came out of the cities of the same period. One might get the impression from reading my account that it was a very happy time, and it was, for me.

Because we were children, the many worries that beset our parents were only a semi-perceived background to our young lives. And because we were all in the same position, financially and socially, we were not embittered by having to struggle against the social restraints that existed in the cities. During the worst years of the Depression in the grain-farming west there was not a great difference among family incomes because, in terms of dollars, there were practically no incomes at all. The village community depended on the countryside, and the countryside was broke. Some business continued to be done because people still had to buy some of the clothing they wore, a portion of the food they ate and parts to repair their machines so that another crop could be offered to the gods of drought and grasshoppers. But a great part of it was done without the benefit of hard cash; horses were traded for machines, eggs for flour and sugar, pigs for clothing and fuel. Wheat put through a hand-cranked meat grinder made a good, wholesome porridge, naturally flavoured with wild mustard and stink weed seeds unless one was very careful.

And so, as far as we youngsters knew, that was the way things were always done. It was only later, when we were older and able to understand what our parents had gone through, that we began to understand the Great Depression. By that time, most of us had moved into the beginning, at least, of the age of plenty. We had suffered without really knowing it and had survived without recognizing danger. Here then, for the benefit of my grandchildren and those who grew up on the prairies during the Great Depression, is an attempt to describe just what things were like in the "olden times" – all of sixty to seventy years ago.

I wish to thank Douglas Sprague and Gerald Friesen, both professors of history at the University of Manitoba, for their critiques and encouragement in the preparation of this work and who were instrumental in putting it on the road to publication.

Dinsmore in 1913, from the southeast, eight months after its birth, shows
the rapidity of construction of prairie villages of the era. Main Street runs
from lower left past near side of hotel. Some buildings facing east, left of
the large white shop unit, were destroyed by fire in the late 1920s. Courtesy
Nelly (Cone) Sveinson, Victoria, B.C. (Commercial postcard)

Hope Jones in the family's first car, 1916. She drove it to a country school
as a van for nearby farm children before Dinsmore's school opened. Her
four-year-old son Dale once bounced out of the folded-down top on to the
dusty road, slightly injuring a thumb. Photograph, taken on the farm where
they lived for four years before Lou went into business in the town, shows
the "bald prairie" that welcomed pioneers.

The foundations of prairie growth – pioneers and the railway – about 1917. The railway trestle at the Mogan farm in the glacial valley east of Dinsmore later was replaced by fill. L. to r. standing: Mrs. G.W. Mogan, Hope Jones. Seated: Bob Mogan, Kathern Jones, G.W. Mogan, who was later a business partner of the author's father in the growing village.

Chautauqua children's parade, mid-1920s. The annual week-long visit of Chautauqua was the highlight of the village's entertainment year. The Union Bank later became a branch of the Royal Bank of Canada but closed its doors early in the Depression.

The Jones family home in 1925 as built in 1917. The tall pole supported one end of a long antenna for early radio. Boys are Harlo Jones's brothers Deane and Dale.

Bare chests! Dinsmore businessmen defy convention at Watrous around
1935 before swimming trunks with no tops became publicly acceptable
for men. L. to r.: Len Clarke, general-store owner; Lou Jones; Tom
Davidson, Dinsmore Hotel owner; and Bill Harper, hardware merchant.

Hope Jones's American family in Topeka, Kansas, 1938. L. to r.: Hope's
brother, Dr. Harlo Woods; Harlo Woods's wife, Louise; Harlo Jones;
Hope's father, Dr. F.J. Woods; Harlo Jones's cousins Frederick and
Mary-Louise; Hope Jones; Harlo Jones's grandmother, Rosetta Woods.
Dr. Woods Sr. went to Nebraska as a boy in a covered wagon; by the early
1930s he regularly drove his car the 1,200 miles to Dinsmore from his
home in Lincoln. In his 70s he became a Canadian citizen, saying that
Canada was the only country with a future!

Propeller-driven snowmobile, built by mechanic Dean Hay about 1937,
frequently carried the doctor to country patients when winter roads were
impassable. The Chevrolet dealership, owned by James D. St. Remy, and
Frank Chow's cafe in the background were levelled by fire in 1939.
L. to r.: Bob Mogan, Jack Leach, Dale Jones.

Harlo Jones at fifteen with boyhood chum and lifelong friend Stephen Bleakley. Jones didn't grow to his mature height of five foot ten until he was nearly eighteen and so was "Squirt" Jones to bigger boys.

Late 1930s Sunday afternoon with teenaged boys "all dressed up with nowhere to go" – except the Chinese cafe. With faces visible, l. to r.: Ken Dowson, United Church minister's son; Chetwin Popplewell, insurance broker's son, killed while serving with the RCAF during the Second World War; Stephen Bleakley, doctor's son; Bill Harper, hardware merchant's son; and Ken Hagerman, a country youth taking senior matriculation in Dinsmore High School.

Harlo Jones at fifteen with his mother, Hope. The felt hat, button-down collar and tie, and suit with breast-pocket kerchief differ from what most of today's teenagers would consider Sunday dress.

Hockey in Dinsmore rink in the mid-1930s with Harlo Jones's older brother Deane playing goal, resulting in a broken nose for him. The goal judge's position was a risky one, while the principal hazard for spectators was frostbite.

Harlo Jones with his sister, Kathern, in 1924. She taught him to read and write when he was four and five years old, so when he started school he spent only three weeks in grade one.

Harlo Jones with Ethel Cloake before he entered the RCAF in 1942. They met on a blind date New Year's Eve 1941 and married in 1946 after he returned from the war and she had graduated from Saskatoon City Hospital as a registered nurse.

Threshing machines about to be manhandled from flatcars in early 1920s.
Heavy steel plates (bottom left) bridged the gap between car and platform.
In only a few years most threshing machines were rusting away or scrapped
and replaced by combines. Gone too were the straw stacks in which
children delighted to play.

The Jones family home (right) in 1942. Foliage returned after the dry
years ended. From the upstairs side windows Harlo could see from his
bed the nighttime activities on Main Street. Auto theft was so rare that
car doors were left open on hot days, and keys often were left in ignitions.

Dinsmore Consolidated School Number 2349, attended by Harlo
Jones through senior matriculation. The original four rooms later were
divided into five to provide a grade-twelve classroom. The full
basement play area was walled into two, one side for girls, the other for
boys and two hot-air heating furnaces.

Grain elevators in Dinsmore, one of the very few prairie towns with seven of them – a source of pride in the town for youngsters. Early in the Second World War they handled the area's first million-bushel grain crop.

Pioneer Hardware (left) and Clarke's general store facing Main Street, in buildings owned by L.E. Jones and connected to his Ford and farm-machinery dealership around the corner on First Avenue. All were destroyed by fire in 1949.

Lou Jones's business establishment housing Ford and farm-machinery dealerships, parts department, electric-power plant for the village and morgue. Harlo Jones as a teenager pumped thousands of gallons of gasoline through the hand-powered "gas pumps" while working for his father on Saturday nights and in summers.

HARLO

Graduating class of 1940. Graduates (in alphabetical order, not all present for photo) were Jack Bennett*, Muriel Conn, Jean Grant, Jean Green, Omar Clark Theona Holt*, Evelyn Johannessohn, Harlo Jones (far left), Jean McDonald, June Mogan, Mavis Nicholson, Clarence Purcell*, Jack Usher*, and Herb Way. O.A. Ness, principal and maths and science teacher for grades nine to twelve, is fifth from right. (Asterisks denote pupils from other schools who took grade twelve or wrote their final examinations in Dinsmore High School.)

O Little Town

Prologue

TODAY, CANADA HAS ONE of the most mobile populations in the world. Statistically, everyone moves at least two or three times in a normal lifetime. The moves tend to be within or toward the urban environment, within a city, from one city to another or from the farms to the cities. The origins of the generation that grew up in western Canada during the Depression were not consistent with these statistics; our fathers and mothers came from the cities and farms of England, Scotland, Ireland, the United States or eastern Canada and, less often, from the farms of Scandinavia or the Ukraine or Finland. Their moves were from city to country or from one rural environment to another. And the land they came to was new, most of it still unbroken. It lay just beyond the end of the rails being spiked to ties on dozens of branch railway lines that enmeshed the prairie countryside in a few short, booming years of settlement of the virgin prairies just before the First World War.

Our fathers and mothers built the village in which we grew up. The few trees that existed, they planted. The wells from which we got our water, they dug. The piles of rock around which we hunted gophers, they had cleared. And all of this happened while one generation was growing up. Some of the older children of this generation had been born in the lands of their fathers and mothers, but only the oldest because these pioneers were themselves young. And most of the children born of this first generation eventually joined the migratory march into the cities.

The village of Dinsmore, Saskatchewan, about which I write, was born in 1913, sixty-three miles straight-line distance south-southwest of Saskatoon. No natural feature marked the spot or attracted people to the location other than the land itself. There was a gentle, almost imperceptible, downward slope of the land to the north away from the Coteau, known to us simply as "the hills." These hills were part of the terminal moraine of the last great continental glacier. The land was so featureless that on a clear day ten or fifteen miles was a reasonable visibility distance and, when the villages had been built, the grain elevators of two or three of them could be seen shimmering in the mirages. There was no intersection of trade routes, no river highway, no promontory or wooded vale that told settlers this was the place for a town. The river that gave it birth was a river of steel and the only prominent feature used to determine its location was the survey marker stating the distance back along the tracks from the last townsite or siding – roughly a half-day's drive for a team of horses pulling a wagonload of grain.

The surrounding land was both good and poor, but at that time it was all just land and no one knew that some of it was better than the rest, or that some of it should never have been broken. To the west, about a half-mile from the town, running from the north along the road allowance, was the border between the "heavy" and "light" land. West of this border was "gumbo," dark in colour and largely free of stones. In wet weather it had the consistency of grease, and as it dried after a rain it passed through a stage when it was like thick, gluey dough. It balled up under the hooves of horses, rolled up on the wheels of wagons and tractors and automobiles, jammed under fenders and eventually forced almost anything to a stop. This was the best grain-growing soil and except in the very worst years it seldom suffered a complete crop failure. Unfortunately, during the Dirty Thirties, what crop there was, too often fell prey to grasshoppers or army worms.

To the east of this borderline the soil was lighter in colour and full of stones. Beneath it was a light grey clay, which would sustain little growth and which set like concrete. Because this clay, when removed from the basements dug for the village, usually was spread over most of what were to be backyards, garden plots were markedly unsuccessful. This light soil also carried pockets of gravel used both in building the grade for the railway and in constructing foundations of the village buildings.

Roughly a mile and a half to the east of the village, and running from the northwest, was an old glacial runoff valley, which held a few small lakes that dried into alkali ponds during the dry years of the thirties. It eventually deepened to run into the valley of the South Saskatchewan River some twenty miles to the east, at the site of the present Gardiner Dam.

When we were in high school we learned that the village stood on what once had been the shoreline of a giant glacial lake that meandered westward for perhaps a hundred miles and collected in its bottom a silty sediment. This sediment eventually became the best wheat-growing soil in the world. The lighter lands to the east, with their stones and gravel, were the legacy of the shoreline, which must have fluctuated considerably during the years when the glaciers were melting. There the glacial streams collected gravel, then shifted while the gravel was covered with a few inches of light soil, and then dwindled away once the final outpouring of the great lake slashed the long valley leading to the present river.

During the first years of farming, the soil was abused sadly, but the day of reckoning was to come. Crop after crop was sown and nothing was done to restore the soil. Stubble and straw were burned recklessly. When the dry years came, the finely pulverized and unbound soil had nothing with which to anchor itself and simply blew away in mile-high black clouds borne by the unceasing prairie winds.

The railway meandered along the southern lip of the glacial valley, vaulting over the intersecting coulees on trestles and fill, and maintaining its grade through a few deep cuts. Then a mile east of the village, it burst out on to the flat prairie land without even a minor obstacle before it for nearly 100 miles.

The location of the railway determined the plan of the village. As it entered the townsite it branched once, then again, so two parallel sets of track aligned themselves with the main line to hold and be used for shunting boxcars. Along their south side grew up a row of grain elevators, eventually seven in all, as well as a loading platform, a small stockyard with a loading chute, and several coal sheds. Later, oil tanks mushroomed beside the tracks as distillate and gasoline became the working fuels. Across the tracks, and dead centre on the line of elevators, stood the railway station. It served triple duty as the passenger terminal, the freight and express shed, and living quarters for the station agent and his family. Through this station arrived the families and personal belongings of every pioneer family in the village and district except for the few who were there before the railway.

Again parallel to the tracks and on the north side, opposite the elevators, a dusty trail became a street with a few shanty-housed businesses. This was later officially named Railroad Avenue, although I don't recall anyone ever calling it that. Later, another street, known always by the typically North American name Main Street, took off from the first at right angles, just opposite the station agent's back door and quickly supplanted the first as the business street of the town. Main Street headed approximately north. Because everything related to the land in western Canada was laid out on the square, so was the village, but the square for the land was rigidly based on the Dominion Land Survey system with all boundaries and roads aimed at true north or at right angles to it. The square for the town, however, derived from the railway, which had given it birth, and the main street ran straight as an arrow toward some indeterminate point about fifteen degrees west of true north. This deviation was a source of constant wonder to us as children. Everything in our experience ran either north-and-south or east-and-west. So, to us, did Main Street, ignoring the fact that the nearest town to the north showed its lights straight off the end of the street while every map showed it bearing sort of north-nor'west.

By the time we had reached the age of remembering, the town was there as solid as two-by-four framing and clapboard siding could make it. Along Main Street were most of the businesses, the majority huddling together in the first block north of the station. This was "downtown" on a street that totalled three blocks in length. Here were, in our time, the bank (which closed its doors in the early years of the Depression), the Chinese restaurant, the poolroom and barber shop, two general stores, the butcher shop, the drugstore, a hardware store, a real-estate office and a Chinese laundry. Farther along, in the second block, were the hotel, an insurance agency, a printing shop that published a weekly newspaper but that closed down early in the Depression, a theatre, the Masonic temple, a farm-machinery agency, and a little one-and-a-half-room building called the Restroom. Beyond these, the third block boasted homes and at its northernmost end, a church, the location and construction of which guaranteed that when the winter winds came sweeping across the prairies, few would sleep through the sermons.

Railroad Avenue collected its share of houses and the south end of the hitching rail. First Avenue, a block to the north, had houses too, but it was devoted principally to the town's essential "industry." Along it was the livery barn, the town well and fire hall, the blacksmith shop, a couple of combined garages and farm-machinery agencies, two or three vacant lots on which machinery marked time between owners or quietly rusted away, the telephone exchange, the two-sheet enclosed curling rink (which was enclosed), the skating rink (which was open) and the lumberyard. Second Avenue contributed a church at either end, the Orange Hall, the school, several more houses, two tennis courts added in the 1930s and, appended to its east end and dead in line with the middle of the street, the tiny hospital. Third Avenue didn't really exist other than as a dusty trail that separated the village from a stretch of prairie grass containing a soccer field and two baseball diamonds, which collectively comprised the "sports grounds." Beyond that, if you ruled out the glitter of lights of similar villages on winter nights, there was nothing of interest until you hit the wall of ice that we imagined surrounded the North Pole, labelled on school maps as the Arctic Circle.

That was the entire village, roughly two blocks wide by three blocks long, discounting appendages such as the hospital, the railway station and elevators, or the particularly adventurous offshoot of First Avenue that carried four or five houses almost a block to the west on an extension of the street that bowlegged around a particularly muddy spot every spring when the snow melted and on those rare occasions when it rained.

What else can one say? It would be dramatic to declare that the village was safely ensconced between the CNR on the south and the United Church on the north, the Anglican Church on the west and the Roman Catholic Church on the east. Physically, this would be quite true, but by our time the formation of the United Church and the onslaught of the Depression had closed the doors of both the Anglican and Roman Catholic churches, while the solid Presbyterian congregation, which met in the Orange Hall, was driven into a sort of spasmodic paralysis to which it slowly succumbed. One is left to assume that a good many souls in the village were left to find their own way through the world.

But if one really had been looking for the soul of the village, one would have done better to look in the waiting room of the curling rink or the talk sessions in the warm haven of the fire hall on cold winter days, or the semi-official town meetings around the huge home-made boiler-plate heating stove in one of the garages. Or someone might have come close to finding it in the discussions, not knowledgeable in terms of books but growing wise in wheat-farming experience, that took place in the harness room of the livery barn among steaming mackinaws and sweaty horse collars and plug-tobacco smoke. Perhaps this soul might have been guessed at, although the members of the Ladies Aid Society would have paled at the thought, in Saturday-night conversations in the poolroom – or even in the Ladies Aid meetings themselves. But as I reflect now, it seems to me I found it years later, tucked away in the dusty pages of ledgers that recorded that venerable Depression institution, the charge account.

Here one could find evidence of individual foibles and collective desperation, insincerity and complete trust, the records of the quitters and the stayers. It is true, certainly, that some who kept those accounts were guided by self-interest more than faith, but at the same time one could note patience, tolerance and the firm belief that a better day would come. I think there was more behind it than self-interest. There was a powerful belief in what they had built, a faith in the future that to them meant that the country would prove itself and justify their faith in it. Some cut their losses and left, but the majority, and these seemed to include most of those who had been among the first there, went deeper and deeper into debt in order to sustain what they and others had built. This was the real soul of the place, a rock-like determination that, in spite of the foibles of human character and the blows of contrary weather and insect plagues, the village and country eventually would justify every ounce of faith of those who had built it up from the sod. Some might call it just plain stubbornness.

So there it stood, perhaps a hundred acres of flat prairie land that now had a name, an identity and, hopefully, a future. I was born there in 1923, just in time to have true memory begin with the Depression. The town didn't shrink much during those years, nor did it grow. Some unfortunates gave up the struggle and fled to God-knows-where, but hardly had one of them disappeared before someone else, perhaps another unfortunate where he had come from, moved into the breach, filling both the house and the gap in the community. But these were few in number and did not change the tale. They were rather like birds of passage, while the rest of us, in what may be an inappropriate simile, were more like the boat's crew and would float or sink with it.

The Homes

IN THE BEGINNING no one knew how to build a prairie house. Houses had to be built quickly and of materials that could be imported easily and cheaply. The answer, of course, was wood. Occasionally the first people to move on to the land wintered for a year or two in homes built of prairie sod, which a thousand years of supporting buffalo grass had turned into a layer of earth and fibre several inches thick and as tough as a carpet. But that was on the farms, and the village was of wood. Except for the concrete foundations, wood provided the sub-structure, the frame, the floors, the outer walls and the roof. Plaster was used inside, spread on wooden laths nailed to the studding.

The first designs were simple. Usually the plan was almost square, with the kitchen, parlour and bedroom on one floor, or with the kitchen and parlour on the ground floor and sleeping quarters upstairs. The house sat on a foundation that was set a few inches deep in the prairie soil and, often a basement was eventually excavated beneath. Few of the basements had concrete walls at first. Wide shoulders of earth were left inside to support the foundation and the weight of the house, and sometimes a concrete floor was laid. Men would hitch a team of heavy draft horses to a fresno, which was a steel scoop about three or four feet wide and a foot and a half deep with handles protruding from the back on each side by which a man could guide it and adjust the angle at which it bit into the

earth. Rocks were dug out with pick, shovel and crowbar. The earth removed was loaded into wagons by hand. Thus, excavating a basement
could take several days. A modern front-end loader can move as much
earth in a single scoop as a man working with a team and fresno could in
several hours, depending on the nature of the ground.

And the houses grew. In a manner still honoured on the prairies, one
house might be moved to become part of another, or a porch built on
here and a shed there. A growing family might require an added dormer
to provide another room upstairs. Wood may not be as enduring as some
building materials, but it is versatile and easy to alter.

The houses had one other thing in common. They were built from
men's memories and so had no characteristic prairie style. Often they
looked like the houses one might find in the American midwest, or like a
narrow slice from a row of English row houses. None were built to accommodate the prairie winter, and so invariably they were draughty and
cold. Extra doors, so appropriately named storm doors, were added. Storm
windows, too, went up on the outside every autumn, to provide a dead
layer of insulating air between the inner window panes and the frost-
chilled outer ones and to reduce the drafts. But even these measures were
not much more than stopgaps in reducing the bitter iciness of forty-below-
zero temperatures driven by winds sweeping unchecked across hundreds
of miles of prairie. But then wood came to the rescue again – in the form
of shavings.

Clean, sweet-smelling white shavings arrived in the village by the
boxcar load. Strips of siding were torn off the houses, and men with curls
of shavings hanging from their hair and whiskers poured bagful after bagful of them into the walls between the plaster-bearing laths and the outer
walls, and then spread them several inches deep across the ceilings under
the roofs. For the first time, houses began to feel at home on the prairies
– the ever-present chill of winter was at least subdued, if not completely
defeated.

There was nothing to check the prairie wind except what people built.
There was neither refuge nor escape, no groves of trees to provide shelter,
no stone walls or hedges marching across the country behind which one
could find shelter or make progress. Unless there was a house nearby, one
was at the wind's mercy. The Canadian prairies were in those days among
the inhabited regions of the world, truly a place where *home* had a meaning

in the most elemental sense. To a child, who after a few hundred yards of struggle would arrive sobbing, breath torn from its lungs, eye lashes and brows ice-coated, and with face and fingers and toes aching, home was a haven sweet beyond description.

So the village grew and became home to a small cluster of families, a cluster so small that everyone knew not only their neighbours, but also everyone else in the village, almost as well as they knew their own family members. The houses stood on their little squares of prairie, and each of us, as children, knew every room in every house, every kitchen cupboard and every inhabitant, from the newborn baby being bathed on the kitchen table to the old grandmother who traded us pull taffy for the first fuzzy-stemmed crocuses in the spring.

The population of the village was under 200. During the years of the Depression it varied only slightly. No new houses were built, but those already standing were seldom empty except for very short periods.

A new family was absorbed into the community within minutes it seemed, and the children would be part of our baseball and hockey teams almost from the moment of arrival. Little attention was paid to where they came from, or their circumstances.

My own family numbered six – Mother, Father and four children. My siblings, two brothers and a sister, had beaten me into the world by several years, my brothers being twelve and ten, and my sister nine, when I was born; I was a product of a miscalculation, as my mother amusedly disclosed to me after I had reached adulthood.

There were about thirty youngsters in the village within two or three years of my own age, almost equally divided among girls and boys. As we reached our teenage years, we were greatly concerned about the genders of members of a new family. We would speculate on the athletic ability of the males. But after the boys were assessed, there was a strange reluctance for us to leave the vicinity until the girls had been surreptitiously inspected too. We were not strangers for any length of time. After all, most of us would have been able to tell the new children more about the inside of their own house than they would know themselves for some time.

Each house stood in its own yard, sometimes but not always fenced, and divided into front- and backyards by the house itself. The front yard was a patch of prairie grass, green in spring but rapidly browned by the blistering sun of the dry years to a colour uniform with the dusty soil. So it remained, until the following spring. Without running water, there was no hope of maintaining a lawn. Backyard gardens suffered similarly. There was success with some early vegetables such as green onions and radishes, but anything that took a long time to mature usually lapsed into a state of drooping despair.

Here and there, yards were planted with poplar trees or Manitoba maples. Few had achieved a height of more than ten or fifteen feet before the drought years, and they seemed to gain little more during the thirties. Just before the dustbowl era, the village planted Manitoba maples along the streets, and these valiantly put forth a few leaves each spring before succumbing to the hot sun and lack of moisture. Surprisingly, many recovered a few years later when moisture became more plentiful, and they developed into sturdy trees, but for most of their early years they were little more than tough saplings whipping restlessly in the wind, dangling a handful each of dried and toughened leaves.

Many yards were graced with the only bushes that seemed able to survive on the prairies – caragana, lilac and honeysuckle. Caragana was used for hedges in town and by the mid-thirties as snow catchers in country fields. Used as hedges, the bushes were most often trimmed into proper hedge shapes; as snow catchers, they were allowed to grow unchecked. Early in the summer they put forth their flowers, shaped like miniature snap dragons and vividly yellow. Sometimes, if the petals were pulled out gently, a small drop of sweet syrup would cling to their bases, which we sucked with delight. Later in the summer, the seeds appeared in small pods like miniature green peas. When picked at the proper stage of flexibility, these pods could be made into whistles.

My family had one of the most unusual hedges in town. For most of the year it looked the same as any other, but for part of the season it bore wild roses instead of caragana blossoms. There was a reason. When the hedge had been planted, the young plants were set out in soil brought from the old glacial valley. Wild-rose seeds lay dormant in the soil, then grew invisibly in the network of caragana branches – until they blossomed. We made no attempt to remove them. They were pretty.

Lilacs fared well, even during the dry years. In the spring, the air around the village would be heavy with the scent of lilacs as they flowered, both purple and white varieties. A row of them separated our front yard from the back, and these did particularly well, perhaps because of their proximity to the back door of the house where they got the benefit of waste water, which was always thrown to some thirsty plant. But the lilacs, too, had a stranger in their midst. At the end of the row, where it joined the caragana hedge, there sprang up a large chokecherry bush, which, I imagine, was imported as a slumbering seed in the same soil brought in for the hedge. It might have yielded enough berries for a quart or two of jelly except that we children usually got them first.

Honeysuckle had its advantages and disadvantages. It managed to weather the dry years well, and large bushes covered the fronts of several houses. The blossoms were tiny, pink and bore a lovely fragrance, but they ripened into twinned red berries of the very squashiest nature. One had to be very careful when entering the house not to track on to the carpets a muddy compound of squashed berries, honeysuckle seeds and prairie dirt – or heaven help the offender. We found also that the berries worked well in bean shooters, adapted from the ceramic insulators used at the time to carry electric wiring through walls, and found their targets with a delightfully splattery effect. I doubt that our mothers shared our enthusiasm for this practice when we came home with well-splattered clothes or great splotches in the region of the pockets where we carried the juicy ammunition.

Some houses encouraged a partial covering of ivy. One variety at least did well and provided shade on verandas and porches. It grew a dense network of pencil-sized branches bearing large shady leaves, dark green in summer and rich shades of red in autumn. These also provided a haven for multitudes of birds, who nested almost against the windows, giving us an unexcelled opportunity to share their home life. Occasionally a nest of hornets would build its paper house in the shelter of the vines against a window, providing a cross-sectional view of their activities. But many of the houses were bare of vegetal adornment and stood angularly on the flat land like children's blocks on a bare floor.

There were other kinds of living quarters, too. Some shops had been built so the proprietors' families lived in the same building, either in quarters at the rear or upstairs. This was the case with the bank, the drugstore, one of the general stores, the Chinese restaurant, the laundry, and the tiny shoe-repair shop, whose bachelor operator worked in one room at the front and lived in another at the back, and who possessed, by the way, the most marvellous privy in town.

A few bachelors lived in the hotel and in one-room shacks. Why they were called shacks I don't know, unless it was because they had only one room or because the town looked upon bachelors as something approaching natural reprobates and thus felt their dwellings deserved a no more respectable title. In fact, each was a one-room house constructed in exactly the same way as the other houses in town. Later, when we were in high school, similar dwellings became a respected institution. Students who had finished the highest grades in their country schools took up residence in existing or newly constructed shacks in the village during the winter while working on their matriculation.

Halfway along the main street was another strange residence, which, during our early school years, we approached with caution. This, as a painted sign on its front proclaimed, was the "Restroom." It was built originally as a haven for farm wives visiting the village. After several miles in a cutter, or a bobsled on a cold winter day, they could retire to the Restroom to wait while their husbands finished their business. Here they could brew tea in the small kitchen and visit with women from other farms whom they might not have seen, or might not see again, for several months.

I am not sure why this function disappeared, but it was probably related to the state of the village's coffers during the Depression. The Restroom became a rental property and the home for several years of two of the female teachers, and this was the reason we steered shy of it. At that time the respect given to teachers – and the discipline exercised by them – did not stop at the boundary of the school yard!

The loneliest homes in town must have been the living quarters of the few Chinese men who ran the restaurant and the laundry. During most of the thirties, the restaurant was inhabited by varying numbers of Chinese. One, the owner, was a fixture in the village. He had been there almost from the time of its beginnings and was still there long after I had gone. To us, I am ashamed to say now, they and their restaurant were known collectively as "the Chinks." To children, the term was only a name and was not used opprobriously, but I can't say the same for all of our elders. The variation in the numbers of restaurant and laundry employees seemed to be related to the prosperity or poverty of other prairie villages and their ability to support similar establishments. The restaurant owner would describe his employees variously as "cousins" or "nephews."

They seldom remained long enough for us to get to know them other than as faces seen occasionally through the glass panes in the swinging doors to the kitchen. They remained quietly in the background, did cooking chores, and seemed to spend all of their spare time perusing the Chinese newspapers that arrived with every mail train.

Immigration laws forbade the Chinese bringing their families to Canada. We, the children, accepted them as they were, feeling only that they were "different." When small, we believed the myths we heard, such as that the Chinese would do terrible things to you with carving knives if you tormented them, which, I am afraid we did, particularly on occasions like Halloween. Fact never gave support to the legend, and most of us considered them our friends.

Years later I had many long conversations with the owner of the restaurant when business was quiet. I thought of him as one of the real "gentlemen" in the town, and I came to have considerable affection for him. Still, it was a tremendous surprise to me when I came home on leave during the war to have him take me aside and show me proudly a photo of his son, who was a pilot in the Chinese Nationalist Air Force. That was when I first knew he had a family.

The Chinese man who ran the laundry disappeared from the scene when I was still very young. We youngsters knew him only as Checkers, because that was his favourite game. He taught many of us to play the game on a homemade checker board using pop-bottle caps for checkers. In my memory he was quite an old man, small and wizened.

One custom of the Chinese that we appreciated was their generosity at Christmas, when they handed out to almost everyone in the village small blue China pots of candied ginger, each pot webbed in a straw net and sitting on its individual black wooden base with a matching blue China cap covering its wide cork. These were accompanied, for the children, by handfuls of dried lychee nuts and, for our mothers, diaphanous silk hankies. They were very kind to the people in our village, but how terribly lonely they must have been when they locked their doors at night and their thoughts returned to their homes.

Although the Chinese man who owned the restaurant failed often to see the humour in many of our pranks, he did have a sense of humour. He certainly needed it. And he never needed it more than when calamity befell him relating to one of the problems common to all the homes of the village.

The problem was that there was no sewer system and so no indoor plumbing. In the summer, outdoor privies sufficed and, except on the rare occasions when it rained, little inconvenience resulted. Winter, however, was a different problem and a much more serious one. Twenty-below weather is not conducive to moonlight strolls in dressing gown and slippers. Nor were bare fir outhouse seats, chilled to a like temperature, at all comfortable. So most homes had an indoor toilet for winter use, and so did the restaurant.

This winter luxury took the form of the chemical toilet. In most houses it was in the basement or some other suitable space. The living quarters in the restaurant were upstairs, as was the toilet. The essential element of the chemical toilet was a large galvanized bucket, which had to be carried out and emptied at suitable intervals. It took a real sense of humour on the part of the restaurant owner to survive the teasing that followed when one day he missed the top step – and all the rest of them too, for that matter.

Outhouses were considered common property by the children. We knew each one as well as we knew everything else in the village. We knew, for example, which families were too "stuck up" to make use of providentially supplied items such as catalogues and newspapers, and who discouraged young visitors by keeping their roll of toilet paper in the house. There weren't many of these families, and their aim was achieved. Their outhouses were sneered at and avoided. Some, a very few, kept their outhouses padlocked. To us this was the ultimate in indifference to the needs of one's fellow humans.

Some of these little buildings were havens of contemplation and citadels of knowledge, with stacks of interesting newspapers and magazines. Most were two-holers and so to the uninhibited young they offered not only education but interesting discussion, speculation and debate. Great plans were made here, and, likely as not, it was under such companionable circumstances one might make the decision, for example, whether to spend those hard-earned savings on the bicycle light from Eaton's catalogue or the one pictured in Simpsons'. You can be sure that we boys were careful always to use the pages of the catalogue near the front, which depicted only such uninteresting items as women's dresses, household linens and so on, and to preserve carefully the back sections, which displayed the really important things, such as sporting goods, rifles, hard-ware and a seemingly infinite selection of toys and games.

There was a side benefit to this community understanding about priv-ies. Children were spared untold hours of agony. When one walks the city streets today and sees a child suffering the obvious pains that only one relief can assuage, one must regret the disappearance of the outhouses, one to a building, which were always available to mothers of infants in distress.

There were phenomena associated with these otherwise strictly utili-tarian edifices that caused us to form preferences for other reasons. In one, someone had carefully torn squares of newspaper and hung them from a piece of wire, ready to hand. This had the appeal of convenience but was avoided under leisurely circumstances because one could seldom find the conclusion of any item one might start to read. In another, facili-ties for hanging removed clothing were first rate – a major consideration for youngsters bundled up for winter. But the most fascinating of all was the solidly constructed one behind the shoemaker's shop. This might be entered for its intended purpose, but usually we went into it in the inter-ests of scientific research or, occasionally, espionage.

Some fortuitous quirk of fate had caused a tiny knot in the wood, right in the centre of the door, to fall out. Also fortuitously, it faced east-ward between two buildings fronting on Main Street. If one applied one's eye to this knothole, one got a limited view of what went on outside. But if one faced the back wall and cocked one's head almost upside down, there, projected in miniature, was a prospect of a large part of Main Street, in living colour! When the sun was high, the building was a giant pinhole camera. There was more than one occasion when dire physical violence was avoided by taking refuge in this most excellent of jakes, meanwhile keeping posted precisely on the tactical situation outside.

Just as there was no sewage system, neither was there running water in the homes. Potable water was available to all from the town well, which was able to meet the demand even during the driest years of the thirties. Where this water came from is a mystery, but it was contained in a gravel formation some sixty feet below the surface, and the supply never dwin-dled. As soon as children, particularly males, were old and large enough to manage it, carrying water became a never-ending chore. Each house-hold had at least two galvanized pails, the sizes suited to the carriers, and once or twice a day, depending on the number in the family, meteorological conditions and other factors liable to affect the consumption of water, the carriers brought water from the well in the centre of town to their homes – and heaven help the one who forgot! The water from this well was cold as ice, clear as crystal, and hard as flint. I don't know just what mineral salts it contained, but there was enough dissolved limestone to build up a heavy, cream-coloured layer in a kettle almost overnight. This water tasted better than any other we encountered, perhaps because that's what we grew up with. City water, which had been settled, filtered, treated and otherwise mishandled, to us tasted flat and unpalatable and was deemed completely incapable of quenching a real thirst.

When nature smiled, and the expression didn't necessarily refer to sunny weather, water for other purposes was collected when it rained. Many houses had basement cisterns into which rainwater was conducted from the roof via eaves troughs. The cisterns were galvanized metal tanks perhaps six or seven feet in diameter and five or six feet high. In the kitchen, a hand pump delivered water for all purposes other than human consumption. Houses without cisterns had wooden barrels or steel gasoline drums for collecting rainwater. These devices provided delightfully soft water that would be the envy of most city dwellers today – when it rained. When there was a long period without rain, a large tank on wheels pulled by the local dray team filled the cistern with hard water from the town well. Homes that used cisterns usually also had underground cesspools into which used water could be drained from the kitchen sink. Because it was a gravity arrangement, the cesspool could not accommodate water from basement operations such as laundry, so this used water had to be carried out by the bucket, another chore to which youngsters fell heir.

There was another use for the soft rainwater. If it rained long and hard enough to wash the roof thoroughly, clean rainwater was collected and used for some cooking, particularly for soup made with ham and navy beans. Psychologists might call it the "old oaken bucket" effect, in which things long-remembered were always best, but in my memory there never was a better bean soup.

The absence of running water and sewage systems meant that there were few bathrooms – that is, rooms for taking baths. Houses with cesspools might have built-in bathtubs, but most had only either a galvanized laundry tub or a portable "tin" bathtub that was stored away and brought out for the family's Saturday night ablutions. Water was heated on the stove in a large copper boiler and had to be dipped by hand, at least when the quantity in it made it too heavy to carry. Every kitchen had its wood-and-coal-burning cookstove, which supported, at one end, a reservoir holding perhaps seven or eight gallons of water. This was heated continuously by the fire in the stove and provided hot water for washing, shaving and house cleaning.

The Saturday night bath in the winter was an experience calling for considerable fortitude. In our home, the bathroom was on the north side of the house and because of the prevailing winds seldom reached a comfortable temperature. One would put an inch or two of near-boiling water from the copper boiler into the tub and then retreat to the kitchen to undress beside the big cookstove. When ready for the plunge, one dashed for the bathroom carrying a quantity of cold water, added this to that already in the tub until the combination reached a bearable temperature, and then followed it as quickly as possible. Water was a precious commodity, so one seldom had more than two or three inches of it in the tub. The result was that one sat for agonizing minutes, arms wrapped around a shivering body while bottom, legs and feet toasted. One realized that a blissful comfort could be gained momentarily by splashing hot water over the body, but knew that in seconds it would chill to near freezing and draw every last calorie of heat from the quivering flesh, but it had to be done. A few minutes of this torture and one leaped out, grabbed a towel, and rubbing frantically in time with chattering teeth, dashed for the warm sanctuary of the kitchen stove.

As one would expect, there were hazards involved in this close proximity to a nearly red-hot stove. I still bear a brand on my left hindquarter obtained when, as a child, I bent over and turned from a starting position too close to the draft knob on the side of the firebox. This brand is in the shape of an inverted *L*, the cross stroke having been created by the turn and the vertical one by the ensuing rapid ascent. When the pain had subsided I was quite proud of this new embellishment, because it had taken the shape, even if upside down, of one of my initials. Naturally, it became my conviction, firmly expressed when displaying this brand to my friends, that every true westerner should be branded. I can't say there was any enthusiastic agreement.

In every life there is a focal point for a great many memories, and I would be willing to give odds that, for a great many of those who grew up on the prairies in the thirties, the kitchen cookstove was that focus. Homework was done and games were played on a table as close to it as conveniently possible. Clothes were put on and taken off within its comforting radius of warmth. Sometimes candy simmered on it in the winter evenings while we stood by with cups of cold water and tested its state at much too frequent intervals to get little semi-liquid blobs of the mixture as a preview of the coming delights. With the stove lids removed and using a simple wire basket over a bed of coals on the grates, we produced the popcorn maker *par excellence*, and we would stare, blinking at the heat on our faces, at the bright pinpoint flashes of flame as bits of popcorn husk drifted into the coals. Or we could watch in fascination as water, dripped from a finger one drop at a time, performed an erratic dance on the hot stove lids, skipping about in a dwindling sphere until it disappeared in a final puff of vapour.

The factor that broke down this intimacy with the kitchen stove was the advent of insulation in houses. Without insulation in the walls, whenever the wind blew strongly, even with convection type central heating, the upwind side of the house was nearly impossible to heat and the kitchen was the only really warm place. Then, with as many of the family gathered about as closely as possible, the oven door was opened and we sat with our slippered feet on it to read or study.

In a house such as ours, with two floors, the upstairs was truly Arctic at times. One morning, one of my brothers was accused of gross exaggeration when describing the coldness of his room the night before. He disappeared for a moment and returned with a water tumbler containing about a quarter of an inch of ice. It had frozen while standing beside his bed. But with the introduction of insulation, the outermost regions of the house became habitable, and life moved from the kitchen to other rooms of the house. Now it was only when the bitterest of winds blew that it occasionally became necessary to seek refuge again by the kitchen stove.

Our home was equipped with a coal-fired and convection heating system, and one of the hot-air registers opened into a corner of the dining room where a rocking chair stood throughout the winter. There often was considerable competition in the family to appropriate this cosy seat. One evening I sat there toasting myself for two or three hours, reading a book and huddled over the register so as to get the full benefit of the heat.

When bedtime came and I arose, my mother took one look at me and fairly shrieked in amazement. The visible parts of me had turned bright red. The lesson was that, if one were just coming down with the measles, long exposure to a steady blast of hot air would make the symptoms luridly visible.

The cookstoves and furnaces provided youngsters with another set of chores. Two or three times a year a wagonload of pine or poplar firewood was dumped in the backyard. Most of this had to be split to provide suitably sized pieces for the firebox of the stove or furnace. Then the split wood had to be piled neatly in the basement or woodshed. Most of the boys and a good proportion of the girls were proficient with a splitting axe. No one who has done it will forget the feeling of satisfaction when, in the cool clear sunlight of an autumn day, one watched the clean halves of split logs fall on either side of the axe head and breathed the resinous perfume of the newly split wood.

But occasionally one encountered a load of wood riddled with knots that seemed to have been grown specially to vex the young axe wielder. In that case, the youngster who had to split it prayed that most of the load was made up of sticks under about two inches in diameter, small enough so they could be used without being split. But bigger ones seemed to be bound together with steel straps. They not only refused to split but seized the axe head in a tenacious grasp and refused to let go. Continued pounding seemed only to imbed the axe more firmly, and one would pry and pound and pry again, breathless with frustration, until it was finally released. When one split straight-grained wood, one was Paul Bunyan slashing through leagues of forest; when the wood was knotty, imagination ran more to the labours of Hercules.

But even then the chore wasn't ended. If one developed providential ways, one would split some of the wood into a good supply of approximately one-inch-thick sticks for kindling for the kitchen fire every morning. If one hadn't so much forethought, as was usually the case with young boys, making kindling became a nightly chore. Just before going to bed, one took the coal bucket, split the kindling for the morning, smashed the large blocks of furnace coal with the butt of the axe head to make stove-sized lumps, and freighted the whole business to the kitchen where it would be ready for Father when he got up. And one wakened with apprehension clutching at the heart if the first sound one heard was the ringing of the axe, because this meant the kindling had been forgotten and a soul-scorching encounter with an irate father was only minutes away.

Another daily chore associated with the kitchen stove was the removal of ashes, usually done in the morning before going to school. Full length under the grates was a metal tray about two feet long and six inches wide and high. Several layers of newspaper were placed on the kitchen floor, and on this, directly under the ash-compartment door, was the dustpan. After the ash pan had been withdrawn, a special ash rake was used to scrape out ashes that had fallen into the ash compartment outside the pan.

Others had more amusing experiences with cookstoves. One related to a town bachelor and his shack. For some time he cooked and heated his home with a somewhat rusted small stove, but there appeared one day a different one, big, black and shiny, with a white enamelled oven door. He was very proud of it and showed it to us lovingly when we made one of our frequent visits. But he had a bad habit. In those days of prohibition on the prairies, it was probably the most reprehensible habit in the books. He drank – not often, because liquor was far too expensive and too hard to get. But when he did drink, it was a real bender often accomplished by consuming what he called "rubbydub," a nearly lethal mixture of rubbing alcohol and soda pop.

On this occasion some of us had dropped in to his place on the way home from skating and found him somewhat overtaken by these unusually strong spirits. It seemed to him a good time to extol to us the virtues of his new stove. He teetered around it, pointing out all its good points and finally announced its capping virtue: it had unbreakable lids. Perhaps some of us indicated doubt, but, whatever the cause, he decided to put the issue to the proof, and, taking his hammer, he rapped one of the large lids a sound blow. It broke. He apologized profusely and explained that that particular lid had come from another stove and was not the unbreakable kind, so he whacked another. It, too, broke – and so did a third.

Overtaken by the treachery of it all, he lashed out at the lids one by one, determined to find one that couldn't be broken. He didn't, and soon the shack was littered with broken pieces of hot iron, and smoke from the stove had driven the rest of us out. For some time after that, the top of the stove was covered with a motley assortment of pieces of tin and grease-pail lids until, from somewhere, another set of stove lids appeared. He made no claims that they were unbreakable.

In many homes the cookstove was retired temporarily during the heat of summer. Its place was taken by a kerosene or gasoline stove that could be lit only when required, thus helping to keep the kitchen temperature within livable limits. Our family had a three-burner stove fuelled with high-test gasoline, which was brought from the hardware store in a two-gallon can, and which worked on the same principle as a modern naphtha-fuelled camp stove. On one occasion my mother was refuelling the stove and failed to notice a bit of almost invisible blue flame in the generator bowl. As she poured gasoline into the tank there was a sudden flash, and flames engulfed the tank of the stove and the gasoline can in her hands. With great presence of mind and self-control, she carried the flaming gasoline can across the kitchen, out the door, across the porch, and tossed it into the garden where it burned itself out harmlessly. Meanwhile, the fire at the stove burned itself out for lack of fuel. But even an involuntary start on Mother's part when the initial flash occurred would have meant spilled gasoline, probable serious burns to herself, and perhaps the destruction of the house. Instead, all that remained to attest to her courage and calmness was a patch of scorched earth in the garden. Miraculously, she received only very minor burns on her hands.

Another feature of most village homes was the family dog. In our home there was a succession of them through the years ranging from mostly-collie, through terriers to German shepherds and even a Pomeranian. My older brother was responsible for this canine succession. He seemed incapable of resisting puppies, and they were constantly appearing from his cap or overcoat pockets. Mother was able to keep the dog population to one-at-a-time only by exercising the firmest of wills. But once a dog had been accepted into the bosom of the family, it was just as much a member as we were. It had the run of the house and, if it were small, found its most comfortable and loving refuge in Mother's lap. And when one returned from skating at a sub-zero outdoor rink, there was nothing more comforting in the foot of one's bed than a nice warm terrier.

One fox terrier was crazy about my father. On short car trips he took her along. Her place in the car was on the back of the front seat just behind Dad's shoulders with her nose sticking out the window into the wind. Fortunately, automobile speeds in those days were not too great, so the occasional whack on the nose she got from a flying grasshopper was passed off with a mild yelp. But gophers! If she spotted one close to the road, she was gone no matter what the speed of the car. I don't remember her ever catching a gopher, because her quarry would always disappear down its hole with a flicker of its tail, but she seemed to delight in the leap through the air, the wild roll across the prairie grass until she regained her feet, and the plunging dash in the general direction of the gopher. I say "general direction" because when her roll ended she was usually disoriented.

Unfortunately, this love for accompanying Dad in the car eventually led to her demise. Usually when Father went to get into the car, she danced along beside him, and often, if the car window was open, she leaped in before he could get his hand on the door. One day while the dog lay sleeping, Dad went out and started to get into a car on the opposite side of the street. Some sixth sense wakened her and she made a mad dash through the door and into the street, and was struck by a passing truck.

For a few days she fought for life, and we all hoped and prayed for her recovery. At first she seemed to be getting better, but after two or three days she weakened rapidly. Her death was marked by one of those incidents that make the passing of a pet so heartbreaking.

Through the years, while occupying her favourite evening spot in Mother's lap, Mother would say to her, "I'm going to bite your ear, Trixie," and take the tip of one of the silky ears between her teeth and give it a gentle nip. A few days after the accident, as Mother held the small broken body, she said again, "I'm going to bite your ear, Trixie." The dog looked up at her, wiggled its ears, and died.

Another of our favourite dogs when we were very young was a giant St. Bernard. It was owned by one of the town businessmen, and its life went back past the beginning of my memory, but its end was too well remembered by us all. This dog truly had the patience of an animal Job. He carried us on his back, pulled us in wagons and on sleighs and toboggans, suffered us to pull his ears or to hang from his fur, and all without the slightest protest. One summer day a group of us stood near where he lay sleeping in the sun, we engaged in boyish chatter and paying no attention to the dog. Perhaps in his sleep he dreamed of being attacked but, whatever the cause, suddenly he leaped up and seized one of the boys by the leg, drawing blood.

Hearing the clamour, the dog's owner appeared and asked what had happened. When we told him, he took the dog by the collar and led him into his shop. A moment later, from behind the shop, we heard the sharp crack of a gunshot. We all understood the necessity for what had been done, but we were sad, and the sadness remains with me to this day.

Sometimes it would have been hard for a stranger to figure out which boy owned which particular dog. A youngster would go down the street with one dog at his heels and would return a short time later with another romping beside him. But, when the sun went down during the long prairie sunsets, the dogs sorted themselves out and loped quietly along the streets or alleys to their own abodes. There they slowly climbed the steps, sniffed the air, looked around and, after making the three traditional canine circles, slumped with a sigh against the back door to await sleep and another day.

Meanwhile, inside the house, when homework was done and the supper dishes were washed up and put away, the radio became the focus for the evening, especially in winter. In the summer we spent most of the long evenings outdoors and, in those latitudes and under clear prairie skies, evening light lasted long after the bedtimes of smaller children, and the winking of the first stars was the signal for the older ones that it was time to go home. In the winter, though, darkness fell long before supper time, and it was on those long evenings that the radio became such an important feature of prairie life.

Because the village did not have twenty-four-hour electrical service, the radios were battery powered. Behind each one, on a piece of linoleum or some other floor protection, stood a six-volt lead-acid battery connected by sharp spring clips to the power leads of the radio. With the early sets, there was also a collection of other types of batteries; large B batteries and smaller C batteries were wired into the various circuits. Most families owned two of the heavy six-volt batteries if the radio was to be in continuous service. One battery was always being recharged on the "battery line" in the town's night-time-only power plant. We changed to a freshly charged battery every two or three weeks, and it was only when we had grown to considerable stature that we were entrusted with the task of transporting batteries back and forth. Firstly, there was the hazard of spilling acid in the house or on ourselves. Secondly, they were almost as heavy as lead, that element making up a considerable proportion of their total structure. Thirdly, they were very expensive in terms of the cash money available to most families at the time, so to drop and break one was a major disaster.

These battery-operated sets provided magnificent reception under the conditions of the time. Radio had swept the country with the rapidity of television a generation later. The first crude sets attempting to pick up some of the few stations broadcasting at the time came in during the twenties. By 1930, every family had one, and broadcasting stations had sprung up like mushrooms throughout the continent. Because each battery-operated radio was an independent unit, not linked into any other electrical system, and because there were so few static-generating electrical applications in the village, there was practically no interference. Reception from far distant stations was marvellous.

The present widely held apprehension about the invasion of Canada by American culture must have started in those days. This ignored the fact, of course, that a good proportion of the population of our part of the country had come from the United States in the first place. It can be said, however, that the radio invasion was a complete success. The stations we listened to were KSL in Salt Lake City, KOA Denver, WCCO in Minneapolis and St. Paul, and WHO Desmoines. Those call signs still roll out of my memory as easily as the ABCs, which I learned around the same time. The entertainment programs we listened to were almost all American – the "Major Bowes Amateur Hour," "Edgar Bergen and Charlie McCarthy," "Bing Crosby," "The Shadow," "Fibber McGee and Molly," "Jack Benny," "Fred Allen" and, somewhat later and one of my mother's favourites, the Metropolitan Opera broadcasts from New York. Somehow or other, we resisted becoming Americanized, while those of us of American origin soon became fervent Canadians.

Local stations, such as CFQC in Saskatoon, provided weather and market reports, news, soap operas and the all-important hockey broadcasts. The noon hour had a sequence of fifteen-minute serials, and these dictated the order in which we sorted ourselves out on the way home from school for lunch. The girls took off like a shot with the noon bell in order to miss as little as possible of a series named "Big Sister" and it was, to them, a catastrophe of the first order if the teacher ran late at noon. We boys could stroll home at a more leisurely pace because "Tarzan" didn't come on until 12:30. It wasn't until later that the incongruities in the productions became apparent to us. We were so enthralled by the stories, that we failed to notice, for example, when the narrator's statement like "The man of the forest strode silently across the jungle floor" would be followed by a sound effect more closely resembling a squad of storm troopers on the march.

Just as today's children would find it difficult to imagine a world without television, I would have difficulty trying to envision our world of the 1930s without radio. We children didn't find the news a matter of great import at that age, but Sunday dinner without Jack Benny or Charlie McCarthy was unthinkable. And it was dangerous for anyone to utter a sound during the broadcast of the grain quotations. But radio opened up the world to us in many ways. Who of my age will ever forget Admiral Byrd's broadcasts from Antarctica or Adolph Hitler's fulminations?

The long winter evenings I remember with a feeling of utter peace. Mother read a good deal, anything from the *Free Press and Prairie Farmer* to philosophy. Dad was an early riser and a hard worker, so he often dozed for a few minutes after supper over the newspaper before setting out again to accomplish something to do with his business or to curl. He was an avid curler, and curling took precedence over anything else. But on a snowy evening when he was home he might ask Mother if there was any extra cream in the kitchen and send us outside to scrape up a big panful of fresh, clean snow. Then, with a mixing bowl and a big spoon, he whipped snow into the cream, added a little sugar and vanilla, and Presto! we had ice cream. Or he helped us make popcorn, which, when richly buttered and salted, we ate in ice-cold milk.

Sometimes we made candy. My sister often made fudge, but only Dad could make pull taffy so that it didn't crystallize into a sugary mess. He knew just when to take it in buttered hands, just when to pull, stretch, fold and pull it again until its golden colour paled to a creamy silver, and when to snip its stretched lengths with buttered scissors so that pillow-shaped pieces fell on to a cookie tray to harden and be enjoyed for several evenings to come.

Another time Dad would look up from his reading and ask, "How about an apple?" This was the signal for me to lift the counter-weighted cellar door, which doubled as the pantry floor, and venture into the cold, musty, earth-walled basement where, back in a corner with Mother's shelves of preserves and the potato bin, there was always a box of McIntoshes or

Northern Spies or yellow Winter Bananas. The apples picked up some of the musty odour from the basement on their skins, but the coolness kept them firm and delicious. A quick wash and they were ready to eat, and Dad's was delivered to him along with the salt shaker so he could flick a few crystals of salt on it before each bite. And so the evenings went on until the hands of the clock signalled bedtime and we were sent off with the admonition to turn the lights out as soon as we were in bed and "Don't read all night."

The lights would go out at midnight in any case because the village didn't have twenty-four-hour service. The town electric lighting plant had been installed by my father in the early twenties, and he operated it until after the Second World War. The daytime consumption of electricity did not economically justify full-time operation, so "the plant" was started at dusk and ran until ten minutes after midnight. Monday and Tuesday mornings it operated from 8:00 a.m. until noon for washing and ironing. Saturday nights in the summer, when most of the village's business with the farmers was done, it operated until 1:00 a.m., and when there was a community dance in the theatre the lights went out at 2:30 a.m., a half-hour after the dance usually ended.

Many of the houses had no electric lights, and even those that did, maintained a complement of oil lamps for use after midnight or on those occasions when the light plant might refuse to operate. Two of the town's businesses had long rows of big glass-celled storage batteries in their basements, which were kept charged by wind-driven, propeller-equipped generators atop high steel masts. These operated at thirty-two volts and permitted the hotel and the restaurant to install electric refrigerators and have continuous lighting available. The ultimate power source was the wind, and there was no lack of wind energy on the prairies. Some farms had similar systems, mostly home made, utilizing generators and batteries from Depression-retired automobiles, driven by propellers hand carved from carefully selected pieces of plank. But our home's lights, and most of those in the village including the street lights, went out when the plant shut down at ten past midnight.

My bedroom window faced south, and from it I could see the better part of two blocks of Main Street. On clear winter nights when it was cold enough that the packed snow rang underfoot, I would lie in my bed looking down the street and waiting for Dad to come home when he worked late. Often it would be so still I could hear him close the door of the shop and his footsteps resounding on the firmly packed snow before he came into view around the corner of the hotel nearly half the length of the main street away. Nothing else in the village stirred. After he had come into the house and gone to bed, an automatic device rigged on the Fairbanks Morse semi-diesel engine would shut it down, its deep "chug-chug" would die away, and utter silence would descend over all. If it were a moonlight night one could scarcely distinguish a difference in the light level when the street lights went out, and all of the buildings in my view would stand silent, stark and ghostly white while the snow picked up the rays of the moon and reflected them in a million glittering blue-white flashes. So silent would it be that when the hard-packed snow contracted with the falling nighttime temperature, the sound rang out like a pistol shot.

All the moods of the weather and seasons I observed from that bedroom window and wove into a million fantasies. When the great blizzards blew, driving solid sheets of snow past the window, I was in the Antarctic with Scott and his band of gallant men or suffering the lonely vigil of Admiral Byrd in his solitary poisoned outpost. Perhaps we, in our icy winter, were able to understand better than most what those men had faced.

In summer, the leaves of the Manitoba maple in the corner of the yard by the street light fluttered restlessly in the wind, peopled by a host of fairies and hobgoblins pursuing their unearthly ways. A rare rainstorm changed the scene to the forests of the Amazon, only tantalizingly shown in the latest issue of the *National Geographic* magazine. And there was time, too, to absorb the night sights and sounds of the village.

When winter began, a small storm shed was placed on the front of the Chinese restaurant, out of my sight at the far end of Main Street. The door was closed by a weighted rope-and-pulley arrangement, and on a still winter night I could hear the run of the pulley as the door opened and closed. I would lie waiting until the late wanderer came into view, wondering who was abroad at that hour. Every figure in the village was familiar, and to see someone was to recognize who had gone to the cafe for a late package of cigarette "makings."

A familiar and well-loved sound, now gone forever, was that of the big steam engine of the midnight way-freight standing on the tracks at the far end of the village in the dead of winter. The engine seemed to pant as it stood there, with a repeated "ump-chuff . . . ump-chuff" as the automatic valves opened and closed. Background to this was the continuous high-pitched whine of the generator, which seemed noticeable only in winter. There would be shouts of the train men to one another, carrying clearly on the still air the full length of the village, and the scrape-clink-clank repeated along the length of the train as the train men checked for "hotboxes" on the axles of the freight cars ensuring that they were adequately lubricated.

When the men had finished, the engine would give a couple of low, rather apologetic moans on its whistle, the bell began to clang, there was a heavy "chuff. . . chuff. . . chuff, chuff, chuff" as the driving wheels spun on the icy rails before gripping, a series of clashes as the slack was taken up in the boxcar couplings, and the train moved off into the night, never seen, but as clear in the mind's eye as if one had been standing on the platform at the station all the while.

In the spring, melt water collected along the tracks, and one went to sleep every night while the air reverberated with the croaking of hundreds of frogs, perhaps stilled temporarily as a team of horses trotted by, harness jingling, only to be taken up with hundred-fold vigour after the team had passed.

All of these things were part of our home. The houses and the village were our home. And the shops were our home, and the curling rink and the theatre and the livery stable. No spot in the village was specifically forbidden to us. There were occasions when we did things we ought not to have done and someone in authority would declare that such and such a place was out of bounds to us. But it seemed that the prohibition lasted only as long as the memory was particularly vivid, and then everything lapsed back into its normal state. We knew every corner of the village with an intimacy that can only come from belonging, and this sense of belonging was so strong that years later, raising a family of our own thousands of miles away, when we spoke of returning to this village, we spoke of "going home."

The Outdoors

SUMMER OR WINTER, a great deal of our time was spent outdoors, probably because, except for the waiting room of the rink, the livery barn and the fire hall, there was no indoors in which we could give full scope to our imaginations. In the shops and businesses we were frequent but hasty visitors. We might venture into the dark gloom of the poolroom, but we weren't supposed to be there until we were eighteen and so our explorations were brief, guilty and most often terminated by dire threats on the part of the owner about what would happen to us unless we made ourselves scarce quickly. He put it much more colourfully. Our introductory lessons in profanity came early and were very thorough.

In the winter, the weather dictated the style of clothing we wore. When we were very small we were well cocooned, almost to the point of immobility. As we grew, the clothing became more practical and eventually achieved a quite efficient compromise between warmth and mobility. But putting it all on was a major chore.

One began with long woollen underwear that buttoned up the front and across the flap at the back. The three back buttons were a problem, especially the one in the centre, which was invisibly elusive. Over the underwear we wore a heavy shirt and whipcord or corduroy breeches, which we called "breeks." In theory, these laced snugly from mid-calf to knee; in fact, they started out that way each morning, but before many minutes had passed this portion accordioned into a series of bumpy ridges just below the knee. In practical consideration of our abrasive existence, the knees of these breeches often were armoured with leather patches. Heavy wool stockings, knee length, were pulled on over carefully over-lapped underwear cuffs in an attempt to achieve smoothness, but soon they, too, had the broken-accordion look. A long-sleeved woollen pullover completed the basic layers. This ensemble, with a pair of shoes, comprised our normal schoolroom attire. Our school building obviously was de-signed from plans that originated in the American midwest or perhaps southern Ontario, with great windows almost the full length of every room. This was admirable from the standpoint of light, since there was no aux-iliary lighting, but this advantage was gained at a great price in heating efficiency.

To prepare for outdoors we added more layers: a cardigan or a hip-length jacket as a precautionary insulation, then a woollen scarf, and over all a heavy, usually thigh-length coat of the mackinaw variety or, some-times, leather.

Our greatest problem was finding outdoor footwear, and many com-binations were tried in attempts to beat the cold. Shoes had to be big enough to accommodate heavy woollen socks. In very cold weather, a second pair of socks, usually Dad's heavy grey ones, might be pulled on over the shoes. In another combination, woolly bedroom slippers were substituted for shoes, and they, too, were covered by another layer of socks. On top of whichever combination had been selected came mid-calf, four-buckle galoshes. Although these were probably the most essential item of all, they could be infuriating. Because they were usually put on after all the other outdoor attire, it seemed to take an exhausting effort, tugging and stomping, to get them on, and another, equally exhausting effort to bend over and get the buckles fastened. These buckles were the multiple slot-and-tongue variety, and it seemed the tongues got into the wrong slots with infuriating regularity. And when it came time to take them off, tongues and slot strips frequently were encased in solid blocks of ice.

For a few years, some of us were fortunate enough to have a particu-larly glamorous type of footwear. Early each winter, some of our fathers went on hunting expeditions in the northern Saskatchewan bush. There they would trade with the Indians for deerskin moccasins. These were things of beauty, and we wore them proudly. The deerskin had a smoky aroma, and the very soft suede texture was achieved, we were told, by having been chewed by Indian women. On the insteps and on an inch-wide flap surrounding the back from vamp to heel were gorgeous designs worked from hundreds of tiny glass beads and porcupine quills. To the top edge, somewhat in the fashion of the leg of a boot, was stitched a flap of soft deerskin, which was overlapped around the ankle and lower leg, and tied in place with deerskin thongs. We were very proud of this exotic footwear and regretted it when our mothers insisted we cover them up with overshoes. But our mothers were wiser than we, and they knew that the soft deerskin would not only wear out rapidly unless protected from scuffing, but would also absorb water from melted snow, thus increasing the risk of frostbitten toes. Sometimes we were able to compromise by wearing low rubbers, which allowed the decorated flaps to hang over the sides. Inside an overshoe they were delightfully warm.

As we approached our mid-teens, a leather boot that came halfway up the calf was the vogue. We would have preferred boots that were almost knee-height, like those the Mounties wore, but we considered the mid-calf variety a reasonable compromise; in our imaginations they came to our knees. The droopy corduroy breeches were coaxed to stand out at the sides in the best imitation possible of the wide flare of the gold-striped blue breeches of the RCMP. In fact, the boots were not as warm as the combinations we had worn before, but we were willing to risk frostbite in order to achieve what we considered to be sartorial perfection.

Surmounting all was the aviator-style helmet. These came in several varieties, but we preferred a type that had a fur peak, which normally stayed up out of the way, held in place against the front of the helmet by a dome fastener. When needed, this flap could be unsnapped and brought down to cover a good part of the forehead and, when walking or skiing into a ten-below-zero wind, it was invaluable. Anyone who has faced such a wind will remember the piercing knives of pain it could drive into an unprotected forehead.

There was another, similar type of helmet that we tried but soon discarded. Its romantic style appealed to us because the front was graced by a pair of goggles like an aviator's. These could be unfastened from the helmet and repositioned over our eyes on dome fasteners. Unfortunately, the positioning of the dome fasteners never seemed to make for a fit snug enough to exclude our warm breath, so the celluloid lenses would frost over almost instantly.

Besides being a very efficient form of headdress for prairie winters, the aviator-style helmet was a symbol of adventure and romance, just as the jet-pilot's "bone-dome" helmet appeals to today's motorbike-riding teenager. Our clothing displayed our hero worship. Our feet were the feet of Indian scouts, from knee to waist we were Mounties, from waist to neck we were lumberjacks, and from the neck up, aviators. Who could want more?

In summer, we delighted in wearing as little as possible. When we were very young, a pair of bib overalls was our sole article of attire. This was acceptable to us because grown men wore them too, but by the time we got to be ten or eleven, we wore only a pair of shorts. We charged about the village on tricycles, which we imagined to be anything from a horse to a DeSoto convertible. Soon our skins became the colour of aged walnut and our hair was bleached almost white by the blistering prairie sun. As our mothers used to put it, we were "brown as berries," a simile I was never able to fathom, because in my experience berries were either chokecherries or saskatoons and were green, red or purple.

Some time during my early teenage years, "whoopee pants" enjoyed a short popularity. These were cotton trousers, usually black, with a thin red, yellow or green stripe down the side of the leg widening into a six- to eight-inch triangle above the cuff. When today I hear derisive comment on the attire of teenagers, I remind myself of whoopee pants and girls' "beach pyjamas" with three or four yards of material around the bottom of each leg, and I keep silent.

Footwear in the summer was a pair of ankle-high sneakers, worn as often as not without socks and, as a consequence, they were somewhat aromatic. Often, after we had gone to bed, they were spirited away by our mothers to be washed or at least set outside to air. When sent to the general store to purchase a new pair of these, we devoted most careful attention to the sole – not, as one might think, to determine which one would wear the longest but to discover the ones with the most intricate tread patterns. These were needed, we told ourselves, for the best possible traction for quick getaways from tight spots, but in truth we were fascinated by the patterns they left in the dust of prairie streets and roads.

A cardboard version of the pith helmet was standard headgear for a few summers. With these we were following Roberts to Kandahar or patrolling the deserts of Mesopotamia and India, defending the globe-girdling frontiers of the British Empire of which we were proudly a part. Eventually this headgear gave way to the baseball cap. There was hero worship associated with this, too, but the overriding consideration was that we adopted bicycles for our chief form of transportation, and the baseball cap would stay on. Unlike the modern high-fronted version, these had a crown that fitted snugly to the head. With these our efforts ran to decoration, and the peak, carefully trained to snap upright, displayed like a billboard our names, nicknames or initials, carefully drawn and painted on the black peak with white paint.

Seldom did the real world offer us adventure equal to our flights of imagination. During those Depression years we were physically almost as isolated as were the plains Indians who had inhabited the country before us. Probably the greatest event that could occur, to prove we were part of a world of almost unimaginable wonders, was the arrival of an airplane. If one was heard while we were in school, no teacher could keep us at our desks. All would crush to the windows to try to catch a glimpse of the marvellous machine. If it appeared it was going to land, the teacher would have been courting outright mutiny by attempting to keep us indoors. On the very few occasions when aircraft actually did land, they nearly always put down on the expanse of prairie grass to the north of the village known as the sports grounds. This bordered on the schoolyard, and the plane would hardly have stopped rolling before it was surrounded by the whole school population, followed rapidly by most of the rest of the inhabitants of the village. We youngsters would examine it minutely, every strut and flying wire, whatever we could see of the engine, and we might even run our hands along the smooth surface of the propeller, that being just about the only part of the doped fabric craft that didn't have Hands Off stencilled on it in bold black letters.

Most of these flights were associated with medical emergencies. A doctor would be flown from Saskatoon to assist our town doctor with an operation or, if the patient required special treatment, he or she would be carefully bundled up and flown to a hospital in the city. The aircraft that performed this function most often was a Stinson Detroiter, a high-wing monoplane with a fuselage of midnight blue and wings of bright orange. It went by the name of Lady Wildfire, and I am sure it was known to every boy within a 200-mile radius of Saskatoon, where it was based.

On one occasion, a doctor from Saskatoon flew himself to our town in a silver biplane with two open cockpits. Instead of landing east or west on the length of the sports grounds, probably because of the wind direction he chose to land headed north. Because the space in that direction was much more limited, he made his approach very low, and the first we were aware of his presence was when the aircraft flashed past the school windows only slightly above our eye level and took the top three or four feet off the poplar trees bordering the north side of the school grounds. One poplar tip slashed the fabric on the underside of one wing from leading to trailing edge. While he was engaged in his medical errand, we wondered how he was going to get his aircraft repaired. When he returned, he inspected the damage carefully, opened his black doctor's bag, extracted a roll of surgical adhesive tape about four inches wide, applied a long strip of it over the slash in the fabric, climbed into the airplane and flew away!

On another occasion when a doctor arrived in the Lady Wildfire, the aircraft had to remain overnight. Because our doctor's wife was also his operating-room nurse, his son and I were detailed to entertain the pilot. No words can possibly express our awe at the good fortune that permitted us to pay close attendance on one who to us was Icarus or Hermes personified. Now I can admire his patience in answering the questions we fired at him by the hundreds. Later, he even let us in on the entertainment of the gods; he taught us to play a card game called hearts. I went home that night with imagination soaring. For days afterwards in our games we were Bishop or von Richthofen or Collishaw. In time perspective, these events happened within a decade of Lindbergh's famous solo flight across the Atlantic.

It is difficult to overstate how important the airplane was for boys of that time. It was the Greek legend, the flying carpet of the Arabian Nights and Tom Swift all rolled into one. The tragedy of it came later, during the Second World War, in the number of my childhood companions who died while realizing their dreams of flight.

Most of us were fascinated by airplanes, and a new stock of do-it-yourself models in the village drugstore was sure to draw out hoarded earnings. If these didn't exist, fathers and mothers were harried with heart-rending pleas for nickels and dimes, supported by solemn promises of faithfulness to household chores and homework.

A superior feature of the model kits of those days was that they kept youngsters occupied, not just for a few minutes while completely finished and coloured plastic parts were stuck together, but for hours and even days. Each model kit contained plans with templates, and one began with a block of balsa wood on which the side profile of the fuselage had been stamped. First with a knife, then with a broken razor blade and sandpaper, the block was trimmed down until it fitted the templates. Wings were cut to shape and cautiously sandpapered to the proper camber. Struts were sliced from a strip of straight-grained bamboo provided, and finally all of the parts were assembled and stuck together with glue, a tiny glass vial of which came with each kit. These models rarely exceeded six or seven inches in span and length, and all were First World War aircraft – Spads, Nieuports, Fokkers. Four or five of us, mounted on bicycles and each with a model in one hand, "flew" around the streets of town executing formation changes as we went, propellers on the tiny models whirling in the wind as we squinted our eyes against imagined slipstream and searched the skies for enemy aircraft diving on us out of the sun.

Later we graduated to rubber-band-powered flying models. Every spare hour for days would be devoted to cutting ribs and formers, spars and longerons, to be built up with supreme care into a framework of featherlight balsa wood. This was just as carefully covered with tissue paper, trimmed, steamed and doped to drumhead tautness. Too often the finished craft was broken beyond repair at the end of a single flight. One, a thirty-inch span model of a Stinson Reliant on which I had devoted days of effort, stubbornly refused to fly properly in spite of everything I did to balance it. One winter day, months later, I decided to fit it with skis. For some reason these contributed just the exact amount of aerodynamic balance it had needed, and it flew beautifully, gliding in to perfect landings on hard-packed snow.

When not involved with airplanes, we spent endless hours playing with our other love, the automobile. One vacant lot on the main street became a network of highways, filling stations, and garages made from wooden cracker or apple boxes. Old exhaust manifolds dug out of scrap heaps, buried until their ports were flush with the ground and the exhaust end draining into a hole became oil pits and drains for car washing. Highways were constructed to rigid standards with shoulders properly sloped, ditch sides squared, curves banked and all road surfaces covered with a good layer of dust. To us, a toy car hand-pushed along the road had to raise a dust or it wasn't realistic, but try as we might, we could never raise clouds of dust that would simulate satisfactorily those grey-black clouds stirred up by real cars on the dirt and gravel roads of the day.

By the time we had reached our early teens, firearms were a part of our lives, and it was every boy's ambition to own a twenty-two rifle. My first was obtained on a swap from an older farm boy. It was almost toylike, a Stevens single-shot model with a rolling block. It had a broken firing pin, but a few minutes in the blacksmith shop with an old bolt was all it took to fix it. It was probably a good thing that the only cartridges we could afford were the low-powered "shorts" because I doubt if the rifle could have stood up safely to firing anything more powerful. But thousands of rounds went up the fourteen-inch barrel, and a combination of familiarity, sight filing and intuition about its performance made me a pretty good shot with it.

Shooting was an expensive sport, but it could be turned into a source of revenue and a business proposition. A box of fifty .22 shorts cost twenty-five cents, an astronomical sum usually achieved only on a partnership basis. Gopher tails brought a bounty of one cent each so, if we bagged forty out of fifty shots, we had funds for another box of shells, a bottle of pop each and a bag of candy to be shared equally.

We could find all the gophers we needed along the grass verges of country roads without going more than a half mile or so from the village. Some areas of prairie grass that had never been ploughed were alive with them. As we approached the selected area, the gophers would scurry down their holes, but we knew that in a minute or two, overcome by curiosity, they would stick their noses out again.

Our method was to lie down quietly at a good shooting distance from the hole and wait silently. When the gopher stuck his nose out we would whistle a soft chirping sound and the gopher would sit straight up to get a better look at the source of the sound. That was his last mistake. But the mistake was ours unless the shot was a fatal one. A wounded animal would dive back into its hole and the tail with its one-cent bounty was lost forever.

Another procedure we used was to "drown out" our quarry, but this could be done only in the spring when there was water around. A check was made to ensure that the hole into which a gopher had disappeared had only one exit or, if there were two, that the second was plugged with a stone. A few cans of water were poured into the hole and the gopher would emerge from its supposedly safe lair, drenched and frightened. Before we were of an age to have rifles, the gophers would be caught in binder-twine snares as they emerged. But the end was the same; the gopher lost its bushy tail and we were one cent richer.

When I look back now and consider my present revulsion to killing animals, I wonder how we could have been so callous about it. But to us, then, it was just another natural and accepted part of our lives. Gophers were a pest that destroyed crops and the holes they dug endangered horses, *ergo,* they must be eliminated. In those days of scarce money, the profit motive also was a strong one. With the advent of poisons to control gophers, however, the bounties were removed and our source of income was lost to us. We were given another chore, however – walking along the grassed edges of fields with a bucket and a piece of stick, depositing a spoonful of poisoned grain at the edge of each gopher hole.

A farm-boy school companion had a much more lucrative business. He shot and skinned rabbits, and a rabbit pelt in its winter white would bring as much as twenty-five cents. But the odds weren't always with the hunters, and one of my closest brushes with death on the prairies came about after a rabbit hunt.

One winter Friday afternoon, as we had pre-arranged, I rode with my friend in the school van to his home about four miles from town. At daybreak the next morning, after the farm chores were done, we started our hunt on skis. The hunt was singularly unsuccessful. We saw only one rabbit, and on the flat prairie a rabbit can easily spot a hunter and stay out of range. By mid-afternoon we were back at the farm, and I started to ski to the village alone.

Hardly had I left the farm when a sharp breeze sprang up from the east, almost directly in my face, and as darkness fell the temperature began to drop to about ten degrees below zero Fahrenheit. I had elected to ski back directly, cutting across the fields to make the distance about two and three-quarter miles rather than the four it would have been if I followed the roads. As I went on, the wind increased in strength until it was blowing up clouds of snow that reduced visibility to nil and each stride forward became a struggle. I tried various methods of locomotion. Walking backwards with skis over my shoulder was no good because the snow in the stubble was too deep; walking forward was almost as difficult.

Skiing was the best way to make progress but that, too, was torture. We had no proper ski harnesses or boots, just a toe strap over our overshoes, and so a sideways-tilted ski meant a tumble into the snow. Neither did we have proper ski poles, only a long stick such as a broken hockey-stick handle. Under way, ski points would tangle in invisible clumps of Russian thistle or tumbleweed hidden in the stubble-held snow. My scarf, wrapped around my face, soon was a solid sheet of ice from my condensed and frozen breath. Snow particles hammered into my eyes as I attempted to search for anything visible in the darkness. I had no idea of direction other than to keep facing the wind and pray it didn't change direction.

I had reached the point when I thought it would be a relief just to lie down in the snow and dig my way out of the wind, then the wind seemed to eddy and my skis dug into something. It dawned on my numbed senses that I had bumped into a snow-covered straw stack. I knew, too, that there should be one roughly on the track I was trying to make toward home. On its lee side, the snow swirled in suffocating eddies, but at least there the force of the wind was broken.

My first thought was that if I could set fire to the straw it would not only keep me warm, but it might attract attention as well. However, a search of my pockets confirmed what I already knew – I had no matches.

With one of my skis I cleared away some of the snow and tunnelled my way into the stack until I had a burrow deep enough for my whole body. In only moments I began to feel warmer. I remained in the straw stack for perhaps an hour and, feeling almost comfortably warm, decided I should make another effort to reach home and supper. I donned my skis, slung my rifle and again headed into the wind. Its fury had abated not one whit, and it was not long before I began to regret having left the haven of the straw stack. But soon I encountered the fence surrounding the village cemetery, which I knew should be directly on my track. I took shelter for a few minutes huddled in the lee of one of the larger tombstones and then, with my confidence restored (I hesitate to say "spirits"), I started on the last short leg of my journey. Soon I began to see village lights through breaks in the drifting snow, and a few minutes later I was safely home. But I know with all certainty that, had I not been fortunate enough to run into the straw stack, my story would have ended in the middle of that blizzard-swept field of stubble.

Prairie winters conjure up the sensation of smothering engendered by the chill onslaught of a sub-zero wind ripping into one's lungs. It was a feeling we had often as youngsters had on our skiing expeditions out to what we called "the old hills."

Why they were called the old hills I don't know; there were no new hills with which to compare them. They were the slopes of a glacial valley that had been eroded across the plains, and our point of access to them lay about a mile and a half east of the village. They provided the only downhill slopes for miles around suitable for skiing, and the vertical elevation from their tops to the valley floor was only a matter of seventy or eighty feet.

These expeditions nearly always took place on bright Sunday afternoons, and the plans were hatched in Sunday school when we were supposed to be joining in the hymn singing. Sunday school was over at noon so we would meet at the back of the curling rink at about 1:00 p.m. This gave us time to go home, eat our lunch, get rid of our hated Sunday-best clothes and put on the layers of outdoor clothing we would need for the expedition.

These skiing jaunts were the only form of outdoor activity resembling entertainment we were allowed on the Sabbath in winter. The common public room of the curling and skating rinks was closed and padlocked on Sunday, but occasionally we defied convention and made our way through the fence of the open-air skating rink via one of the openings used when clearing the ice of snow. This necessitated donning our skates in an unheated pump house on the edge of the rink. The Sunday school superintendent of the time seemed to have an unerring detective sense, and so we were frequently rousted out and sent home, sure that anyone we met could tell that we were branded sinners.

Whatever the reason for the dispensation, we did plan and execute most skiing trips on Sundays when the sun was shining brightly on a new fall of snow and the temperature was not too forbidding. Often we were deceived about the temperature on those still, bright winter days, however. It would only be proved to us how cold it really was when we had played our way a mile or so along the valley and had to make our way homeward as the sun dipped below the horizon, taking its scant warmth with it. The eternal west wind freshened in our faces as we started home, weary and with our clothing soaked by melted snow and the sweat of a hundred climbs up the valley slopes.

We learned from our adventures, however. At the head of the valley stood an old abandoned barn. It had no windows or doors but it did provide some shelter from the wind. After having skied down and climbed up hills all afternoon, always getting farther from town as we found one more slope that looked better than the last, we would arrive back at the old barn soaked and chilled. Here we would change into dry socks and mitts we had cached there on our way out, and we would chew up the handful of raisins or candy we had brought with us to revive our flagging energy. After we had learned these tricks of winter survival, we could make our way home with far less discomfort.

Not all of our winter activities required so much in the way of endurance, and the only parallel to the struggle home on skis was that resulting from sleighing. One of our favourite sports was to hook our sleighs behind a cutter or bobsled as a farmer started home from the village. The farmer would usually oblige by briskly trotting the horses for a short distance before settling them down to the long trudge home. To us, it seemed we were flying over the snow, and the temptation was great to hang on too long, resulting in a long, cold walk back. The worst circumstance was when, through sheer treachery, we were hauled far out into the country before being liberated. We soon learned to decline an offer from certain of the farmers to hold the rope, and we trusted to our own devices. We accomplished this by having an extra-long rope on the sleigh, which was looped around some convenient brace on the bobsled and taken back to the sleigh where we could hold the end ourselves. When we had gone far enough, we had only to let go of the end of the rope and it would slip around the brace, leaving us stopped as the bobsled went on its way. Only occasionally would the rope snag on something, and even then no harm was done if the farmer was cooperative and slowed the horses to a walk while we got free. But if the devil in him was stirred by our plight, we were in for a lengthy trudge home.

One younger farmer used to come to town frequently on horseback, and then we got the biggest thrill of all. He would trail his lariat from the saddle horn while we held the end on a half turn around the front of the sleigh. Off he would go at a gallop with us shrieking behind, half in joy and half in stark terror, squinting our eyes against the wind and vainly trying to dodge the clods of snow flying from the horse's hooves. It was like a roller-coaster ride through a snowball fight.

Occasionally we would have natural ice to skate on. This didn't happen too frequently, but sometimes in the spring there would be sufficient melt water to fill the sloughs, and a hard frost would provide a beautiful skating surface. One of these was along the south side of the railway tracks to the east of the village, and one memorable spring we had a marvellous skating area. It was shaped like the side view of a saucepan, the pan portion perhaps a quarter of a mile long by 100 or 150 yards wide, while the handle stretched off to the east along the tracks for nearly a half mile. The ice was strong enough to support the weight of the entire population of the village, and many of our elders, whom we had never suspected as being skaters, came out to glide over the glassy surface – on Sunday!

Sometimes the lakes in the old glacial valley froze over smoothly enough for skating, providing ice extending for over a mile. But lack of foresight could make this chilling. One could go like the wind downwind but then had to return bucking the same biting breeze. One also to be careful of lurking reed beds waiting only for a skater's weight for the ice to give way. The lakes' bottoms were soft alkali ooze, which stank to high heaven. Skates so coated seemed to retain the smell forever.

Another phenomenon associated with slough skating was "rubber ice." When the sun began to melt the ice in the spring, patches would become almost elastic, bending perilously under a skater's weight, and returning to its original position after one had passed. We would seek these out, responding to the fascination that any form of risk seems to have for children. Our ventures would become more and more daring until the inevitable happened and one of us went through the ice, to the sardonic delight of the rest of the group. Once one was in the water, it was almost impossible to regain the surface as the ice would break away at each attempt to step up on it, and the disgruntled victim would have to break a lane through the ice toward the nearest shore.

Although the slough along the railway tracks seldom reached the size it did that one memorable spring, it provided us each year with a considerable expanse of water into which we could fall. We had only to build rafts of railway ties and we were off to the Spanish Main. The chief method of propulsion was poling, but in the few spots where the water was too deep for the makeshift poles we could find, a piece of board served as a paddle.

The finest raft design, we discovered, used three ties nailed together by bits of board with about two inches between the ties. A piece of board that extended some fifteen inches beyond each side was nailed on at one end and provided some stability and resistance to tipping. Almost all of us had knee-high rubber boots as standard attire in the muddy spring season, but the normal hazards of these maritime ventures meant that we seldom arrived home with dry feet.

A much larger type of raft – perhaps six or eight ties fastened together – would support four or five of us, provided we kept ourselves more or less evenly distributed over its surface. These larger rafts were our dreadnoughts, while the smaller ones were the destroyers and cruisers of our fleets. The ballast of the railway tracks supplied an inexhaustible supply of ammunition stones for naval battles. In these, the object was not to hit the enemy crews but to have the projectile land in the water close enough to splash them. Because these adventures usually began before the ice was all gone, it was often a chattery-toothed group of youngsters that made its way home.

Sometimes the section hands who maintained the tracks would attempt to restrict or prohibit our use of the ties, but their effort was most often half-hearted and not taken seriously by us. Had the ponds been bigger, this dispersion of their working material could have been a serious inconvenience, but the main body of water was beside the tracks, and to get home we had to disembark on the railway embankment, the most convenient place being the spot where the ties were piled originally. At any rate, they bore our depredations patiently.

When the ponds dried up we had another use for the ties – for building log cabins. When the railway crews unloaded a new stock of ties, they were piled in neat cubes beside the loading platform along the right of way. By re-piling them with interlocking ends, we were able to create cabins, which looked little different from the original piles. One, in particular, was a masterpiece with three rooms and a garage for our bicycles. By continued practice, several of us could approach at full speed, reduce velocity in a skidding turn that aligned us with the garage entrance and let the bicycles continue into the garage, while we ducked aside into the cabin, all disappearing completely in seconds.

Such cabins naturally led to the formation of secret societies, the membership of which varied from day to day as the participants in the game changed. Membership rites might include initiation trials such as smoking a "peace pipe" or occasionally a cigar. Often these rites ended in complete dissolution of the society for the day due to sudden illness of many members.

One cigar, an Arabella, did many of us in. This brand was favoured by a man who worked for my father, who seemed always to have a box of them under a counter. When he was busy, it was easy to filch one of these for our rites. It wasn't until several years later that I learned he had been aware all along of these thefts and would wait in grim anticipation until we returned, pale and sweating, to add to our discomfort by suggesting nauseating prescriptions as cures for the mysterious malady that had laid us low.

In the autumn, our cabins would serve a more utilitarian and humanitarian purpose. One day we would return to our secret hideout to find it inhabited by strange men. These were the hoboes, or tramps, as they were incorrectly called, who rode into the country every fall as non-paying passengers on freight trains from the east, looking for work in the harvest fields.

Our first reaction to them was fear, and the wildest stories were circulated about their depredations. But after a few encounters, we found that they were mostly men just like those we knew in our own village and countryside. They seemed to enjoy talking to us, as if having youngsters around made their temporary encampment more like home. And they always had two stock questions: firstly, was anyone hiring harvest hands; and, secondly, did we have any tobacco? Some would strike it lucky and get jobs for three or four weeks stooking and pitching sheaves for the threshing rigs, but the trains brought them to town in seemingly endless streams. The leftovers would hop another freight headed west and go on to the next village and the next in their quest for a few days' work.

If they were occasionally thieves, it was only because they had to be to survive. We would watch them prepare their suppers. On a small bonfire would be set a tin jam can filled with water in which there might be a couple of potatoes and an onion or two. I am proud to say that sometimes the potatoes and onions had been supplied from our pockets because we knew which gardens could be raided with the least risk.

Some of these unfortunate wanderers came up with unique ways of earning a few cents. For example, some would collect glass jars and newspapers and, by making a sort of *papier mâché*, transform the jars into flower vases resembling sections of tree trunk complete with rough bark and knots. Another form of free enterprise was looked upon with considerable disfavour by the railway. This consisted of the manufacture from wire of such items as ornamental and hanging flower baskets, wall broom holders, and other small items. What the railway objected to was the fact that the wire came from their fences, this being of a suitable gauge for the purpose. These items the hobo entrepreneurs peddled from door to door and, in spite of the scarcity of money, there were few homes in the village that didn't have several of them.

I am surprised now as I recall how high-spirited and friendly most of these men were when, in fact, they must have been close to desperation. They seemed always to have a smile and a wave for us when they rode by, sitting on top of the boxcars or in the open doorways with their feet dangling outside. It is remarkable, too, that, considering the hundreds of them who passed through our village during the depths of the Depression, I do not recall them having committed any crime more serious than filching a few vegetables. There were a few safes blown open in village businesses during the Depression, but it was obvious that these were raided by professional thieves and not the migrant work-seekers.

For that matter, our own "crimes" probably would have exceeded theirs both in number and magnitude. Happily, the attitude toward such things was much more practical then than it is today. There was scarcely one of us who did not become involved at some time or other in an incident that today would have found its perpetrator enrolled in the expanding company of "young offenders."

When we were in trouble, as we quite often were, we received swift and direct punishment from the person we had offended. We were desperate to ensure that our parents didn't hear about the case lest the punishment be repeated by them in exactly the same fashion. On the whole, it was a good, workable and effective arrangement. Punishment was swift and pretty well adjusted to the seriousness of the offence without need for police, courts or legal battles. The person offended had the satisfaction of administering the punishment, we didn't become juvenile-delinquency statistics, and the next day we were all friends again. I cannot help but wonder how many of our foremost citizens today would have worn the label of juvenile delinquent had his neighbours not been willing, forty or fifty years ago, to take his correction into their own hands. I believe it is almost impossible for any lively youngster to grow up without becoming involved in some peccadillo, which could now be classified as juvenile delinquency. I have to face the fact that I grew up in a population of 100-percent juvenile delinquents – now all successful businessmen, farmers, engineers, doctors, geologists, teachers – and not a single one in prison!

One activity that kept us from getting into more trouble was our propensity for making things. We were particularly fond of making "elastic guns," for a time. These came in two forms – rifle and pistol, the former made from three-quarter-inch board and the latter from laths.

To make a rifle we took a suitable piece of board to the owner of a hunting rifle, preferably a carbine, and persuade him to let us trace its outline on the board. With a coping saw we cut the board to this shape, extending the barrel six or eight inches and omitting only the trigger guard. Just ahead of where the trigger guard would have been, six notches were cut about a half inch deep and shaped like a conventional jack-o-lantern's teeth. Then the whole thing was trimmed, sanded, and sometimes varnished and decorated to our individual taste. Into the muzzle end a nail was driven, to which was attached a piece of heavy cord long enough to follow the bottom line of the rifle back past the notches. Next, an old inner tube was cut into rubber bands about half an inch wide. A rubber band was placed over the muzzle end and stretched back to the first notch over the cord, then another to the second notch and so on. By pulling the cord gently, we could release the rubber bands one at a time, and they would fly twenty or thirty feet. A strong pull of the string would release all six of the bands with a "scattergun" effect.

Pistols were made by using a piece of lath about fourteen inches long for the barrel and three shorter pieces at right angles to it at one end for a pistol grip. To the butt, a spring-clip clothes pin was bound by an inner tube elastic to give it additional gripping power. One of the ammo rubber bands was stretched from the muzzle and secured in the grip of the clothes pin. By squeezing the pistol grip, we could release the stretched band, and it would fly for perhaps fifteen feet. The range of both weapons varied with the length of the barrel and the elasticity of the bands. These weapons provided us with many hours of amusement, both in their manufacture and in the ensuing games of cops and robbers or cowboys and Indians, with the added advantage that cries of, "Bang! You're dead," were supplanted by the certainty of a hit given by the rubber projectiles.

Thus, many of our amusements were "homemade," including carefully copied game boards of many varieties, from checkers to Monopoly, in ignorant defiance of copyright laws. It seemed that only weeks after a particularly interesting new game appeared, homemade copies of it would make their appearance in most of the homes in town inhabited by children. I don't think the marketers of the original games lost much in the deal because most households could not have afforded to purchase them. Jigsaw puzzles became popular in those years, and we made our own versions of these by gluing an attractive picture from a calendar or magazine on to a thin piece of board and then cutting it up with a jigsaw. The big disadvantage of these was that the interlocking joints were omitted so there was always the risk that a bumped table would wreck a nearly completed puzzle.

Statistics on juvenile delinquency are not the only ones that show differences in the lives of children then and now. In the light of today's statistical knowledge of the hazards to young lives, I am often awed by the fact that we survived at all. Take the matter of swimming pools and the various infections we guard against so zealously today. Places where we could swim during the hot summers were few and far between. When we were very young there was a swimming hole beside the railway tracks a half-mile west of the village. Actually, it wasn't much more than an extra wide and deep spot in the ditch, created when earth had been removed to grade up a road crossing over the railway tracks. One corner of it, perhaps fifty by twenty feet in size, held water that lasted into the early days of summer and that we shared companionably with a few farm animals. When we boys went swimming no thought was given to bathing suits and so any epidermal disease that might have been lurking in the water had maximum opportunity to attack us. I don't remember any other than an occasional case of the "itch," however.

The biggest risk we took was to our modesty, if the village girls should come along. Even if we saw them coming, there was no place to hide, so we would stay quietly in the water until they were about to enter it, at which time we would announce that we had no bathing suits. This was usually enough to send the whole covey fleeing helter-skelter back to the village, but the more daring of our number would display a "full moon" or "bottle on the table" to their disappearing backs.

The tables could be turned, however, as was proved when one girl, bolder than the rest, defied our announcement and led the whole group of girls into the opposite end of the pond, and no amount of threatening on our part could make them leave. As a consequence we, not nearly as bold as we had pretended, had to remain huddled in the water until they had finished their dip and departed. To add insult to injury the bold Lysistrata who had led the foray, just before leaving the water shouted tauntingly at us and, to our shocked amazement, waved her bathing suit high above her head in triumphant defiance. Before we could recover our senses, she had slipped it back on and they were gone.

As the dry years persisted, several farmers dammed small gullies to collect water, and these replaced the puddle by the railway tracks as our swimming holes. The nearest was about two miles from the village, and so the value of a swim on a hot summer afternoon was largely lost by the time we had walked back to the village. This problem was relieved some-what when we became equipped with bicycles. And, as we grew older and automobiles began to sport finishes that required more care, we were fre-quently able to find someone who wanted his car washed in return for transportation to a swimming spot.

One of these small dams came to be particularly favoured by us, and we visited it frequently for a period of years while indulging our penchant for skinny dipping. One day, however, the farmer upon whose land the dam was situated came driving up, quite obviously in a rage. He berated us severely and told us that henceforth there would be no more nude swimming because there was one window on a stairway in his house, nearly half a mile away, from which we could be seen by his daughters. He didn't take kindly our suggestion that he should tell his daughters not to look out that window, and I have wondered since how this situation came to light after all the years we had disported ourselves in the buff in that same spot. Nevertheless, we complied – with the odd exception.

It wasn't often that we had run-ins with adult authority about our games and sports. In fact, the attitude of all the adults was most tolerant. One could imagine, for example, a building owner being irate over us playing games such as auntie-aye-over on one of his buildings, alleging damage to shingles, but no one objected. There was one building in par-ticular around which many of our games centred, a large machine shed set well back from the property boundaries on all four sides, providing good games areas. Its owner, who assumed a gruff and peremptory manner with children and of whom we were all secretly afraid, I realize now was one of the kindest men in the village where children were concerned. He never stopped us playing any of our games on his property.

His machine shed was our favourite spot for auntie-aye-over. In this game, both boys and girls took part. The group was divided into two equal teams, one on each side of the shed. The object was to throw a soft rubber ball over the roof, preceded by shouts of "Auntie-aye-over." If the ball failed to reach the peak of the roof and rolled back, the throwing team shouted "Pigtail!" to let the other know that a false start had been made. When the ball came over, it was necessary for someone to catch it before it touched the ground. If this wasn't accomplished, that team then threw the ball over with the same warning shouts. However, if the ball was caught, the receiving team divided and ran around the ends of the building, each member holding his or her hands as if concealing the ball. The opposing team's members would break and run for the side of the building just vacated, but if any one of them was struck by the ball hurled by the person who had caught it, that person had to join the thrower's team. The game continued until one team or the other had all of the players and thus could see-saw back and forth for hours.

Another game, played always in the vicinity of this same machine shed, was a particular favourite. It was run sheep run, a modified form of hide-and-seek. Someone was selected, by any one of a dozen possible methods, to be It. This process could take up a lot of the evening by the time all the arguments had been settled, but eventually the game was begun. A large stick, two or three feet long, was used as a goal, and to begin the game, this was thrown as far as possible by one of the participants. The person who was It had to retrieve the stick, lean it in a certain spot against the machine-shed door and, as in hide-and-seek, count for a specified period with his eyes covered by his arm against the door, after which he was at liberty to search out the hiders.

It was not necessary for him to catch his prey physically. If he saw one of the participants he had only to shout, "Come to my boneyard . . . ," naming the victim. But all of those who had been caught could be set at liberty if one of the players could reach the stick without being seen by It and hurl the stick away again while shouting, "Run sheep, run!" at the top of his voice. Everyone captured up to that time could dash off and hide again while It was retrieving the stick. Any player who merely ran off and hid without making any attempt to seize the stick, thereby exposing himself to the risk of being caught, was considered to be a poor sport, and a new game might be begun without his ever having been found.

Because we seldom had enough youngsters to make up two complete teams for outdoor sports, many of our games were modified versions of the originals. One such was scrub softball.

When things were dull, someone would suddenly shout, "One for scrub!" This would be followed by a chorus of voices calling out numbers more or less in sequence. Great arguments often took place about who had called which number first, while the person who had called "One" would stand by in fidgety impatience, waiting for the argument to end and for the game to get under way.

Those who had called "One" and "Two" were the batters. "Three" was catcher, "Four" the pitcher, "Five" first baseman, and so on. Because any number could play, there might be several outfielders instead of the conventional three. The batters stayed at bat until they were put out, after which they had to take their places in the field behind the last number in the sequence. Because there was no umpire, there was no such thing as a base on balls, and a batter stayed at the plate until he had three strikes or a hit. When a batter was put out, all the other players advanced one position, the catcher becoming one of the batters, the pitcher becoming the catcher, and so on. This game had no end, and so it continued until the first stars began to twinkle in the turquoise of the evening sky, signalling the time for us to go home.

Another day it might be suggested that we go for a hike. These hikes usually had the alkali lakes in the glacial valley for their objective and often were planned in relation to some event such as the ripening of the chokecherries, one of the few fruits native to the prairies. The berries grew in clusters, each one about the size of a small pea. Most of the volume of each berry was taken up by a hard seed, surrounded by a thin layer of edible pulp with a deliciously tart flavour, which we described as "puckery." Eating a quantity of these could generate a large thirst, but with our childish lack of foresight we would gobble them up as we found them and worry about the thirst later. When we came upon a good spot, on the shaded northeast-facing slopes, the trees could be milked of the clusters, and our hands, lips and mouths were stained a lurid purple by the juice.

Planning for these hikes was a spur-of-the-moment thing. The decision being taken, each of us would go home, persuade our mothers to let us pack lunches of peanut butter or jam sandwiches in tin jam or lard pails and we were off. One day we might take our elastic guns and play at posses chasing bands of rustlers around the gullies and bushes. On another, we would wander the pathways made by cattle on the hillsides, watching the crows or seeking out the beautiful cactus flowers that grew here and there on the sunnier slopes.

It was between two and three miles from the village to the point where we most often gained access to the valley, and the distance seldom seemed long – on the outward journey, at least. While there we would log several more miles as we raced up and down the paths lacing the clumps of low bushes. By the time we began the homeward trek, it seemed often we were scarcely able to put one foot ahead of the other, and the road home seemed endless.

Added to our weariness was the problem of thirst. Whether or not it was the berry season, we seemed invariably to wind up with an almost Mesopotamian craving for water and so directed our homeward steps to one of two farms that were more or less on our route. One was uninhabited but still had a functioning well used to water cattle and horses. This well was equipped with a windmill, as were most of the farm wells of the era. Atop the tower, the blades of the big fan would be turned so their plane paralleled the direction of the wind when the pump was not in use. At the base of the tower, a lever-and-cable arrangement swung the guiding tail to a position at right angles to the fan blades that aimed them into the wind. With a groaning rattle, the connecting rod, between the gear box at the top of the windmill and the pump, would begin to move up and down, and cool water would pour from the pump spout into the watering trough. If there was no wind, a pump handle could be attached in a few seconds, and two or three of us swinging on it together soon had the water flowing. We drank from our cupped hands, and water never tasted better.

Another frequent objective of our hikes, in the same valley area but about a mile farther from the village, was a place of mystery – "the old stone house." Actually, there was little mystery to the place, beyond that of why its original owner and builder had expended so much work on it only to abandon it and never return. But, because it was abandoned, it seemed to us to have an eerie air about it. It was situated on the west side of the valley, a few hundred yards back from the steepening valley slope. A slough had formed in a low spot and had persisted for many years because it was surrounded by willows ten feet high and by two or three small groves of poplar. On a rise overlooking this pond the owner had constructed his little house. We were told he was a bachelor immigrant from Scandinavia who spent untold hours building up the little homestead and then disappeared, most probably back to his homeland.

The land was stony with rocks ranging in size from fist-size to slabs eight feet long, none native to the country but part of the debris left by retreating ice-age glaciers. With these stones he had built his house. It was tiny, a two-room cottage, stone to the bottom of the window ledges with wood and shingle above. It looked very "old-world." But the strangest feature of his homestead was the fences. Around the house, across the land, through the willows and everywhere ran stone fences, long continuous piles of assorted stones and rocks, unmortared and perhaps four feet thick at the base and three to four feet high. These he had built alone, and in the process he had moved hundreds of tons of rocks of all sizes and shapes. Behind the house stood a stone table, six or seven feet long and four or five feet wide, its top a solid slab of stone about fourteen inches thick and weighing several tons. How he managed single-handedly to set it atop its stone supports one can only guess.

Behind the house he had planted raspberries. By the time of our hikes these had gone wild and covered a considerable area of what at one time had been his garden. But they bore quantities of fruit, and these were the objective of some of our sorties. I have some lingering recollection that a neighbouring farmer perhaps had prior rights to them and was not too happy about our raids on the fruit, but there was no direct confrontation. The whole site was an ideal playground, its character completely different from that of the surrounding bare prairie.

It was on one of these expeditions to the old stone house that I had my first and most memorable encounter with chewing tobacco. Having played in the vicinity for several hours and eaten copiously of raspberries, we stopped at a farm on the way home for water. We arrived as one of the young men of the farm returned from a jaunt on his saddle horse, so we and the horse were watering at the same time. Having quenched his own thirst, the farmer got out his chewing tobacco, sliced off a piece for himself and then another for the horse, who accepted it with obvious eagerness. The plug was then offered to us.

At first we declined, but this refusal prompted a reaction of simulated hurt feelings from the young farmer, who insinuated that we didn't think his tobacco was good enough for us, and he even hinted that we were afraid to try it. The clincher was the horse. If a little old saddle pony could chew tobacco, we should be able to as well. These arguments worked on me, so I accepted a piece. Unfortunately, no one had told me that one did not chew up tobacco and swallow it. The result was catastrophic.

We still had about a mile and a half to go to the village, and how I survived it, I will never know. We had gone scarcely one or two hundred yards from the farm when my stomach was compelled to unburden itself of the tobacco as well as a couple of pints of raspberries. Sitting on a rock in the middle of a pasture, watching my friends disappear in the distance, I believed I was destined to end my life right there. I was sure no one could be as ill as I was and live, let along walk a mile and a half. I decided then that I would leave the delights of chewing tobacco to overly pampered saddle ponies.

By this time, saddle horses were becoming a rarity in our area. There were still considerable numbers of work horses on the farms, but their numbers had begun to dwindle. Besides their relative mechanical inefficiency, which saw nearly all of them replaced within a few years by tractors and trucks, there was also an acute shortage of feed. When crops could not be grown, neither could feed for horses. The prairie grass, which had grown knee-high when our fathers had first come to the country, grew to a bare two or three inches in height during the Depression years, and by mid-summer that growth was dried out and thin. On some farms there were a few sloughs that grew quantities of feed in moisture collected during the spring thaws, but these were comparatively few and far between, and the farmers who had them were lucky.

There was still some market for horses in eastern Canada and the Maritimes so, as the years went by, more and more horses were traded in on tractors and other farm machinery. The horse dealers who handled these transactions collected the animals until there were enough to justify a shipment, and then they were brought to the little stockyard beside the railway tracks, loaded into cattle cars and hauled away to the markets in the east. They were one of the few remaining farm products that sometimes could be sold for cash.

These shipments provided a few of the young men of the village and district with their one opportunity to see some of the rest of Canada. With each trainload of horses shipped, a small crew was required to feed and tend them on the long journey east. The young men who were hired to do this were given the opportunity to travel across the seemingly endless miles of rock and bush north of the Great Lakes. Some found work in the east and never returned except for occasional visits, but most were back in a short time and regaled us with stories of their adventures "down east."

We derived one great benefit from our close association with farm animals. We never had to be told about the birds and the bees. Because of all the controversy about sex education one hears today, and much learned speculation on the age at which children are ready to know about such things, I have searched my memory carefully and cannot remember a time when I was unaware of the basic mechanics of sex, what the sexual apparatus was for, and what the end product was. Even as small children we would have considered anyone woefully ignorant who didn't know that the purpose of having a stallion service a mare was to get a foal. And we were quite unconcernedly aware that the same process had applied to us. Consequently, it seems to me that the dangers of offering sex knowledge to very young children lie in the imaginations of adults, not in the minds of children to whom such a thing can be as normal and natural as the sunrise.

Nature

IT IS A POPULAR MISCONCEPTION that the prairies contain little interesting plant and animal life. It is true that during the Dirty Thirties much more attention was given to plant and animal pests than is given now – Russian thistle, tumbling mustard, stinkweed, gophers, grasshoppers, army worms – because they represented a very real threat to the economy. But there was unique beauty to be appreciated as well.

The wild crocus was the prairie herald of spring. Its short, grey-green furry stems pushed upward and produced blossoms before the last snow had melted from the ground. In spots of undisturbed prairie grass where the sun first warmed the moist earth, crocuses would appear in small clusters, opening their delicately veined mauve petals to reveal centres of brilliant yellow. We picked them by the hundreds in spring forays into the countryside along the railway tracks.

The tracks provided access into the country while the roads were still quagmires of melting snow, ice and mud. The first bright, warm Sundays of spring saw many of the villagers out walking along the gravel and cinder embankments. From the tracks we would sight the glowing patches of crocuses and would pick our way cautiously toward them, doing our best to avoid puddles and mud. Stem and flower together, the wild crocuses seldom topped three inches but, packed in a shallow container, they made a substantial centrepiece for many a Sunday dinner table.

Two summer flowers that seemed to flourish in the cinder-strewn gravel ballast of the railway tracks were the buffalo pea and the purple-topped "Scotch" (Canada) thistle. The plant we called buffalo pea grew six or eight inches high, had vivid green leaves and bore small, brilliant yellow blossoms shaped like miniature sweet peas. These, too, went into bouquets we carried home. The Canada thistle's rich purple blossoms provided another splash of lovely colour on the "dull" prairies.

Dandelions spread like wildfire across the plains during the dry years and seemed to be one of the few plants that thrived even under the worst conditions. Strangely, they were not often seen in open areas of prairie grass in the country, but in the village, ditches between the gravelled streets and plank sidewalks were matted with them. The secret of their successful growth was their roots, which penetrated straight downward as far as they had to go to reach moisture. Little was done to eradicate them, and to children the brilliant yellow-gold blossoms were appealing. In moist shaded spots where ditches went under sidewalks they grew to enormous size with flower stems a quarter of an inch in diameter, more than a foot tall, and with giant yellow blossoms as big as a child's palm. With their faces flat to the cloudless sky they seemed to absorb the sun's heat. We would retrieve this captured sunlight by placing the plucked blossoms face downward on our curled fingers to feel the warmth being re-radiated from them. The split stems provided little girls with additional curls to hang over their ears, with the bonus of giant yellow "earrings."

When the dandelions went to seed, we spent hours watching their tiny parachutes drifting in the breezes and, standing on a rock or some other local elevation, would blow them off from their stems to see how far we could get them to drift. Walking into a large patch of them while laying about with a stick, a small boy would almost disappear in the resulting clouds of millions of flying dandelion seeds. Some might think we were spreading the nuisance, but we were only hastening what the prairie wind would have done in any case.

Of all the weeds that bedeviled the prairies during the dusty years of the early thirties, none could compare to the Russian thistle for the hatred it generated. It would establish itself wherever there was a bare patch of ground. It began with small, soft green spikes that were not a risk even for bare feet, but as summer progressed the plants grew into large balls up to three feet in diameter with a dense network of hard, dry branches supporting millions of sharp spiky seeds. When the seeds were mature, a gust of wind would break the main stem and off they would go, bounding across the fields like beach balls, spreading the seeds for the next generation as they went. In severely infested fields during the drier years, a strong wind would create a moving layer of grey dust and bounding weeds. Obstructions such as fences, farm machines or other growth in ditches caught the weeds, which then created their own windbreaks, capturing blowing dust and burying them. In this way, fences became continuous ridges of "blowdirt" four and five feet high, trapping more and more dust in their lee, filling ditches and encroaching upon farmland.

The only means of control available at the time was summer fallowing, but even fallow fields would be covered with the weed. In this case, farmers resorted to burning, using tractors and harrows. This could be a very uncomfortable procedure.

One of my brothers and I were sent to burn thistle on a field that was thoroughly infested, using a tractor and several sets of harrows, which acted as a giant rake. When the harrows had filled with thistle, they were ignited, and flame would sweep through them at an astonishing rate, creating its own draft through the matted stems and burning with a searing, crackling heat that must be experienced to be believed. In a few seconds a heap of thistle fifteen feet wide and six or eight feet high would be reduced to little more than a shovelful of smoking ashes. And here I learned, once again, the truth in the old adage about the difference between youth and experience.

At the time, I was thirteen or fourteen years old, and my brother was in his mid-twenties. We had agreed that the work would be equally divided. One of us would drive the tractor the mile length of the field while the other walked behind with a pitchfork, picking up the clumps of thistle that tumbled off the harrows and using forkfuls of thistle to spread the fire across the mass. At the end of the field we would change places. With apparent generosity, my brother allowed me to have the first turn on the tractor, headed south. I soon learned that his motive was far from generous.

The tractor was an old Fordson, which one rode with one foot on each side of the transmission housing, bringing the body close to the heat of the engine. The sun poured down and the wind was from the north. When we struck a large patch of thistle, it piled rapidly on the harrows.

Then the flames took hold and sheets of fire leaped through it, billowing fifteen feet in the air, and carried by the wind over the tractor. Hell must be cool by comparison. On reaching the other end of the field, we traded places. It was with murder in my heart that I watched my brother ride back, the breeze in his face, while the flames now streaked back to where I walked behind with the pitchfork. I have wondered what temperature was reached in that heat sandwich with sun and flame above, tractor and baked earth below, and me in the middle.

Other weeds were nuisances, but not on the same scale. Tumbling mustard added its contribution to the piles of blowdirt along the fences. Stinkweed presented a considerable hazard to those who kept cattle for milking; its unpleasant flavour was unmistakable in the milk. A variety of foxtail grew in low spots, and we were told that when mature its spearlike seeds with points barbed like porcupine quills could work their way into the tongues of grazing animals.

When the foxtail was green, the brush was soft and provided us with ready-made ticklers with which to annoy the girls in school. A large patch of foxtail had its own beauty as the brushes shimmered silvery green in the breeze. But when the foxtails had ripened, the hairs of the brushes became javelins, which, once stuck in our clothing, hung on tenaciously and worked their way inward. Extracting the points from our clothing was best effected by removing the garment and pulling the points through from the inside; their barbs frustrated attempts to pull them out backwards.

Other weeds also used our clothing to spread their seeds. Hard burrs clung to us and seemed almost impossible to remove from woollen stockings. Sticky burrs fastened themselves to our trousers and gummed our fingers in gooey messes when we tried to pull them off. But burrs were not too plentiful and with care we could usually avoid them. Unfortunately, they seemed to thrive in places of great interest to us, such as the nuisance ground.

The nuisance ground was the dumping place for anything anyone wished to discard and that could not be got rid of conveniently by burning or any other method. Here were tin cans, old car bodies, machinery parts, skeletons of horses and cows, bottles – in short, anything adults didn't want but that fascinated youngsters. Many a happy summer afternoon was spent prowling the debris, or sharpening our aim with slingshot and thrown stones on the hundreds of old bottles available for target practice. The rusting metal, decaying cardboard and decomposition of 100 different kinds of matter provided an environment in which the more obnoxious types of weeds seemed to thrive, so our expeditions there often ended in long sessions of de-burring before we dared go home.

Some plants teetered on the borderline between being useful and being a nuisance. Sweet clover in a grain field was a nuisance; where it grew in ditches along the road allowances in quantity, it was valuable fodder. But whether or not it could be harvested, its sweet perfume was appreciated by all. When it was in bloom, its lovely scent would waft into the windows of the car as we drove by, and everyone would comment.

Another visually appealing ditch flower was the brown-eyed Susan. At times, ditches would be lined with them for hundreds of yards, and tens of thousands of golden-yellow-and-brown flowers nodded in the wind and bowed to us in the slipstream of the car as we passed. White daisies, too, added their bright salutes to passers-by.

The grounds of the old stone house on the edge of the big valley provided the shelter needed for some of the more delicate wild flowers. Tiny violets and purple vetch hid in the stones and grass. Here, too, wild roses abounded, their delicate blossoms nodding beside the fences where their dark green foliage contrasted with the myriad of colours in the stonework. Last year's bright red seed pods had dried in the sun to shrivelled, raisin-skinned balls, which could be peeled to yield bits of tough, sweet flesh for us to eat. Yellow buttercups grew here too, and with these we tested one anothers' chins; if the flesh under the chin reflected the yellow of the buttercup it was taken as proof positive that the chin's owner liked butter.

Animal life abounded in the deserted precincts of the fence-laced farm. In the bushes and pond, small amphibians and reptiles made their homes. Farther up the slopes on dry ground, weasels oozed their sleek bodies around the stones in the fences. Higher, on the open prairie, gophers riddled the ground with their burrows, while here and there the comparatively giant holes of badgers punctured the terrain. In isolated patches of low bush, coyotes made their lairs. Rabbits, wearing their brown summer coats, sat stiffly still, assessing the situation with twitching nose, ears and eyes before bounding away in an erratic zig-zag. Occasionally a skunk, beautiful in black and white, ambled across our field of view, unconcerned by any activity around and given a wide berth by us.

Snakes were rare. The yellow-and-green-striped garter snake was the only variety we saw, and in the summer heat they usually favoured the cool, damp ground around the pond where they sought both comfort and prey. We would watch with fascination as one of these little snakes, with a body diameter of no more than three-quarters of an inch, made a meal of a frog that looked twenty times too big for the slender jaws. Sometimes we would poke at the snake until it regurgitated a half-swallowed frog. Then came the marvellous part. The snake would make for safety and the frog would be left on the ground, inert and apparently dead, but in a few moments it would revive and hop away, apparently none the worse for having been half-eaten alive!

Another time we might spend a lazy afternoon in the warm spring sun watching the antics of a family of young gophers. When they emerged from their burrows in the spring, the young ones had not yet learned that the world was a dangerous place for small animals, and, as long as we remained still, they paid little attention to us. If they did perceive us, instead of dashing away, they would face us on all fours, front legs bowed and bright eyes staring intently. The bushy tail flickering occasionally betrayed the finely tuned nerves ready to trigger instant flight. If we remained immobile, or even whistled softly, it seemed to us a look of amazed curiosity appeared on their faces and the front legs would curl under their chests as they raised themselves half-erect to get a better look at the strange beasts confronting them. Another moment and the back would straighten and they would sit perfectly erect, ramrod straight, surveying us from the four or five inches of height their young bodies permitted them.

They frolicked in the sun like all young animals do, dashing about, nipping at one another, seemingly playing a form of tag. One might stop suddenly to nibble a bit of vegetable matter and be bowled over as another, following closely behind, failed to stop in time. But then a sudden move on our part would end the game, and in a split second all would disappear into the multitude of holes that dotted the prairie. They seemed to work on the principle of "Any port in a storm" and dashed down the nearest hole available. I have wondered often if they got their families straightened out or if mother gopher just took into her care any number of youngsters who happened to tumble into her home.

Because we nearly always had dogs with us when we went into the countryside, we had to keep them under close control if we wanted to see much of the wild life. But once in a while some near-sighted animal would make a mistake that was nearly fatal. One day in early spring my older brother, some friends and I rode out into the country in a truck of Model T vintage accompanied by our family dog of the time, a white fox terrier. While driving across an open stretch of prairie, we encountered a jack rabbit, still in its winter white, which hopped away from us. The terrier, unable to stand the sight of the rabbit getting away, took off after it and, to our surprise, the rabbit stopped a couple of hundred yards away and then began hopping toward the dog. This unexpected turn of events so surprised the dog that it skidded to a halt. The rabbit approached until only a few dozen yards separated them when the dog, completely confused, gave voice to its frustration with a sharp bark. The rabbit, startled by this hostile sound coming from what it had taken to be another rabbit, bounded into the air and raced off across the fields, soon outdistancing the dog, while we sat in the truck, helpless with laughter.

Occasionally, automobiles were used to pursue animals in earnest, as in the case of coyotes. These were deemed a great nuisance to farmers, particularly those who kept chickens or turkeys. If the coyotes got too numerous, a hunt was organized. When a coyote was flushed out the chase began, and it was usually a wild one. A coyote that is really stretching can make forty miles an hour and keep it up for amazing distances. The object was to draw almost abreast of the coyote on its left side so the gunner could shoot it from the right front seat with a shotgun. But the coyote is a canny beast and seems to know instinctively that natural and artificial barriers such as ditches and fences are impassable obstacles to a car, so invariably the animal would make for one of these. Safely on the other side, he would slow to a trot, and when the car came to a halt so would he, sitting just outside shotgun range to regain his breath. But then a hunting rifle was brought out, so in the end the coyote usually lost.

If there was a form of wildlife we envied when we were young it was most truly represented by the birds, and of these the hawk was the most graceful expression of freedom on the wing. Lying on our backs under a cloudless sky, we would watch them soaring silently, high over the blistering land. Sometimes it was possible to watch a single bird for what seemed hours as it made circle after circle, dipping a little, then rising again almost to the point of invisibility, with never a detectable motion from its outstretched wings. We would speculate on the purpose of this apparently aimless circling, which seemed to us to be at much too great a height for hunting. We preferred to think that those flights were made just for the fun of it and could imagine the cool rush of air beneath the wings as the bird soared through the brilliant blue of the heavens.

More of a nuisance to us were the kingbirds that nested around the village, often in the same spots year after year. One pair in particular nested in the eaves of the house next door to ours and held tyrannical sway over the whole backyard through which I used to take a shortcut to a friend's home. Fearless, they swooped upon anyone who came near their nest and sent small children fleeing in terror.

Another winged denizen of the plains was the red-winged blackbird. Wherever there was a slough or ditch with a bit of water and a few willows or cat-tails, there would be a pair or two of these beautiful birds in residence. We admired their glossy black colouring set off by brilliant red wing patches and anticipated their presence at our swimming holes.

But if there was one bird that symbolized the prairies to us it was the western meadowlark. When we heard its beautiful song trilling across the countryside, we knew spring had truly arrived, and everyone gave glad ear to its lovely chorus, telling us over and over again, "I left my pretty sister at home." From atop a telephone pole or fence post its song would peal, proclaiming its dominion over the patch of prairie grass where its nest was cunningly hidden and where the female hatched the brown-speckled eggs. So cleverly hidden were the nests that it was almost an accident to find one, its position revealed only when the mother bird skittered away from our approach. Sometimes an egg was taken to add to someone's collection, but usually we left the nests alone. All prairie children had a special place in their hearts for this joyful singer.

The song of the meadowlark will be for me always the most characteristic natural sound of the western plains. When we return to visit, my wife and I cannot refrain from looking at one another with smiles of pleasure when the first is heard. To us it is a proclamation that we have returned and that our presence has been duly noted by whatever guardian angels look after the animals and children of the prairies.

Duck hunting was a popular sport because the village was on one of the main flyways of migrating waterfowl, and any body of water could be almost black with ducks on their southward migration in the autumn. As we grew up we watched with a certain envy as our older brothers and fathers returned from hunts with several green-headed mallards each to prove their prowess.

My first duck-hunting adventure took place when I was about fourteen. A farm friend had scouted a reed blind and mat in one of the alkali lakes, and at dawn one morning we took up station on it, he with a double-barrelled twelve-gauge shotgun and I with my second brother's four-ten. The lake was alive with ducks. Suddenly someone on the other side let go a shotgun blast. The ducks took flight over us with a roar of wings. In his excitement my friend leaped up and pulled both barrels of his gun. The next sound was a resounding splash as he landed on his backside in the water. I turned to see his head, two feet, and two hands holding a shotgun, above the icy stinking water. By the time we extricated him I, too, was wet and covered with smelly alkali mud. Our hunt ended with two chattery-toothed would-be Nimrods making their way home in the frigid autumn dawn.

Some hunters, my father among them, had their own secret hunting spots, found during years of exploring the prairies within several miles of the village. One, in a coteau valley holding a small circular slough surrounded by willows, was a marvellous spot for prairie chicken. My father, brother-in-law and I once bagged seven or eight there in little more than an hour. We approached the willows from outside the circle and flushed several chickens, getting two or three. The birds flew across the slough to the willows on the other side, and we repeated the procedure, walking around the slough outside the willows. For some strange reason, the prairie chickens just flew across the slough each time they were flushed out rather than leave the area. We had reached the place by leaving the roads and driving a goodly distance across and around the prairie hills, and the spot was so secret that years later neither my brother-in-law nor I was able to find it again. However, one's attitude changes, and I have not fired a gun at a living creature for fifty years.

Another winged occupant of the bushes along the alkali lakes was the crow. Dozens of them built their scraggly nests in the bushes and trees, and in the spring, when the fledglings were almost ready to fly, we would try to get one to take home for a pet. These attempts were unsuccessful, with one notable exception. One boy succeeded in raising one, and it was a village fixture for at least one summer. It learned to speak one word quite distinctly – *hello*.

The bird had a favourite perch on a sign that overhung the sidewalk in front of the hardware store, and we took great delight in watching the puzzled reaction of passing adults when they were greeted by this apparently disembodied voice. One might back up a step or two and shout a greeting into the hardware door or even retreat several steps to the door of the general store in search of his unknown greeter while we youngsters, seated on the curb farther down the street, squealed with delight. But the bird developed another habit, which eventually led to its demise. Many of the residents of the village were startled out of their wits when the friendly bird swooped down to land on their shoulders or heads, and, although we were convinced that his intentions were always of the best, he did frighten some people and particularly some of the younger children. So one day he disappeared and we never saw him again. But it was a sad day for us when we learned he had been shot as a nuisance.

By far the most numerous avian residents of the village were the sparrows. These little grey-brown birds, even in a village as small as ours, must have numbered in the thousands. For the most part, they made their homes in the grain elevators and the stables, and no attempt to eradicate them had the least success. When some of us acquired air rifles, we were occasionally invited to eliminate them from an elevator, and, although we destroyed many, we could never detect any diminution in the total population. They did no harm beyond soiling every surface in the elevators with their excrement.

Much more occasional visitors were the tiny, jewel-like humming birds. We would see only two or three in a season, and the best place to watch for them was at a nasturtium bed along the south side of one home. Whether it was the same birds that returned to this spot year after year or whether it was different ones I cannot say, but at one time during the summer they would put in their appearance at that particular flower bed.

During the driest years, ducks had difficulty finding lasting bodies of water for nesting, and occasionally we would find a family of them on one of the dams or dugouts we used for swimming holes. Great consternation would reign in the duck family if we ever arrived to swim before the ducklings were able to fly, and I'm afraid we didn't do much to soothe the mother duck's fears. The better swimmers among us were able to overtake the ducklings and would gather up one in a hand and carry it to shore. The mother duck would quickly herd the rest of her family to safety. But we would not hurt the little one and after stroking its downy back we would allow it to waddle back to the water and rejoin the family. After a time the duck family would ignore us and continue its normal life at one end of the dam while we swam at the other.

If the shortage of water caused problems for the ducks, the insect-eating birds must have been in paradise during the dry thirties, for those were the years of the grasshoppers, peaking in 1938. If there was any member of the animal kingdom that the western farmer loathed with an unparalleled detestation, it was this flying, leaping, crawling, chewing, spitting agent of destruction. They ate the crops, befouled the laundry, clogged auto and tractor radiators, contaminated the harvested crop, spooked horses, wrecked gardens and even, during the worst years, blotted out the sun as clouds of them darkened the sky. Any shallow shovelful of prairie sod taken at random in those days would contain dozens of their egg clusters. Efforts to control them seemed futile, but we made the effort anyway, in the form of a sawdust-based poison spread broadcast along road allowances and on unused patches of prairie, using spreaders made from the rear axles and differentials of retired Model Ts and resembling the modern rotary fertilizer spreader.

It was impossible to escape the loathsome creatures. When we walked on the prairie, they leaped up our trouser legs, holding to the flesh with their grasping claws. When we rode our bicycles, they flew up in clouds from the road ahead of us, wings rattling, flying into our faces and falling inside our shirts. More annoying, when trapped or annoyed they exercised what I assume was a defence mechanism, spitting "tobacco juice." This brown liquid exuded from their mouths, soiling anything with which it came into contact. When riding in the car, it was almost impossible to have a window open or soon dozens of them were crawling around inside, and they were even known to chew holes in the upholstery.

Automobile fronts soon were plastered with the pulp from their broken bodies, and this hardened into a coating of filthy enamel that was nearly impossible to remove. Radiators could be plugged almost completely in the course of a relatively short drive, and, if the car had been driven at a fairly high speed, grasshopper bodies were wedged deeply into the fins of the radiator where they baked and solidified in the heat. Getting them out was a tremendous task. Under these circumstances, the twenty-five cents each a couple of us might get for washing a car was truly well earned. We learned to protect the fronts of cars with screens made of wire window screening mounted on homemade metal frames. These covered the entire forward-facing area of the car except for the windshield. The modern commercial bug screens are the direct descendants of those crude anti-grasshopper barriers.

But the black shadow of these pests fell most ominously on the farms and crops. There were times when the air resounded to the clatter of their wings, and, looking up, we would see huge black clouds of them sweeping across the sky to descend on any patch of green growth visible. In minutes, the ground and vegetation would be crawling with grasshoppers, and in not much longer than it takes to tell about it, every green stem was being gnawed to destruction. Even when there were not enough of them to completely destroy a crop, they continued to play economic havoc with the remainder. When the grain was harvested, a large part of the product that trickled into the hoppers of the combines consisted of the dismembered bodies of the beasts, which were swept into the machinery as it made its way across the thinly stubbled fields, adding to the grading and dockage penalties assessed against the farmer when the grain was delivered to the elevator.

Just as devastating was the plague of army worms that swept the district in 1936. We were amazed, mystified and intrigued by this phenomenon as it moved across the countryside like a green-grey carpet, from south to north, stripping every living plant on its way. No obstacle diverted the tide of caterpillar-like creatures. Strips were ploughed around the village six or eight feet wide in the hope that the expanse of bare earth would divert them, but to no avail. They swept over the strips as they did over the buildings or any other barrier in their path. They were found high up the sides of elevators that stood in their way. Heavy trains were unable to start because of the greasy pulp of crushed worms on the rails.

A friend and I found our own method of combatting them. We discovered that gasoline sprayed on them would cause them to curl up and fall off whatever they were climbing, so we equipped ourselves with a pair of oil cans that could project a stream of liquid when a lever was pressed. I am sure that when we had finished there was not a single army worm anywhere on his father's garage, outside or in. I am also sure now that if his father had returned and driven his car into the garage before it had time to air out completely, the result probably would have been catastrophic.

There were other insect pests – sawflies and tent caterpillars, for example – but none could compare in damage to the destruction caused by the plagues of grasshoppers and army worms that ravaged every living plant in the country. The army worms disappeared, as did the grasshoppers, and no assault of comparable magnitude has been launched by them since that one terrible year. But no one who witnessed that creeping carpet of devastation will ever forget it. After it had passed, it was as if some world-straddling giant had drawn an immense brown blanket over the face of our earth.

The havoc wrought on the plant life by these insect plagues left the land nearly bare. The sun and lack of rain dried the earth to the consistency of talcum powder, and the prairie winds completed the destruction of thousands of acres of land as dust storms swept the country. When a calm day occurred, it would always be followed by a windy one, and the oncoming blasts could be seen marching across the country toward us, heralded by a billowing black wall rising from ground level to the basement of heaven itself.

These dust storms began to the west of us and could be seen advancing while they were still tens or scores of miles away. A seemingly solid black rampart would move out of the west, gradually moving closer and appearing to increase in height as it neared. Closer and closer its leading edge approached, dimming the light of the sky before it finally enveloped everything, eclipsing the sun. The air was filled with swirling, stinging particles that penetrated every crevice, every crack in every doorway and window frame, and dust piled itself on floors, window sills and furniture. Outdoors, anything that broke the force of the wind precipitated its own drift of dust until, in places, it was piled to depths measured in feet. Farm machinery disappeared in mounds of powdery dirt, as did hedges and fences. A wry joke of the period declared that, unless the blowing stopped, Saskatchewan farmers would have to pay Alberta land taxes, even though all the best land had now moved on to Manitoba!

In spite of the plagues, animal, mineral and meteorological, that beset the country and worried our parents, in my childhood memories, the summer days seemed to glide by in a never-ending blaze of sunshine; only in a very few memories does rain play any significant part. But thunderstorms on the prairies could be swift and terrible, and too often the sudden torrents were combined with wildly destructive hail storms that slashed to tatters the last remote hope farmers might have for something to harvest. These storms seemed always to take place in the early evening, and so we were usually out of doors when they first appeared.

A typical sequence might begin early in the afternoon with a few puffy white clouds scattered across the sky. As the temperature continued to mount with the sun's heat, these small clouds would evaporate before our eyes. On such a day it would be much too hot for any strenuous activity, and several of us might lie in the shade of a building or of the big billboard on Main Street advertising Model A Fords, staring at the piercing blue of the sky and calling up images to match the small clouds drifting from west to east. One cloud might look like an elephant, then a curled cat and then a cluster of mushrooms until it finally dwindled to a smokelike wisp and disappeared into the dry, hot air.

On the evening of one such day many of us had gone to the sports grounds to watch a soccer practice. Not long after, giant thunderheads began to appear in the west. These were watched with a mixture of hope and fear, for they could bring life-giving rain or they could grow into terrible instruments of destruction with cyclone-force winds, driving rain and pounding hail. This one could be seen advancing across the countryside while still miles away and, as we watched, its top soared into the sky, flattening out into an anvil of ice-crystals. Clouds of dust were whipped up from the ground as the storm marched toward us at fifteen or twenty miles an hour, pushed by the steady west wind. Suddenly, silence. A dead calm settled around us, and the light from the western sky changed to a fearful amber tint as the rays of the lowering sun tried to pierce the dust. Everything seemed to stop. Not a blade of grass stirred. Everyone gazed fearfully at the ominous sky. Then came a puff of breeze, and then another a little stronger. These came from the east, exactly the opposite direction from which the wind had been blowing a minute before. The light now was a violent orange, and the men on the football field moved into frantic action, gathering up discarded clothing, as the strengthening easterly wind began to suck dust and dried grass toward the cloud like a giant vacuum cleaner. We children stood in naive fascination, intrigued by the spectacle, until one of the men dashed up to us and shouted, "You kids get home now! Go on! Get going! You'll get hurt if you stay out here."

It wasn't his words so much as his tone that eliminated any notion of dissent we might have had, and, mounting our bicycles, we made for our homes as fast as we could go. Scarcely had we left the football field when there was a tremendous flash and roar, and a bolt of lightning crashed into a summer fallow field to the west, showering up dust and smoke like an exploding artillery shell while its white light was blinding in contrast to the yellow gloom through which it had slashed its way.

As I arrived home, the first drops of rain splattered down, huge drops that fell between gusts of the strengthening wind and splattered the sidewalks with blotches the size of baseballs. I went into the house to find my mother and sister standing at the upstairs west-facing windows, watching the spectacle. Within a matter of seconds the rain was pouring down, driven almost horizontally by roaring gusts of wind, now from the west again, and the weight of the wind-driven drops stripped leaves from the trees as they struck. The light was indescribable, a mixture of rusty orange and purple, as the ponderous might of the cloud lowered itself around us, its guts rent by nearly continuous brilliant white flashes of lightning. Then came the hail.

First one or two isolated hailstone rattled against the windows. Then their tattoo accelerated, and we watched as the first few hailstones bounding in the street became dozens, then hundreds, and suddenly the ground was white with them while the air for two feet above the ground was filled with bouncing pieces of ice.

"Hold the windows," Mother commanded. We placed the flats of our palms against the west-facing windows and were shocked to feel the glass panes vibrating like drumheads as the hail pounded against them. Now it was utterly dark outside and the only perceptions remaining to us were the pounding of the hail against our palms through the thin sheets of glass, the maniacal howl of the wind, the flash of lightning and the nearly continuous roar of thunder.

How long the hail continued I don't remember, but it couldn't have been more than five or ten minutes. The rain and hail stopped like the turning off of a tap. The bottoms of the clouds to the west lifted, and the village was illuminated by the red rays of the setting sun, streaking almost horizontally under the storm's gloomy trailing edge. The ground was covered to a depth of two or three inches with hailstones ranging in size from marbles to golf balls. Water ran in torrents in the ditches and streets, and large outwash fans of sand and gravel formed along the edges of the street where sudden rivulets poured water from the road surface. Our car, in front of the house, stood rim deep in a lake twenty-five feet across and half a block long. Yard and street were littered with slashed leaves and twigs from the Manitoba maples and caragana hedges. Later we learned that there wasn't a blade of any growing crop left standing in a strip from west to east more than a mile wide and as long as our ken. The whole episode, from that first reversal in the wind direction, had taken perhaps a half-hour.

School

PROBABLY THE MOST IMPORTANT service provided by the village was the school, which served an area of approximately 100 square miles for primary education and high school up to junior matriculation. Later, when the school began to teach the senior-matriculation grade, students from farther afield were enrolled, and these boarded in the village or "bached" in small "shacks."

The school building was erected in the northwest corner of the village on a lot that covered more than half a block. The building was one storey, of frame construction, set on a full basement and was painted white with brown trim. The basement was divided down the centre by a wall, which separated boys from girls when classes were not in session. On the boys' side were two enclosures, each housing a large coal-fired hot-air furnace and coal bin. Each furnace heated half of the rooms on the upper floor. When the school was built, sewage facilities were provided in two large outhouses, but later, toilets were installed on each side of the basement, emptying into large tanks, which were chemically treated and periodically pumped out. There was no running water, and drinking water was provided by a portable "fountain" in the upstairs hallway, filled each day with two large pails of water carried by the school janitor from the town well, nearly three blocks away.

The main floor was divided down the centre by a wide corridor, which ran south to north from a wider porch and a vestibule in the front to wide double doors at the back. Inside the entrance on each side were stairways to the boys' and girls' sides of the basement, while opening into the hall near the rear doors was another stairway into the boys' side of the basement, which, for some reason I still do not know, we boys were not allowed to use. On each side of the central hallway were two classrooms. The first on the right housed grades one and two, the first on the left grades three, four and five. The second on the right held grades six, seven and eight, and the second on the left high school grades nine, ten and eleven.

The rooms each had a cloak room running nearly the full width of one end with rows of coat hooks for outdoor clothing and the lunch pails of the country students. During my student days but before I reached high school, the cloak rooms were eliminated from the two upper classrooms, one enlarging the room holding the intermediate grades, and the other, a narrow classroom with seating for perhaps a dozen, accommodating the newly initiated grade-twelve class. At the same time, a small room, perhaps six by eight feet, was framed out of one corner of the high-school room, opening into the grade-twelve room. This was known as the chemistry laboratory, but it really served only as a storage area for chemicals and equipment, which were moved into the classrooms for experiments. Still later, the use of these two enlarged rooms alternated occasionally as the populations of the intermediate and high-school grades grew or shrank.

Each room was equipped with several rows of desks, usually six, of assorted types. The type we preferred had a hinged writing surface that lifted to give access to the book-storage compartment inside. Less liked were those that had an immovable top and a shelflike area about six inches below the lid onto which one could slide books but which required students almost to lie on their sides to select items. Least liked were those similar to the latter type but which were wide enough to seat two students, who were at great risk of cracking their heads together if both sought access to the shelf at the same time.

In the far right corner of each desk top was an ink well, covered by a hinged circular metal lid and containing a semi-cylindrical heavy glass ink container with a capacity of perhaps a quarter of a fluid ounce. When we were deemed old enough to start writing with pen and ink, the ink wells were filled from a large bottle containing about a quart, and we were started off attempting to write using straight pens with, it always seemed, needle-sharp nibs that caught on every imperfection in the paper, splattering ink in all directions. I don't recall any attempt being made to provide each one of us with a nib suited to our own particular hand conformation; rather, we were expected to conform to the nib. Needless to say, ink-stained desk tops, fingers and clothing were common. We filled page after page with individual letters attempting to achieve a flowing script with precise proportions of each letter on, under or over lines pre-printed on the paper. Few of us attained perfection in this art, and I was not among the few who did. As we progressed, we used fountain pens, which we could obtain with nibs more suited to our individual styles. Ballpoint pens didn't appear until long after our school days had ended.

Across the front of each room and along one side wall ran great stretches of what now are called chalkboards but which we called blackboards, because they really were painted black. Along their tops, on window-blind rollers, were large maps, which were pulled down for teaching geography, their legends proudly proclaiming, "The British Empire Shown in Red." On world maps, Canada was by far the largest of these red areas, a fact of which we were tremendously proud, as proud as we were to be a part of "the empire upon which the sun never sets" and which we were sure would go on forever. One had only to look at the imperious features, jewelled crowns and robes of King George V and Queen Mary, in framed portraits above the blackboard, flanked by the Union Jack and the Canadian Red Ensign, to be reassured of that.

The maps served another function as well. Before reaching the grade level at which we were required to write departmental examinations, we were excluded from the room while the teachers wrote their examination questions on the blackboards and covered them with the maps until time for the test to begin.

It often fell to our lot to perform certain tasks associated with the blackboards, such as cleaning them with felt erasers or sometimes washing them when accumulated chalk dust built up to an unacceptable whitish grey thickness. We boys liked nothing better than to be sent to the basement with a half dozen blackboard erasers to be cleaned. First, by pounding them together, we were able to raise satisfactory clouds of white chalk dust. Next we applied them to the eraser cleaner, which consisted of a hooded, vertical, circular hand-cranked brush mounted over a small tray filled with water to trap the dust. With one boy holding the erasers and a second turning the brush as fast as he could, it was possible to generate immense clouds of chalk dust that no amount of water in the tray could suppress. Boys often returned to the classroom with nicely cleaned erasers but wearing a good proportion of the chalk dust on their clothing and hair.

Along the outer wall of each room were windows, occupying perhaps seventy-five percent of the wall space, so the lighting in the rooms was very good, a necessary feature, because the school had no artificial lighting. These also provided the only ventilation, so in the summer they were covered with large screens and in the winter by storm windows with sliding panels. As in the houses, the adequacy of heating in the winter was a function of the outside temperature and wind direction. On bitterly cold winter days, it was not unusual to see students seated near the windows on the windward side of the building wearing their overcoats in classes, while those near the inner walls, where the hot-air registers from the furnaces were located, were quite comfortable wearing normal indoor clothing.

The ducts from the furnaces to these hot-air registers were large, nearly two feet in diameter, with several joints at about three-foot intervals. It was not impossible, therefore, for mischievous boys to get them apart in order to introduce such items as dishes of hydrogen sulphide solution, which the hot air from the furnace propelled into the selected room as rotten-egg gas. One April Fool's Day, some boys placed a repeating alarm clock in the furnace pipe leading to the room being supervised by our science teacher, with the alarm set to go off in mid-class. The timing worked out to perfection. The alarm rang. Searching for the cause, the teacher headed for the hall door. As he reached out to open it, the alarm stopped. He stepped out into the hall, looked around, saw nothing and returned to resume teaching. The alarm rang again. The same procedure was repeated. Only after his second attempt did the teacher realize that the sound was not coming from the hall but from the hot-air register. Two boys were sent to the basement to retrieve the noisemaker while the teacher joined in the general laughter.

I am amazed now at how good humoured most of our teachers were, considering the comparative laboriousness of their task at that time. Except for textbooks, a limited supply of chemistry equipment and their own ingenuity, there were practically no teaching aids – no movie or slide projectors, not even a library.

It is difficult to imagine, in this age of photocopiers and computer printers, how onerous a task it was fifty years ago for teachers to prepare several copies of some material they might wish to distribute to students. The device used was called a hectograph and consisted of a flat tray into which a gelatinous mixture was poured and allowed to set. The material to be copied was hand-lettered or drawn on paper with a special pencil of a bright purple hue. This paper was pressed face down on the surface of the gelatine and was rubbed firmly to transfer the purple lettering or diagram from the paper to the gelatine. A clean sheet of paper then was pressed on to the gelatine and rubbed carefully to ensure complete contact with the its surface. When this paper was peeled off, if everything had been done correctly, it bore a copy of the original but often with imperfections, which had to be touched up by hand. Each succeeding copy was slightly fainter, so the number of copies that could be made was limited. If the handout consisted of more than one page, the whole process had to be repeated for each page. Thus, preparing a dozen copies of a diagram or page of text could be a two- or three-hour job.

The teachers produced all of the school's records and documents by hand. A note to a child's parents or an order for equipment was hand written. There was no secretarial staff, nor did the school possess a typewriter. This state of affairs continued at least until after my graduation in 1940.

I look back on our teachers with tremendous admiration and respect. For grades one to eight, there was one teacher, usually female, to each room, and she taught all of the subjects to all of the grades in her charge as well as maintaining order and discipline. Two teachers divided all of the four high-school grades between them, one teaching all of the non-science subjects: history, literature, languages (French or Latin), English grammar and composition, physiology and hygiene; and the other teaching the science and maths subjects – agriculture, chemistry, algebra, plane and descriptive geometry, trigonometry and, one year, even geology. Their collective competence is attested to by the number of us who successfully qualified and went on to universities and the professions.

One of the great advantages of the system was that our teachers got to know each one of us personally, and they knew our parents and their circumstances, because they shared the social life of the village with them. The principal for most of my years in school had come to the village before I reached school age, and while I was a student the village celebrated the graduation from grade twelve of the class that had begun grade one in his first year there. It is quite safe to assume that he and the other members of his teaching staff knew many of us better, in many ways, than did our own parents. One never heard of such things as psychological counselling in those days, but there is little doubt that a good deal of practical assistance was rendered by teachers on the basis of this intimacy with our lives.

We were particularly fortunate in the teachers provided for us in my high-school years. The principal taught the non-science subjects, and his main interests were literature and history; world events of the day were his passion. He imbued us with a genuine appreciation of English poetry, Shakespeare and English prose. But most interesting of all were his history lectures, which often led him into current events. Because grades nine, ten and eleven shared a classroom, we could eavesdrop on his talks to the other classes, even when we were supposed to be working on assignments of our own, and we benefitted from these digressions into current affairs far beyond the requirements of our own classes. I can still picture him pacing up and down between the two rows of the class he was teaching, hands plunged deeply into trouser pockets, while describing how some event of the day was a direct result of the historical event under discussion. Instead of teaching just dry historical facts, he instilled in us an appreciation of history as the background from which our world derived its political and social colour.

These were the days when Hitler and Mussolini were prominent in Europe, Roosevelt was inaugurating the New Deal in the United States, and names such as Aberhart and Coldwell were familiar in Canada, and there was plenty of political colour in the world for him to share with us. We were very lucky to have had him as a teacher.

For several years we had a science and mathematics teacher of rare ability; he was also vice-principal and later princial. He was in the process of defeating the Depression by teaching in the winter and earning a university degree in summer school, after having won a Governor General's medal in high school. He was a brilliant teacher, who could make even a mathematical dunce like me understand the intricacies of trigonometry and descriptive geometry, and I can still recall at will many "useful num-bers" that he expected us to remember: 1.4142, 1.7321 (the square roots of 2 and 3) and the litany "zero, one-half, one-over-root-two, root-three-over-two, one" (which are the trigonometric sines of zero, 30, 45, 60 and 90 degrees).

He inaugurated the teaching of geology in our high school because that was his major in university. He led highly enjoyable all-day outings as we explored the outcrops of Belly River sandstone and Bearpaw shale along the banks of the Saskatchewan River, seeking – and finding – scores of fossil shellfish, all the while marvelling that our area of the prairies more than once had been at the bottoms of seas. And on a bare stretch of prairie he showed us the derelict remains of the biggest steam tractor ever to make its way to the prairies. It had been used to drill an exploratory oil well, which produced nothing but salt water and probably disappeared during the great scrap-iron collections of the Second World War.

One wonders, with shame for the world and sadness for one's self, what heights he might have reached had the war not interposed. Advanced mathematics and astronomy were among his hobbies, sources of pleasure and intellectual exercise. Because of these abilities he was commissioned into the air force as an instructor of astro-navigation and was killed in an aircraft crash.

One of the more trying personal aspects of our school must have been the complete lack of privacy at any time during the school day. There was no teacher's lounge, no office, no place where a teacher might go to struggle privately to overcome a flare of temper or regain composure after some particularly trying incident, for example. This was particularly true for the female teachers. The two male teachers pre-empted the minuscule chemistry laboratory during recesses, thereby achieving a semi-privacy that we interrupted only on matters of extreme urgency. But there was no place in which the female teachers could take refuge. Successful teachers developed amazing powers of self-control.

Boys were not alone in betraying an interest in things to do with the opposite sex. Early in our high-school years we studied a poem by Rupert Brooke, "The Great Lover," which poetically lists a number of things the poet found appealing. In class, our teacher asked one of the girls, about sixteen years old and always modestly comported, which of the things mentioned in the poem she particularly liked. She replied, "the rough male kiss in blankets," bringing a roar of laughter from her startled and incredulous classmates. The phrase in the poem reads, "the rough male kiss *of* blankets."

A poet came to my rescue on one occasion. Profanity of any kind was strictly forbidden in the school and brought swift chastisement from our teachers. A friend and I were walking along the main hall and were nearing our classroom door when he suddenly elbowed me in the stomach. I reacted with a surprised "Jesus Christ!" at the moment our English teacher appeared at the door. My reaction to her appearance was immediate and the result of one of those flashes of inspiration one sometimes achieves without conscious thought. Almost without pause I continued, ". . . Thou child so wise, / Bless mine hands and fill mine eyes, / And bring my soul to paradise." The teacher's beginning frown changed to a smile of approval, thanks to Hilaire Belloc's short poem "The Birds," which was on our course of studies for that year.

Our school day began at 9:00 a.m. and went on until 3:30 p.m., with fifteen-minute recesses at 10:30 a.m. and 2:15 p.m. and a lunch hour between 12:00 and 1:00 p.m. All of these intervals were marked by the ringing of a hand bell by the principal, outside the front and rear entrances and at each basement entrance to call us into classes, and in the hallway to signal the beginning of recesses, noon hour and the end of the school day. Once in a while, for no predictable reason – perhaps because the two male teachers got into an exceptionally interesting discussion in the chem lab or perhaps were listening on the radio to an exciting moment in the World Series – recess or noon hour would be indefinitely prolonged, to the great delight of the students and the exasperation of any teacher who might have a difficult class ahead that now had to be covered in twenty minutes instead of a half-hour. But how interesting this fallibility of the system made life for us, compared to the clockwork systems today, which divide the periods with mechanical precision, carrying on even through the unlistening hours of the night.

These hours were very convenient for those of us who lived in the village and who could walk to school under even the worst circumstances in ten minutes or less. But for the country students who were transported to and from school in horse-drawn vans, anything up to an hour or even two or three had to be added to the beginning and end of each school day, depending on the weather and the distance of their farm homes from the village. Usually a van was operated by the farm family with school children who lived farthest from the village on each route. Not until near the end of our schooling were the horses replaced by automobiles, into which seven or eight children might be packed; but cars usually were replaced by horses when winter blocked the roads.

The vans were a modified form of the prairie farm wagon, completely enclosed by wood and canvas, mounted on wheels in the summer and on bobsled runners in winter. Comfort was not a feature. Longitudinal benches ran along the sides, and midway between them, in the centre of the vehicle, was a small stove that burned coal stored in a box under one of the benches. Each end was enclosed with a narrow door, the one at the rear for the students to enter and exit, and the one at the front for the driver. Each door had a small window, and the one at the front had a slot through which the reins to guide the horses were passed. In the winter, because the rate of progress of these vehicles when pulled by a team of draft horses seldom exceeded a walking pace, farm youngsters started for school long before dawn, and in the evening it was long after dark before they arrived home again. During the school day, the van drivers wiled away the hours in the small heated office of the livery stable or in farming talk in the pool room and perhaps did some small amount of shopping for their wives. With the shortage of cash in the Depression years, they could do little else.

Considering the viciousness of which prairie winters are capable, it is amazing that the times these vans were unable to make it to school were so rare. Naturally, when there was a blizzard blowing, the country children might not even start out, and the village children greeted these days with delight. Regular classes would be suspended, and we might spend the day reading books or in some much more enjoyable pursuit than our lessons, with the added bonus that school probably would be dismissed early. Sometimes a storm would blow up during the day and we would sit on the edges of our seats, stealing glances out the windows and trying to hear conversations in the hall as the principal and van drivers discussed the possibility of dismissing school early.

One of the worst times for country students, van drivers and horses alike was the change of seasons to spring. During the winter, the trails often adopted a wandering character as the vans took to the fields to make their way around heavily drifted spots on the roads. In the spring, as a result, the vans often were caught between the Scylla of melting drifts on the roads and the Charybdis of bottomless mud in the fields. Often the students had to dismount and walk while the horses dragged the empty but still-heavy vehicles across stretches of bare earth and mud. It was a matter of fine judgement on the part of the van drivers to decide when to change from runners to wheels.

Four to six of these vehicles served our school, and, when we were too young to have watches, the jingle of the harness as they pulled up outside was the signal to us that the end of another school day was only minutes away.

Often the teachers boarded in one or another of the family homes in the village and, for two or three years when I was still a pre-schooler, one lived with us. She was generous with candy and other treats, which she carried in her purse, my access to which probably was granted much too freely. This continued until she once brought home a package of what I took to be chocolate but that actually was a laxative. *Distressing* is probably an overly mild description of the result; I have never been so ill in my life. If anyone is seeking a way to teach an obnoxiously nosey youngster to stay out of a purse, I can recommend this method as being effective – but I suggest a considerably reduced dosage!

While we were in the junior grades, classroom seating was arranged by the teacher but, as we advanced to the more senior grades, we were allowed some latitude. On the first day of school each autumn we arrived at school as early as possible in order to get the seating and types of desks of our choice. We knew which rows of desks would be allotted to each grade and, although these would have been laboriously organized in advance by the school caretaker, we arranged and rearranged them to suit ourselves.

This rearrangement was not quite as simple as it sounds, because desks and seats were screwed to wooden boards or runners one behind another, two or three to each set, so to change one desk meant moving several. The ensuing arguments were usually settled more by might than right. The country students who arrived by van were at a distinct disadvantage in this contest, but often a chum of a country boy would ensure that his friend had a desk "reserved" in close proximity to his own. However, if we had a teacher who had supervised the same class before, our plans were unavailing and we were re-seated in accordance with the wishes of the teacher based on our conduct of the previous year.

The height of the desks and seats could be adjusted by means of a T-shaped wrench, and it became the task of the boys on the first day of school to adjust these to suit each individual occupant, a chore we enjoyed and that took ten times as long to perform as it should have. Occasionally, bolts would be only semi-tightened, so a desk, when leaned on, would drop to its lowest level with a crash, or a girl student might find her seat slowly sinking toward the floor. But before long the desks would be allotted, the necessary adjustments made, and the school year could begin in earnest.

On the first day of the new school year the teachers provided each class with a list of the textbooks required for each subject. If there were new ones, which had not been used in the school before, they were ordered by the students or their parents through the village drugstore, which was the local agency for the distributors. Textbooks that continued in use year after year were sold by the students to their successors in each grade. The purchasers added their names on the inside of the covers or on the flyleaves to those of previous owners, some of whom might have preceded us by several years. These books were carefully inspected for interesting marginal drawings or comments, and it was a sort of detective game attempting to link a particular inscription, especially if it was ribald, to one of the book's previous owners.

The drugstore was also the source for other materials we might need for school – pens, pen nibs, pencils, variously coloured inks, rulers (wooden with a metal strip along the edge and calibrated in inches only), geometry sets with tin protractors and triangles, and the notebooks that we called scribblers. These last came in several varieties, but we always made sure we had at least one whose back cover contained mathematical tables, as well as tables of land measurements, weights and volumes, which saved us memorizing facts such as the number of pecks in a bushel or the number of square feet in an acre.

But school wasn't all just books and lessons. Recesses and noon hours were a time for fun and games. In the winter these were confined almost entirely to the basement, where the younger children played tag, or hopscotch on patterns drawn with chalk on the floor. Older boys might play pom-pom-pullaway, a game in which two facing walls were "safe" territory and a single player designated as It took up station in the centre of the area and attempted to tag any of the others running from the safety of one wall to that opposite. Each person tagged then had to assist It in tagging the rest until all were caught. The first tagged became It for the next game. As can be imagined, this game required considerable physical effort and when the bell was rung to end recess we would return to the classroom out of breath, red-faced and sweating.

Games such as this illustrated the changes of social status in our young lives. When we were very young, we were not invited to participate and, even if we were in the group when the game was organized, we were ignored. When we left the safety of a wall to run across the floor, the older boy who was It would not deign even to notice us, and soon we would drift away to some other group. But one day, one of us would run across the floor and be tagged. From that moment on, his rank in the hierarchy of juveniles had increased and he was accepted as having come one step farther along the road to being grown up. And, of course, from that moment he, too, ignored the smaller boys who were coming along behind him. Interestingly, one boy could occupy several steps in the hierarchy at the same time, depending upon the nature of the activity and the individual's skill in that activity.

From grade six onward, we were allowed to spend winter recesses in the classroom, but our activities were restricted to those of a less physically active nature. Games of tic-tac-toe and hangman were played on the blackboards, or jacks on a desk top, while innumerable sheets of squared graph paper were expended on games of battleship.

When the early warm days of spring arrived, skipping ropes appeared among the girls, first on the broad concrete sidewalk surrounding the flagpole and leading to the school's front door, then moving to the school grounds as the sun melted the snow and dried the earth. For the boys, this was the season for marbles, and several different games were played, most with a strong gambling element as each boy attempted to divest his companions of as many of their dibs and alleys and steelies as he could. Dibs were small clay marbles, glass alleys were larger, and steelies were shiny ball bearings of appropriate size scavenged from machinery repairs. The games were the conventional chip-out-of-the-circle or chip-into-a-hole type plus a few of our own devising and of a more larcenous nature, such as giving odds that a victim couldn't drop a marble from waist height into a hole only slightly larger than an alley in the lid of a tobacco can.

As soon as the ground had dried almost sufficiently, soccer balls appeared, as did softballs and baseballs. Village boys raced home at noon hour, ate lunch as quickly as possible, and dashed back to the school to take part in the games.

During my years in primary and elementary school, there were no organized track-and-field sports. By the time we reached high school, however, the Depression had eased a little, and time was set aside for at least two or three sports days each spring. These began with trials and eliminations in our own school and concluded with a zone sports day involving schools within a radius of thirty or forty miles from some central location.

As soon as the program was announced, boys of the high school were recruited to work on the sports grounds, and never was work a greater joy. Lime lines were laid and distances measured for the sprinting events; pits were refilled with sand for the jumping events; two-by-two uprights were carefully marked at one-inch intervals and finishing nails driven in at each mark to support a bamboo cross-pole for the high-jump events. Finally the big day for the local eliminations would arrive, and the whole school had a day off to participate or to watch. Everyone seemed to be able to find something to do. Sports duffers, such as I, were assigned many tasks – raking the sand pits after each jump, judging toe alignment at the hop-step-and-jump, keeping records, and so on.

Special training or equipment for sports was unheard of. Except for the fact we were all in pretty good condition because of the life we led, there was no special preparation for the sporting events. Nor were there track suits or school uniforms. The boys competed in their everyday school clothes and the girls tucked their skirts up under the elastic leg bands of their bloomers, and that was that. Footwear ranged from farm boots to sneakers to stockinged feet to bare feet, depending on the preference of the athletes and the toughness of the soles of their feet.

Each of us cheered for our particular favourites and friends in each age group as they competed. But our science and maths teacher cheered for all, body and soul. Not a youngster ran or jumped without his complete and utter participation. As a high jumper approached the bar, the teacher tensed; as the one leaped, the other's facial and body muscles became rigid; as the one soared upward toward the bar, the other's body twisted in unison. If the jumper dragged a leg or foot, the teacher raised his to help. By the end of the day, he must have been exhausted. But every competitor felt his tremendous sympathetic energy and knew that at least that teacher was with them all the way.

When the zone finals took place, there was another full-day holiday and every student who could possibly reach the location was there. Transportation for all was by private automobile, most often driven by teachers and by high-school students who were old enough to have driver's licenses, usually the sons of the cars' owners.

For all of us, participants and onlookers alike, it was a great occasion. At no other time did we have such an opportunity to view, assess and discuss strange youngsters of our own ages. For most of the year we were sealed in our little village and had no more communication with children of neighbouring towns than we had with those on the other side of the world. Of course we were convinced that our outlook was worldly, wise and sophisticated and that youngsters from other villages were most definitely of an unfortunate and inferior breed. And communication among the children of the various villages was difficult, if not impossible, to establish. We looked at them and they looked at us, but few sparks of human recognition passed between.

As we began to mature, there was more than a little interest shown in the strange members of the opposite sex, but it would have required an impulse akin in power to an atom bomb to get us to communicate with them directly. We passed and re-passed, stared and giggled, or even ventured a remark at random, addressed to the air in their vicinity, on how unfortunate they were to belong to a village other than ours. But a direct confrontation was unthinkable, if not downright terrorizing. Later we would compare impressions of the blonde with the blue dress from one village or the red-head with the green sweater from another, for example, but, when the day had ended, in our minds they sank back into the limbo from which they had appeared and were forgotten – at least until the next year. When we grew older we discovered that it really was possible to communicate with these exotically strange females.

And while on the subject of this attraction between the sexes, it is worth mentioning the beauty of those prairie girls as they began to become young women. Makeup was a rarity and artifice of any kind almost unknown. Their clear skins, natural bodies, unfettered movements and unaffected poise were a disturbing delight to boys just tremoloing their way into manhood.

The use of outdoor sports equipment in the school rooms was strictly forbidden but, when it did happen and the guilty parties were caught, punishment appropriate to the circumstances was applied. On one occasion two of us were playing catch with a baseball the length of one of the classrooms until a wild pitch removed a baseball-sized chunk of plaster from the wall under the blackboard. We quickly divested ourselves of mitt and glove and assumed nonchalant attitudes at the far end of the room. Another boy came in, saw the damage and picked up the baseball just as the teacher entered. Cowards that we were, we left him to his fate as, in spite of his fervent denials, he was ordered to repair the damage. This he did with plaster and water while we snickered at his discomfiture. Of course, our boyish code of honour would not let him divulge the real culprits.

Cases of extraordinary breaches of discipline were punished with the strap, but this was very seldom necessary. However, one particular incident resulted in every boy in the senior grades of the school suffering this chastisement. The incident took place a day or two after Halloween.

It was customary for some piece of trickery to be visited on the school every Halloween, but usually it was relatively harmless and was quickly forgotten. On this occasion, however, a large freight dray had been taken apart and re-assembled in the hallway of the school. The problem was that, in the process, daubs of grease from the wheel axles had smeared the walls, and some heavier pieces of the dray had come in contact with the walls too, removing areas of the plaster.

Interrogation began immediately, conducted by the principal. Who had done it? No one confessed. I knew that the group I had been with on Halloween night had not been involved, and others claimed equal ignorance. No one would admit involvement. Without a confession, who was to be punished? At this point, the chairman of the school board became involved. After assessing the damage, he instructed the principal that, unless the culprits were identified, every boy in the high school was to have a strapping. We protested. The principal protested. The board chairman was adamant. So, we all had a strapping. It is true that in executing the order the principal really didn't have his heart in it, and the smacks we got on the palms of our hands with the two-inch-wide strap were light. I am sure I detected a sympathetic twinkle in his eye as I got the punishment in my turn.

Beyond the corporal punishment, it had been decreed also that the high school boys would repair the damage. This we did, taking most of a school day to do it and enjoying every minute of it. But the mystery remained, and to this day I do not know who the guilty parties were. I suspect strongly that it was not school boys at all, but rather some of the school's recent and not-so-recent graduates and drop-outs.

The strap was considered to be the ultimate in degrading punishment and, short of expulsion, was the most severe punishment meted out to misbehaving youngsters. But there was one mass punishment whose threat to the junior grades invariably produced whatever result it was intended to achieve. This was the threat to eliminate our afternoon reading session.

Each day, for the first ten or fifteen minutes after the noon hour, the teacher or a student nominated by the teacher would read to the three grades in the room from a book of our own choosing. Loss of this privilege was unthinkable, and the threat stimulated us to imagine afternoons of classes completely unrelieved of boredom to be endured for eons longer than usual.

There was the inevitable conflict in the selection of books. The division took place along lines of gender, the girls begging for one kind of book while the boys groaned in dismay and countered with another proposal. The solution was alternation. This resulted in the boys listening with a great show of boredom and disgust to the trials of Anne of Green Gables, for example, and the girls shuddering in mock horror at the adventures of a modern-day Robin Hood known as the Grey Seal. If the truth were admitted, I am sure we all enjoyed the choices made by both sides, and it was a great day when an exciting stage in the development of the tale stimulated the teacher's curiosity so the reading went on for a considerable period after the allotted time had expired.

All school activities came to a halt at the end of June, concluding with final examinations. These, it seemed, always took place in an agony of heat and sweat, meteorological and mental. For all of the grades up to grade ten, school ended on a particular day, usually the last Friday in June, and the children raced from the school, final report cards in hand, with two months of freedom from lessons in happy prospect. For the matriculation grades, eleven and twelve, school ended for students as they handed in their last departmental examination papers, but satisfaction with the termination of the year was shadowed by the wait ahead for examination results.

The examinations were marked in Regina by a group of teachers drawn from schools all over the province. When all of the examinations had been marked, the results were published in newspapers serving the various areas of the province. Word that "the results are out" seemed to spread through the village like magic, and there was an immediate congregation of high-school students in the village drugstore, which got its newspapers directly from the train, eliminating the wait for papers to be sorted in the post office. Two or three papers were spread on tables in front of the soda fountain, and a half dozen heads crowded around each as we sought our names in the lists set in minuscule type for each subject. Each of us backed away from the papers with whoops of joy when we had found our names listed for all of our subjects, and it is a great tribute to our teachers that very few of us ever were disappointed. With very few exceptions, all of us who had shared classes throughout our school years graduated from high school together.

We may have celebrated our graduation with a bottle of pop or a sundae in the drugstore, but there was no other event to mark this major occasion in our lives. The school didn't stage graduation ceremonies, nor did we have any other special social function. Rather, in my graduating year of 1940, ten months after the beginning of the Second World War, we were more concerned with what was to come next. Some of us went on to university, some to business or teachers' colleges, some went into nursing, and many stayed home to continue helping to run farms and businesses. But many went to war. Two years after graduation, I returned to the village on leave from the air force and found only two of my male contemporaries there, one also on leave from the air force and the other who had been found unfit for military service. And when we two in the air force returned to duty, our friend was left alone.

Church

DURING MY CHILDHOOD, the village boasted four church congregations: Methodist, Anglican, Presbyterian and Roman Catholic. The formation of the United Church of Canada in 1925 absorbed the Methodists and dealt near-fatal blows to the two other Protestant denominations, and the Depression of the 1930s provided the *coup de grâce*. The Depression also closed the village's Roman Catholic church when I was a child, and it did not re-open until the early years of the Second World War.

The United Church soon gathered in almost all the former members of the Protestant congregations with only a few exceptions, a notable one being a particularly stubborn elderly woman, a Presbyterian who vowed to preside over the demise of the United Church even though her equally stubborn husband became a member of the hated congregation and seldom missed a service. But it must be said of the determined old woman that her attitude toward the United Church had no effect on her love of all the children of the village, of any faith, on whom she lavished affection – and pull taffy in exchange for bouquets of wild flowers.

The United Church was built on the west side of the north end of Main Street. It, too, was constructed of wood and was a plain box of a building set on a concrete foundation without a basement. The outside was white-painted siding, and its only distinctive characteristics were simulated gothic points on the windows and an exceptionally steep roof with a small steeple containing a bell at the east end over the front door. Its interior was no more lavish than its exterior. The walls were finished with varnished fir panelling to a height of about six feet, above which the walls and ceiling were sheeted with a fibreboard that had an alarming tendency to bow and droop in damp weather. Down through the ceiling by the front doors hung the bell rope, which, when it rained, carried a trickle of water to be absorbed by the fibreboard ceiling panelling, creating a brown stain that spread slowly, year by year.

There was little decoration. The congregation sat on wooden chairs facing a dais at the west end. This dais, elevated about seven inches above the rest of the floor, was surrounded by a galvanized pipe railing draped with dark green material that enclosed the pulpit, the foot-powered pump organ, and chairs for the choir, which were replaced by miniature chairs for very young children during Sunday school. On one wall hung a bronze plaque, covered by a draw curtain matching those on the railing around the dais, in memory of one of the pioneer members of the congregation. On the west wall, facing the congregation, hung two fibre placards, lettered in gold and beginning to warp from exposure, proclaiming "God so loved the world . . ." and "Suffer the little children . . . ." A paper banner headed "The Cradle Roll" contained the names of those children, year by year, who had achieved recognition by being born and baptized into the congregation. On the north wall hung an athletic-award shield on which each year was inscribed the name of the boy or girl who achieved the highest score in sports events at the annual Sunday school picnic and which had been won with disheartening regularity and almost without exception by the family members of the local doctor.

In diagonally opposite corners, southwest and northeast, were heating stoves, fuelled with wood and coal. The larger of the two, in the northeast corner by the front door, was surrounded by a jacket of galvanized iron, locally fabricated, which served the dual purpose of assisting in the convection heating of the building and protecting people from direct contact with the hot stove. Along the east wall and behind this stove ran a box bench on which there was room for four or five boys to sit out of sight of the Sunday-school superintendent. By custom, this bench was reserved for the boys in the Sunday school of the fourteen- to sixteen-year age group, and for these same boys when they graduated to the evening church services. It was a great day in the life of a young boy, therefore, when he moved into the class that permitted his entry into this select gathering and joined the weekly competition for an anonymous seat behind the stove.

In the box bench were kept the Sunday-school curtains. Their purpose was to divide the single room into six classrooms for the lesson period. In addition, they served multiple duties in the town, for example as stage backdrops for political meetings, or as curtains for amateur theatrical productions.

When it came time during the service for Sunday-school classes, these drapes, ready mounted on ropes, were taken out of storage, and in two or three minutes the rope ends were secured by loops over permanent hooks in the walls, seven-foot poles were erected at the rope intersections, and the church was transformed by one longitudinal and two lateral partitions into a half dozen more-or-less private, but not soundproof, classrooms. Putting up these drapes before and taking them down again after the class period became the highlight of the service for us because, by the time we were old enough to be allowed to do it, we had reached that stage of worldly boredom with Sunday school that seems to strike most boys in their middle teens.

In Sunday school, too, we ran the risk of being trapped into the annual Christmas pageant. As youngsters, it was easy for us to enter into the spirit of it and give it our best. As we grew older, however, and more self-conscious, we began to suspect that some of the things we were asked to do were really beneath our dignity, if not downright childish. This precipitated what was probably my first major revolt against Sunday school, and parental, authority. By this time, I had reached the age of fourteen or fifteen and was assigned a verse to recite, in conjunction with several others, in one of these productions. I recall it only as having been particularly saccharine and juvenile, and I announced to all and sundry that I refused to be a party to such an infantile production. I suppose the Sunday-school teachers didn't take my refusal seriously, probably thinking that a word or two from my parents would put me back on track.

My parents tried to put me back on track, but I stubbornly refused to memorize the verse. I refused even to read it again just in case it might stick in my mind. This precipitated a family row of no little proportion. Mother was adamant that I would speak the piece; I was adamant that I would not. The outcome was that I was forced to join the group that was performing but, as my mind was my own, no one had been able to make me learn the verse. When my turn to recite came, I stood absolutely mute and refused to say a word. The impasse was broken by the superintendent reading the verse while I stood silent. Needless to say, I never again performed in a Sunday-school pageant. To say that I was not embarrassed as I stood there, or that I did not feel shame, would be to lie, but I still think that, as a personal declaration of independence, the rebellious act was worth it.

Most of the time, however, we were much more cooperative and took part in Sunday-school activities with good will. Several of us enjoyed the music particularly and contrived to sit next to one another as often as possible so we could try to work out harmony parts to the hymns. The results may not have been successful always, but we learned a good deal about music from our experiments. We preferred the hymns with a lilting swing to them or those with a resoundingly contrasting part, such as the bass in "Onward! Christian Soldiers" or the harmony parts in "Tell Me the Stories of Jesus." Occasionally our musical fervour would get the better of us and a good harmony chord of barbershop ilk would ring through the church long after the rest of the congregation had paused for breath, causing us to be fixed by a disapproving glance from the superintendent. This gentleman was most definitely of the opinion that Sunday school was not a place for light-hearted amusement.

For most of my childhood, the Sunday-school superintendent on the other six days of the week operated the local lumberyard but, because of his Sunday position of authority, we stood always somewhat in awe of him. He took his position in the Sunday school very seriously and his routine life was exemplary. Perhaps, because of the Depression and the resulting scarcity of business, his occupation gave him time to develop one of his most impressive talents. He was a master at praying. I don't intend to infer that he was praying for business in the lumberyard (although this may have lent some fervency to his prayers) but rather that he took advantage of the time on his hands to compose his prayers for each Sunday. He was not histrionic or given to hellfire-and-brimstone tirades; rather, he prayed quietly, fervently and in a tone of voice that had us youngsters convinced he really did have some sort of private line to the Almighty. He prayed standing, facing us, his eyes closed and his hands clasped below the bottom button of his rather well-filled waistcoat. He rocked back and forth from heel to toe, never to the point of losing his balance but with sufficient energy that we were fascinated; we watched under our eyebrows as with bent heads we paid much more attention to this entrancing spectacle than to the content of the prayers. His prayers, it seemed to the young, tended to length as well, so it was with audible exhalations of relief we heard him arrive at the magic words ". . . Who has taught us to pray, saying . . ." and we were able to launch into a unison rendition of the Lord's Prayer and get on with the service.

As superintendent, he was in charge of the Sunday-school library, a collection of perhaps forty or fifty books that reposed in a locked cupboard in his office at the lumberyard. Most of these extolled God, King and Empire and bore titles such as *With Roberts to Kandahar*. I suspect that most of them were chosen for inclusion in the library by title alone and that neither he nor any other adult ever looked between the covers. This suspicion was confirmed when I borrowed a book with the obviously Biblical title *The Judgement of Solomon*.

What I expected, I don't remember, but what I got I am positive was not what the straight-laced master of the Sunday school intended. The tale described a situation in which a man seduces one woman and gets her pregnant, then marries her sister. The seduction takes place in a berry patch and is described in sufficiently lurid detail that the book became an immediate hit with our teen-aged set. The judgement concerned the life of the child but, like most of the world, we were much more entertained by the seduction than by the final outcome, the details of which escape me now. There was a sudden run on the library for a time but, unfortunately from our point of view, the rest of the library consisted of exactly the type of book one would expect to find in a Sunday-school library of the era.

Another example of this man's rectitude related to one of our money-making pursuits. Whenever there was a dance in the village, we youngsters would scour the vicinity for empty beer bottles, which we would turn in to the beer parlour operator for one cent each. Occasionally our search would turn up a stash of two or three full bottles, which we also considered fair game, and these could be peddled in the next day or two to certain men in the town who always were willing to give us the going price of twenty cents a bottle for our booty – a real bonanza. You can imagine our astonishment when the superintendent's son, one of our peers, told us of finding six full bottles and taking them home, where his father poured their contents out and returned the bottles to him to sell for six cents – instead of the $1.20 we could have got for him. I am sure we considered this a horrible example of interference with the principles of supply and demand and of free enterprise, however morally correct it might have been. To a junior teenager in those days, $1.20 was a small fortune that would buy twenty-four chocolate bars or bottles of pop or take you to six movies at the local theatre.

There was one occasion on which the paths of our fiscal cupidity and the Sunday school crossed. This was the annual Sunday-school picnic, at which one might gain a little hard cash by the exercise of athletic prowess. Unfortunately for me, most of the races were staged by ages, and I was very small for my age. But there were those who excelled at sports and were able to clean up handsomely, since there were dime and nickel prizes for the various events. But even one such as I could pick up a little change occasionally by judicious teaming up with the right people for events like the potato relay, the three-legged race or the wheelbarrow race. Because of my small size, I was greatly in demand for any event in which one of the stronger boys wanted a light partner.

In addition to the appeal of Mammon, the picnic featured free ice cream and lemonade and all the sandwiches and cake one could eat from those brought by the women of the church. The rule for ice cream was one cone per person, at least until all were served. Then it was catch-as-catch-can until the big insulated container was empty. Invariably, it seemed, there was at least one urchin whose ice cream fell off his precariously held cone into the dirt or who, after a moment's inattention, found his ice cream being licked appreciatively by one of the many dogs in attendance. Exceptions to the one-per-person rule were made in such cases, much to the solace of the weeping youngster.

The final event of the picnic was the peanut scramble. Peanuts in the shells were hurled willy-nilly on the ground by handfuls while we children dived after them, snatching up as many as we could and stuffing them in our pockets. In this battle no quarter was asked or given, regardless of age, sex or stature, but judicious aiming of the thrown peanuts by the men in charge ensured that everyone got a reasonable share and there were usually some left over in the bag for those too small or too timid to win their quota by combat.

In a way, we youngsters felt that the prizes at the picnic were, in a sense, only giving us our own back. Every week of the year we were sent to Sunday school, each with a nickel in a pocket or tied in the corner of a handkerchief for the collection plate. By today's standards, the purchasing power of one of those nickels was fantastic; to give them away, for some purpose only remotely understandable when they were so scarce and hard to come by, was probably one of our great lessons in self-denial, particularly on a hot summer day when the appeal of cold bottles of pop in the Chinese restaurant at the other end of Main Street was almost irresistible. If one of us claimed to have forgotten his collection money and later was seen with candy or pop, suspicion was immediate that he had been unable to resist the temptation, and we shuddered at the thought of the punishment that would be visited on him, in the next world if not in this. I remember one occasion when three of us conspired to commit the crime and, unlikely as it was that three of us in the same class of eight or nine would coincidentally forget our collection, carried out the dastardly deed. Immediately guilt began to weigh on our consciences, and I was positive that when the weekly collection figure was chalked up on the little blackboard at the front of the church, the fact that it should have been fifteen cents greater must have been obvious to all. The figure was our personal "Mene, Mene, Tekel, Upharsin," signifying that we had been judged and set aside for future punishment. However, nothing in the way of divine retribution happened to us before we got to the restaurant, so we enjoyed our ill-gotten treats.

Guilt-inspiring occasions such as these were extremely rare, however, although they were experienced by most of us at one time or another. And certainly the moral teaching we received in our Sunday school was instrumental in convincing us that what we had done was wrong, although it must be admitted that the effect of conscience seemed to vary considerably from one of us to the next. Our village, like any other community, had its good boys and bad boys, its good girls and bad girls, the proportionate distribution of each type seemingly little affected by our attendance at Sunday school. Perhaps the most lasting effect on all of us was that when we did those things that we ought not to have done, we knew we were doing wrong.

We were not unconscious, either, of the paradoxes in our society. We knew not only our own contemporaries, but the older generation as well.

We knew which ones had a tendency to sharp business practices, or were stingy, or inconsiderate, or cruel, but who seemed to be just as religious as others when it came to attending church, while some who never set foot inside a church were kind and considerate and exemplary citizens. For children, these paradoxes were difficult to resolve but, fortunately, our Sunday school training also taught us to be tolerant.

One example of intolerant prejudice among our church-going elders rankles still. The church was planning a fowl supper, and the owner of the Chinese restaurant, a regular church-goer, had been invited to carve. Upon hearing this, one member of the congregation who apparently was in a position of some authority opined that he wouldn't eat anything carved by a "Chink" and insisted that the invitation be withdrawn. How the painful task was performed I don't know, but as a result the restaurant owner ceased to attend weekly services. However, at Christmas he would slip quietly into the church and take a seat at the back. I was a child at the time and was told of the incident by my parents some years later. My heart still aches when I recall it.

In the winter, attendance at Sunday school sometimes took much more physical than moral fortitude. In sub-zero weather when the wind blew from the north, it swept unchecked across the fields, hurling itself against the little church, which literally creaked on its foundations. Often the two stoves were barely adequate to battle the chill that had soaked into the empty building, unheated during the week except for Thursday evenings when the choir practised, and then only to the extent that the temperature was bearable for those wearing an overcoat.

For most of the years of my childhood, the church was tended by a youth who had been partially disabled by polio and whose story was an example of how prairie villages of the time "looked after their own." When he was stricken with the disease, at that time almost a death sentence, his treatment was arranged for by the members of the local Masonic Lodge in a special hospital for polio victims operated by their international organization. Later, when he was old enough, he was hired by the United Church congregation as caretaker of the church. Happily, I can add that he went on to a successful career in the hotel business.

While preparing the church, he kept track of the time with a big pocket watch of the variety that could be bought at that time for a dollar. Promptly at ten minutes to eleven he grasped the bell rope and tugged mightily. The bell pealed out from its steeple as a signal to all the towns-people that it was time to start out for the church. Again, precisely at 11:00 o'clock, he rang the bell for a few seconds, and as the last reverbera-tions died away inside the church the organ began signalling the start of the service.

The matter of music for the church and Sunday school was always one of great concern. Fortunately, our village was a truly musical commu-nity and there was always someone willing to take on the chores of organ-ist and choir director, including my mother at various times, the pianist of the local dance band, and several teenagers, including my sister, who took their turns for the Sunday school and later for the church as they progressed to a satisfactory stage in their music lessons. At one time we even had a Sunday-school orchestra, which played all the hymns and which comprised two or three members of the dance band, one or two amateur instrumentalists who usually played only for their own amusement and our village doctor who sang a beautiful bass with the church choir in the evenings and played trombone for Sunday school in the mornings. I was always fascinated by the beautiful tones he could produce with the trom-bone and ached to get my hands on it, but for a youngster even to touch it was to court a dire consequence in the form of the most reproving stare I have ever seen anyone produce.

The pealing of the bell also announced the evening church services at ten minutes to seven and 7:00 p.m. These services were attended only by adults and young people past their middle teens. For the minister, it was the last service in what had been a long and arduous day, for he would have held services in two or three country schools around the village in the morning and afternoon.

One minister, when I was eight or nine years old, carried out these duties in winter travelling by horse and cutter. The horse was stabled in a small barn behind the manse and was tended, harnessed and driven by the minister himself. In fair weather, the minister must have enjoyed those drives, but when the weather turned nasty there was considerable risk involved. He wore a buffalo-hide coat, and a lap robe of the same shaggy material was wrapped around him in the sleigh, but even with these, he was probably cold; a Saskatchewan winter wind could pierce a human to the marrow in a matter of minutes.

Had a real blizzard blown up, there was considerable danger of losing one's way if the tracks drifted over or if one lost sight of familiar land-marks and veered away from the trail. If the snow was deep already, huge drifts could form in practically no time, and then it would be up to the man to help the horse as it floundered helplessly in chest-deep snow. But almost always he was at the church when the evening service was to begin, and there was an aura of snug comfort in the gathering while one listened to the sermon and felt the soothing radiance of heat pouring from the stoves. At such a time, with the black winter night wrapping itself close around the tiny structure and with the building frame creaking and snap-ping in the chill wind, the little congregation could easily imagine itself isolated on some small island of peace and heavenly mercy.

As my boyish thoughts wandered from the scene and searched among a thousand unknown places for a thousand unknown things, I was often lulled into a state of near hypnosis by the drone of the minister's voice addressing itself to the adults. Then there would be a sound, incongruous but well known, and the youngsters would look at one another and grin. The sound was caused by an elderly man who never missed church; nei-ther did he miss bringing with him some candy, which he carried in the side pocket of his suit coat in the noisiest cellophane bags ever made. We would listen with glee as his hand rattled around in his pocket seeking admission to the bag and, in the quiet of the church, the din created by the crackling cellophane was fantastic. Eventually, after what seemed like eons, his hand would emerge and he would slip into his mouth a candy that could be sucked for several minutes. As the man was partially deaf, he never was aware of the diversion he created, nor do I ever recall it happen-ing more than once during a service no matter how long the sermon. But it was a magic moment for us youngsters.

And so the little church, too, constituted an intimate part of our vil-lage home. As the seasons of our childhood rolled by, each week we made our way to the small frame-and-siding building, up to our knees in snow in the winter, leaping the meltwater in the ditches in the spring when crocuses bloomed in the reflected heat from the south wall of the church, or scuffing along the cinder path past the dusty caragana hedge fronting the church in the summer. I can only hope that as many prayers were answered for others as there were for me.

Here and There

HOSPITALS WERE FEW and far between in Saskatchewan during the Depression, so it was a source of pride for the village to have one. It stood alone at the eastern end of Second Avenue and faced west, its front door exactly in line with the centre of the street, thus effectively blocking any future extension of that avenue to the east. It had been built by the town about the time the Depression started and its continued existence involved a constant struggle by the women of the Hospital Aid Society and its board to keep it solvent, staffed and equipped.

It stood in its own yard, surrounded by a sturdy barbed-wire fence to keep out the cattle and horses that grazed occasionally on the prairie grass surrounding it. In front of the front door looped a gravel driveway surrounding a circular flower bed, which was edged with whitened field stones from which, through the years, the whitewash gradually disappeared. In spite of the devoted efforts of some village women, little grew successfully in the bed except for a few straggly geraniums and clumps of pigweed.

The front door opened into a corridor that extended about two-thirds of the length of the building, terminating at a dispensary door. On the left, immediately inside the front door, was the doctor's office, which functioned not only as his private sanctum but also as the diagnostic area, dentist's office and operating room. Here were the dentist's chair, his foot-powered drill, glass cupboards full of shiny dental and surgical instruments, and other mysterious and fearful objects. Farther along on the left were the nurses' quarters. On the opposite side of the corridor were the patients' rooms, the door of each displaying a plaque informing the public that the room had been furnished by one or another of the area's women's organizations. Beyond the dispensary were a back door and the stairway into the basement, which housed the kitchen, furnace room and laundry area.

Fortunately for the village, the doctor who presided over the institution from the mid-1920s to the mid-1940s was a medical jack-of-all-trades. He had served in the Canadian Army Medical Corps during the First World War, where he had specialized in plastic facial surgery and, after coming to our town, he provided the nearest thing to "womb-to-tomb" medical service possible for one man to accomplish. Besides being a medical doctor and surgeon, he was a dentist and, later, a dental surgeon. He ushered most of my contemporaries into the world, set our broken limbs, repaired our teeth, removed our appendixes and tonsils and pooh-poohed our imaginary ailments.

Children were no different then from what they are now, so it was not with any great eagerness that we visited the doctor/dentist's office. My first terrifying encounter with the dentist's chair went off rather well, I thought. I cannot recall just what stage had been reached in the procedure, but it was relatively early in the encounter when I, frightened beyond reasonable control, took advantage of an opening, popped the doctor a punch on the nose, and took off down the street as fast as my six- or seven-year-old legs would carry me. We children always held the doctor somewhat in awe, both because of his position in the community and his natural remoteness of manner. For my part, after that incident I was never able establish a feeling of trust between us. This was doubly strange because, through the years of our childhood and youth I spent considerable time in his home with his son, who was my closest friend.

The close association with the doctor's home was profitable for me in spite of the strained relations between us. The doctor read a great deal and had an excellent private library. My friendship with his son gave me access to the books in that library, thereby contributing greatly to my knowledge and entertainment. I recall one book in particular because I coveted it so much. It was an edition of *The Count of Monte Cristo*, printed on fine rice paper and bound in black leather. I read it several times, and each time having to return it to its owner wrenched my heart. Perhaps, because of that book, I now hate to part with any I have read and enjoyed, and I disliked public libraries because they insist on having their books back!

I did not escape from my next professional encounter with the doctor, but apparently I tried. I was taken into the hospital for a minor operation and, as was usual at that time, was anaesthetized with ether. We youngsters knew that one must be very careful when using ether on an animal, such as a dog with its nose full of porcupine quills, because the dog's terror combined with only a small amount of ether often was fatal. Perhaps in my case the same conditions applied; I was told afterwards that I had died on the operating table. My heart had stopped beating.

How the doctor got me going again I don't know, but I was certainly the rage of the younger set when I recounted to them that I had really and truly been dead for a time. I was forced to conclude, however, that ether must anaesthetize the soul as well as the body, because I had not got to talk with Saint Peter, nor had I even seen the Pearly Gates. All I remembered was awakening to a deathly nausea that continued for most of a day in spite of the ministrations of the lone nurse in the institution.

Usually the nurses worked alone. During those lean years the hospital could afford to hire only one at a time, and there was a steady progression of them. But sometimes, when the workload became too heavy, a former nurse who had married into the community would be called back as a part-time assistant to the resident nurse. And there were times when there was no permanent nurse and the staff consisted entirely of these local conscripts. However, the doctor who was in our village when I was a youngster had a permanent operating room nurse always at his side – his wife.

Socially, the lives of single nurses were closely circumscribed, with the added disadvantage that the hospital demanded twenty-four-hour-a-day attendance to their duties, except on those rare occasions when there were no patients in the hospital. When that happy circumstance came about the nurse could go to the movies, or attend a local dance. It was a difficult life for nurses, and there was little wonder that many stayed only a short time. Others found enough social contact in the village to marry there. Although marriage didn't require their dismissal, most did leave the twenty-four-hour-a-day service and were added to the reserve of part-timers available in times of need.

It was one of the nurses, as I recall, who created a major furore by smoking in public. It couldn't have been more than a few hours after the time she was seen smoking before it was being talked about throughout the entire village, and, if the deed didn't exactly make her a "scarlet woman," it certainly added a pink tinge to her reputation. She, I remember, openly defied criticism by smoking in the Chinese restaurant and in the waiting room of the rink when skating or curling. We youngsters ogled this performance in open-mouthed amazement, whispering comments to one another while we waited for God to strike her dead. He didn't, and the novelty soon wore off.

In spite of all economic vicissitudes, the little hospital survived throughout the Depression and continued to minister to the illnesses and accidents that beset our friends and neighbours. Our family certainly appreciated its existence. Only a few years earlier my mother, to get medical attention for my sister, had to take her about eight miles by horse and cutter to another railway line and another twenty or so miles by train. In the mid-thirties a severe illness in a farm family in winter could be catastrophic.

If the doctor could be reached by telephone, it would be decided whether the patient was to be brought to the hospital or if the doctor must go to the patient. If the former, it could mean that the patient would spend hours bedded down in a sleigh box before reaching hospital; if the latter, it often meant a long journey for the doctor in a cutter across the snowy countryside, often the same cutter the minister used for his Sunday visits to his country congregations. If the weather were very bad, it might be decided that a one-horse cutter was too risky, and a team of heavier horses would be harnessed to a bobsled with a driver to take the doctor to his patient. If the farm home had no telephone, it might be necessary for some member of the family to harness a team, drive an hour or more to town, take the doctor to the farm home and then drive him back to town after he had treated the patient.

Sometimes the case was a difficult one, and the village doctor would decide to send the patient to a city hospital. It was ironic that on some occasions it took the patient longer to arrive at the hospital in the village from a farm home only a few miles away than it subsequently took to transport him or her seventy miles to a city hospital by air. The aircraft usually used, a single-engine Stinson Detroiter based in Saskatoon, was equipped with wheels and skis and had an enclosed cabin large enough to accommodate the pilot, patient and doctor.

As well as being the birthplace for many of the new generation, the little hospital provided death beds for many of the first settlers. One particular death was a sad blow to all in the village and surrounding country. This was the death of a farm woman, a nurse who in the years before the village had a doctor or hospital had provided the medical attention required by families for miles around. She had delivered many of the babies born in farm and village homes, including me, born in the bed in which I was conceived. She was universally loved.

Her death was the first to strike me personally. As a small child I visited her farm, sometimes for several days at a time, and was permitted to perform what to me were very grown-up tasks, such as dropping pieces of seed potatoes into holes that she dug, or assisting her husband with the operation of the cream separator even though when the crank handle went around I was lifted right off of the floor. Her funeral was the grandest in the village during my time there and perhaps to this day. It was held in the village theatre and was attended ecumenically by hundreds from the town and countryside. Every square foot of the theatre not occupied by people was filled with flowers. Later, memorial gates bearing her name were mounted at the local cemetery in one of the most universal outpourings of love and esteem I have ever witnessed. *on my birthday*

A village institution of more immediate significance to youngsters was the town fire hall. It stood near the centre of town to the west of Main Street on First Avenue and consisted of a frame building with a concrete floor. It accommodated the three hand-pulled fire engines and a huge wooden tank some eight or ten feet in diameter and six or eight feet high, mounted on a six-foot-high concrete base, for the storage of the town's supply of potable water. An annex on the west side contained the foundation platform for a windmill, the shaft of which extended through the roof and which pumped the bulk of the water, although in the annex there was also a single-cylinder pump engine that provided power for the pump on those rare occasions when the prairie wind failed.

Because it had to be heated, and also because some member of nearly every family in town had to visit it at least once a day for water, it became a sort of town social centre, for the males particularly. And in the winter it was a convenient place for youngsters to drop in to get warm. Heat was provided by a pot-bellied stove, which was kept burning day and night throughout the winter. Around the stove there were three or four chairs of assorted types, including one captain's chair with a pillow, somewhat the worse for wear, which was the throne and seat of authority of the caretaker.

He was a bachelor of indeterminate age and uncertain background who had come to the village originally as a teamster and drayman, employed by the operator of the livery barn. With the passing of horses from the scene, he stayed on doing odd jobs and finally was engaged by the village to look after the fire hall. Most of the time he was to be found in his chair conversing with those who came for water or who had just dropped in for a chat.

Every village should have at least one personality such as he. He was possessed of a delightful sense of humour, a wry mode of expression and acute powers of observation, particularly where the foibles of human beings were concerned. He applied labels in the form of nicknames to most men in the village with devastating accuracy. And they stuck. Years later the labels he assigned were still in daily use, and many of us had difficulty recalling one or another person's real name.

There was, for example, a businessman in the village who, in the winter, always wore cheap cotton gloves of the type that made the wearer's hands resemble those of Disney's Mickey Mouse. These gloves were always loose and had a tendency to slip off. The man had developed a habit of pushing his gloves back on at every third or fourth step by brushing the backs of his hands downward on the seat of his trousers. In all probability most of us would have taken no notice of this characteristic gesture had not the caretaker one day labelled him "Pat M'Ass." From that day forward he was Pat M'Ass to the young men and boys of the village – but not within his earshot or that of our parents.

The caretaker spoke with a pronounced drawl, completely unlike the speech of anyone else we knew. He did totally unexpected things with the language and was able to convey meanings that went far deeper than the words themselves. Thus, when he spoke of one farmer as "The Squire," his drawl added an opinion on that person's character that would have taken a page of written words to convey. It was devastating when applied to names ending in the diminutive ie, such as Bobbie or Willie. When we said them they were names; when he said them they were character sketches.

The caretaker also had a penchant for "grain and the grape." Because money was so scarce, the opportunities for him to indulge this taste were relatively infrequent – at least after village council, as his employer, took control. Before this, when he was paid at the end of the month the sudden affluence would go to his head in the form of alcohol fumes. The next day he would be broke again, which really wouldn't have mattered much except that he probably had neglected to pay for his board and room at the local hotel. So the elected representatives of the people arranged that his lodgings and sustenance would be paid for first with the balance going to him in cash, providing enough money for perhaps one boozy session and pipe tobacco for the month.

Because there was no liquor store in the village, the preferred beverage for his occasional binge was a concoction he called "rubby-dub," a mixture of rubbing alcohol and soda pop. Why it didn't kill him is a mystery, but I have wondered often if the druggist, knowing his habits, might mercifully have substituted ethyl alcohol for the denatured spirits that should have been in the rubbing alcohol bottle. I hope so.

He smoked continually, sucking on a bent-stemmed pipe with a huge bowl, and it was unusual to see him without the pipe in his mouth. What kind of tobacco he smoked I don't know, but it was sufficiently powerful that on the occasions when we tried it, the results were nearly always disastrous. While we puffed, choked and turned green, he would sit placidly in his chair, a hint of a smile at the corners of his mouth and a thin spiral of smoke arising from the bowl of his pipe, the picture of innocent detachment.

Perhaps the best thing about our relationship with the caretaker was that although he was an adult, older than most of our parents, we could talk to him about anything, without fear, and get an adult answer. Probably a good deal of the information he gave us was flawed, but the main thing was that we could ask him questions we could not have brought ourselves to ask anyone else. He dealt with our questions as though they were serious matters, worthy of consideration. Who else could we ask, for example, if it really was possible to make a buggy whip from a bull's pizzle?

He also provided us with much of our sex education. We never wondered how he, a bachelor, had got to know so much about the subject. Naturally, when we were young teen-agers, sex was a frequent topic of conversation, and when some wild assertion was made he would quietly put down the purveyor of false information and set us straight. To be sure, his handling of the subject of human sexuality was more than a little ribald, but, from the bawdy humour and lurid comment, we were able to sort out a good deal of fact.

At the same time, we got some of our sex education in a roundabout way. There was published at that time a tabloid that carried rather lurid stories of various forms of sexual dalliance amid a plethora of advertisements for "rubber products," which, we soon learned, were not rubber boots or automobile tires. These tabloids were obtained by one of the leading male members of the community who, when he had finished with them, gave them to our friend the caretaker who in turn passed them on to us. I don't believe they did us any harm, but I have often been amused by this situation – we of the younger generation were being "corrupted" unknowingly by one of the community's foremost citizens.

According to some of the older members of the community, the caretaker had been one of the best horse handlers in the country in his younger days, but in the course of his career his legs had been broken an unknown number of times. In addition, he was so bow-legged that he rolled rather than walked down the street, his toes pointing inward on about a thirty-degree angle and his shoulders weaving back and forth through an arc of about two feet. His old injuries caused him considerable discomfort as he aged, a condition he described as "rheumatiz," eased to some extent by his constant and close attendance on the fire-hall stove.

He owned, as far as we could tell, only what he wore or could carry in his pockets. His garb in summer consisted of a pair of black trousers with big police-type suspenders, a heavy work shirt, ankle-high boots and a battered felt hat. In the winter he added an old cardigan. I don't remember ever seeing him with an overcoat or a pair of gloves. Fortunately, his first residence was a one-room shack just across the street from the fire hall, and later he lived in the hotel, which was less than a block away, so he had to spend little time outdoors. Other than tending the fire, seeing that the big water tank was kept full and keeping the interior of the building tidy, he spent his time in his captain's chair, from which, through the window, he commanded a view of the town's main intersection. From this apparently constricted viewpoint he was able to keep amazingly close tabs on what went on in the village, and I have thought he must have had either some form of second sight or deductive reasoning powers that would have made Sherlock Holmes look like an amateur.

I can recall only one occasion when he really lost his temper with us children, and that time we deserved it. There were four or five of us in the fire hall at the time and one of the boys noticed a loop of half-inch rope dangling from one of the overhead pipes, about the level of his neck. While we watched, he stuck his head through the loop and twirled around tightening the loop around his neck. Suddenly he slumped, and the care-taker, with a speed we would not have believed possible, leaped across the room bowling the rest of us out of the way like ten pins. Lifting the boy in his arms, he quickly unwound the rope from the boy's neck and in a few moments the boy regained his senses. The whole group of us was chased from the building in a shower of curses such as we had never heard before and are unlikely ever to hear again. We were forbidden ever to set foot in the place again, and the threats as to what would happen to us if we did were marvels of vituperative imagination. We hurried off, leaving the old man white and shaking in the pump-house doorway. The next day we were back again and were received as if nothing had happened – but the rope was gone.

On the peak of the fire-hall roof was a cupola containing a large bell, fourteen to sixteen inches in diameter, with a tone that sent shivers down our spines. When it was rung there was a fire, and fire, in a village where many of the business buildings stood only a few feet apart and all were built entirely of wood, was catastrophic. It is impossible to describe the gut-wrenching sensation one had when awakened from sleep by the bell's dreadful clangour.

The rope attached to the fire bell hung down outside the south wall of the building, right beside the double doors through which the fire en-gines could be pulled. Whoever discovered a fire would rush to the fire hall and toll the bell as loudly as he could while he waited for the men of the village to arrive so he could direct them to the fire. Too often, by the time people were roused from their sleep, threw on some clothes and reached the fire hall, there was not much need for directions. The few minutes' start that a fire had were usually enough to make it visible from anywhere in town and to guarantee destruction of the building in which it had begun and often several others as well.

A fire in such a village could be hugely destructive. I remember one particularly serious one, in 1939, which began in the upstairs living quarters of a combined general store and garage around 7:00 a.m. one winter morning when the occupant lit a stove that had leaked gasoline during the night. The fire destroyed that building, a two-storey restaurant building, the village post office and a poolroom-barbershop with living quarters at the rear. All the buildings were reduced to ashes before we children had to be in school at 9:00 a.m.

Most often, the town's tiny fire engines were of little help against a fire that had become well established. There were three of these machines, two with single tanks and one with two, all mounted horizontally on steel-rimmed wheels, each equipped with a tongue as well as ropes that could be extended in front so several men could pull each one. Combined, I doubt if they had a total capacity of more than 300 or 400 gallons of water. After being filled with water, each tank had a pre-measured paper bag of soda broken into it, which was dissolved by an agitator crank on one end. A bottle of sulphuric acid was placed under a pressure-tight cap and broken into the tank by means of a lever. With further agitation, the water, soda and acid together released carbon-dioxide, which pressurized the tank and propelled the water through a hose. A metal box placed across the front of each engine contained additional bags of soda and bottles of acid. As soon as the alarm had gathered a few men, they would take off with the fire engines while others went immediately to the livery stable, harnessed a team of dray horses to a water tank mounted on a wagon chassis and took it to the fire hall to be filled as an auxiliary source of water for the fire engines. Someone else would start up the pump engine in the fire hall to ensure that the main tank was kept as full as possible. But all this effort most often was futile except possibly for the morale boost it gave the men who were doing at least something.

There were two other major fires during my childhood that ripped great chunks out of the downtown business area. The first occurred when I was so young I was told to stay in bed, and I could only watch from my bedroom window as the flames ate about half the buildings on the west side of Main Street's principal business block. Three or four years later another fire completely destroyed a large two-storey building containing a general store and family living quarters. This time, the fire engines performed a useful function by preventing the fire from spreading to a drugstore some twenty feet from the building that was destroyed. Burned in this fire, too, was a quantity of binder twine, almost a boxcarful, which had been stacked beside the store and which burned for a day or two almost without flame, pulsating and glowing in waves of intense heat as the prairie breezes eddied around it.

The sites of these fires, after they had cooled down, were great hunting places for young boys. Strange and wonderful were the things we found – blobs of melted glass in weird shapes and colours, machines such as counter scales, cheese cutters and cash registers, still recognizable but now Dali-esque in shape and proportion. Occasionally someone would find a blob of what had been coins, fused into a blackened lump. After one fire a large iron safe was removed from the burnt-out basement, its sides bulged and warped. On it was placed a four-foot cast-iron eagle perched on a globe, which had fallen, undamaged, from the roof of the building. The eagle stood on a street corner on its weird pedestal for several years until, after another fire, a new building was constructed on the site. I was always sorry that the Case farm-machinery company had not adopted the phoenix for its symbol rather than the eagle. It would have been more appropriate! The Case dealership continued across the street from its salvaged emblem.

A few fires were discovered in sufficient time so that even our limited fire-fighting apparatus was able to extinguish them before serious damage was done. One such fire was discovered early in the morning in a large farm-machinery and automobile garage. When the townspeople and fire engines arrived, the fire was contained inside the building, and because the doors and windows were closed the flames died from lack of oxygen. When we peered through the windows, the inside of the building was illuminated by a dull, luridly red glow that looked more like the inside of the firebox of a poorly stoked furnace.

Some of the men rushed to open the doors to get at the fire, but fortunately one of the village businessmen of commanding presence assessed the situation and stopped them. He directed them to break out one or two small window panes farther away from the fire instead, through which hoses could be directed on its source. In a comparatively short time the fire was out, but I have always been curious to know just how great an explosion there would have been had the doors been opened and a rush of air been admitted to that super-heated and gas-filled atmosphere.

Outside the fire hall on the east side stood a wooden watering trough for horses, and through the wall, above the trough, protruded a pipe with a tap from which one could fill a bucket. This was the source for all of the village's drinking water. Carrying water was a task assigned mainly to males, and as we grew, so did the size of the pails we carried. This became a source of income, too, as some of us boys were hired to carry water to homes where there were no children to perform the task. Around the trough in summer was a quagmire created by the overflow from the trough and the action of horses' hooves.

In winter, the spillage caused a build-up of ice, which gradually rose toward the top edge of the trough and which spread out in concentric waves across the sidewalk and into the street. When it snowed, this rise became almost unclimbable or, if one was able to mount it successfully and drew a pail of water, the manoeuvre was fraught with danger. Nearly everyone, at one time or another, landed on his or her seat on the ice while endeavouring to dodge the water from their own pail. Around the mid-thirties a new tank was installed in the fire hall, and at the same time an indoor tap was provided so one could draw a pail of water in comfort and security in the coldest weather. The horse trough has long since disappeared, but I remember well the many times when we were small having to balance precariously on its edge to reach the tap.

For a time when I was very small there was a community drinking cup on a chain at the tap. Later, when the cup had been removed for hygienic reasons, we had to drink straight from the stream from the pipe or from our cupped hands. As we had usually been using our hands for anything from pulling the wings off grasshoppers to petting sweaty horses, there is some doubt in my mind as to which system was more hygienic.

On the west side of the fire hall, next to the windmill, was a concrete paddling pool. It covered an area of about fifteen by twenty-five feet and sloped from two or three inches deep at one end to around sixteen inches deep at the other. When newly filled with water from the deep well, it was icy cold, and even on a hot day one could hardly stand the chill. But since the pool was small and shallow, the water heated quickly under the sun and soon was almost lukewarm. Because of the constant drift of dust from the gravelled streets, as well as the dirt we tracked in, the paddling pool was soon the consistency of soup. In the mornings, after the water had been standing undisturbed through the night, the bottom of the pool would be as slippery as grease with silty sediment. There was no system for chlorination or filtration and so, I suppose, it should have been a marvellous source for epidemics of infections of one type or another. I don't remember any.

The clarity of the pool's water was not improved by the fact that we used it for a number of pursuits other than paddling. If, for example, a frog or toad was discovered in the damp weeds around the pumphouse, into the pool it would go to be a plaything for a time. Or we would watch with fascination the uncannily smooth undulations of a garter snake as it rippled its way along the surface. Toy boats of assorted shape and sizes found their way into the pool, and we were intrigued for a time by one variety, which presaged the jet engine. It had a tiny boiler with a vibrating top heated by a small pan of alcohol. As the top vibrated, squirts of steam were ejected through a tube below the water line to propel the boat along while another tube sucked in more water to continue the action. Of course, the pool often was littered with assorted debris that at one time or another had seemed useful to us – tin cans, stones, sticks and even old car parts that had some momentary fascination for splashing, creating waves, or just annoying someone.

When we were paddling-pool sized, most boys had tricycles as their chief form of transportation. These were constant companions, capable of representing any form of transportation we might desire, from a bronco to a Pierce-Arrow, and our tricycles were never more than a few feet from wherever we might be disporting ourselves at the moment. At the signal provided by the whistle of a train engine at the grade crossing a half mile east of the village, it was a matter only of moments for us to abandon the pool, leap on our tricycles and pedal furiously down the block to the railway station to watch the train come in.

At that time, the railway was a functional institution of fundamental importance, and it is strange now to think that after only some fifty years of useful life, except for the basic function of hauling grain away to the markets of the world, the railway's role in the life of the town has diminished to nothing. In the days of our youth, the railway brought in the lumber to build the town, and its food, fuel, mail, inhabitants, travelling salesmen, newspapers, visiting hockey teams, automobiles, farm machinery and, most wonderful of all, it would take us on board for those magical and rare occasions when we were taken to the City.

The arrival of the tri-weekly (also known as the "try-weakly") train from the city was an event of unparallelled excitement. After our helter-skelter rush down the main street, we would abandon our tricycles by the plank platform and dash to the rail side to watch the giant steam engine come thundering down the tracks toward us, its headlight gleaming even in broad daylight. The measure of our courage was expressed in terms of the distance from the edge of the platform at which we stood. Although our reasoned minds told us the train was unalterably guided by the rails and that the edge of the platform was about a foot or more from any projection on the train, we could not free our minds from the thought that perhaps, just perhaps, the juggernaut might deviate from its pre-scribed course and grind us into oblivion. It was a heart-stopping mo-ment when, standing only inches from the edge of the platform, we watched the massive machine roar past, its main and connecting rods clanking and its huge counter-balanced drive wheels, taller than we, slowing as the en-gineer braked the train to a squealing stop, its express cars at the platform.

A few minutes before the train was due, the town dray would have arrived at the station. This was a large, flat-bedded wagon, decked with oak and steel strapping. It was drawn by a magnificent team of huge Clydesdales with heavily muscled backs as broad as a sidewalk and hooves with prints the size of dinner plates. The dray was backed up against the edge of the platform opposite the rails and, through long custom, the horses stood placidly as the train racketed into the station fifteen feet behind their rumps. On the platform, the station agent pushed the ex-press wagon to the edge of the platform, and it was always a matter of wonder to us that the train's engineer could stop the train with the door of one of the express cars perfectly in line with the wagon.

In the summer, the door of the express car would be opened before the train came in, and scarcely would the wheels have shrieked to a halt before the men in the train would be pushing barrels, boxes and bags out the door to the agent and drayman who stacked them quickly on the wagon and on the platform after the wagon was filled. The unloading seemed to take only a minute or two, while passengers dismounted from the single passenger coach at the rear of the train, always with a long step down to the squat step placed by the trainman or conductor on the cinder roadbed beyond the end of the platform. The conductor, known to all, would exchange greetings with bystanders and, when he saw that the un-loading was completed, would toss the auxiliary step into the vestibule of the coach, call out a long-drawn "b-o-o-ard" and wave a hand signal to the engin-eer. The bell on the engine started to clang and the train began to move.

As the train gathered speed and the passenger coach passed the platform, the trainman would reach out, grab the handrail near the rear vestibule of the passenger coach and nonchalantly swing aboard while we marvelled at this death-defying gesture. Then we stood, squinting into the afternoon sunlight, as the train dwindled in the distance down the tracks, which ran arrow-straight toward the elevators of the next town, ten miles to the west.

Meanwhile, the drayman loaded the dray in neat order, placing together the assorted items to be delivered to the business establishments in the town, things for the farthest business at the front. If there was room on the dray, and there usually was, we rode along on it; if not, we walked along behind or rode on the tailgate. The tailgate was a single metal-edged wooden plank three or four inches high, which, when not installed, dangled swinglike behind on two short lengths of chain.

First call was made at the Chinese restaurant. Here were unloaded wooden cases of bottled pop, cardboard boxes with labels revealing that they contained chocolate bars or tobacco or cigarette papers or chewing tobacco, and, finally, big blue canvas cylinders, heavily insulated and dripping ice water, containing tall, slender steel cans of ice cream from the creameries in the city. Then, weaving across the street, the dray came to the drugstore where similar boxes were carried into the shop, plus bundles of magazines and newspapers, boxes containing big bottles of rich syrups for the soda fountain and others with mysterious and tongue-twisting labels, full of patent medicines and drugs for compounding prescriptions.

Unguided, the horses tugged the dray diagonally across the gravelled street to the next stop, one of the general stores. Here the foodstuffs to be unloaded varied with the season, but in the summer there would be flat cases of cherries or peaches from Ontario or British Columbia and baskets of purple Concord grapes, each basket made from paper-thin wood and each with its own curved handle and a bit of purple net set into the lid through which the fruit could be seen and through which its own little cloud of fruit flies buzzed, accompanying the rich odour of fermenting grapes. At all seasons there were burlap bags or, as we called them, gunny sacks, of dry foods like navy beans, sugar, coffee beans, peanuts in their shells and a host of other products imported in bulk. In the store these sacks were emptied into bins or stood open-mouthed on the floor and their contents were weighed out into paper bags in quantities requested by customers. There were also the tall tapered and slatted cylinders of banana crates, taller than a small boy and packed with some variety of dried tropical grass. We treated these with considerable caution, having heard tales of "banana spiders," which were reputed to arrive in the crates, their bite meaning instant death!

Huge cheeses in circular wooden boxes sewn in burlap were unloaded, as were big cubes of salt for cattle, and children, to lick, boxes of shoes and rolls of yard goods, straw hats and baseball caps, needles and threads and knitting wool, redolent rolls of oilcloth for farm kitchen tables and all of the thousand and one other things a small village and farm community needed.

With their reins looped around a post on the dray, the horses moved on again to the next stop, a garage and farm-machinery dealership, to unload machinery parts still sticky with gobs of red and green paint, and cotton bags containing small parts. At the hardware store there were wooden kegs of nails, big sheets of "tin" (actually galvanized iron), lead-heavy bars of solder and boxes of dry-cell batteries, rolls of wire, bundles of chain and pails of paint, pots and pans and kettles and stove grates and curling irons and coal-oil lamps.

After the town had voted to "go wet" (to the extent of allowing the hotel to have a beer parlour for men twenty-one or older only) the next stop for the dray would be the hotel, where wooden kegs of beer were rolled off the back of the dray and down the steps into the cool, musty-smelling basement. Bottled beer came in cardboard cartons of twenty-four bottles, each bottle in its own grey paper sleeve and nested neck-to-bottom with the others in overlapping layers. These were important to us because when they were emptied we would gather them along the roadsides, and they constituted one of our principal sources of income. Each one turned back to the hotel netted us one cent.

Finally, at the blacksmith shop across the street from the livery stable, the last items were unloaded – wired clumps of horseshoes, cylinders of oxygen and acetylene for the welding torches, bar- and angle-iron of various dimensions in heavy bundles or single pieces, kegs of horseshoe nails and the huge circles of replacement steel tires for wagon wheels. Then the dray would make a U-turn in the middle of the street to halt in a dusty grassed space between the edge of the street and the sidewalk. The horses were unhitched, the traces thrown across their backs, and we would be allowed to ride or lead them the forty or fifty feet to the watering trough at the fire hall where they dipped their heads and sucked up noisy gulps of water around their bits while their tails switched and flanks quivered to dislodge the flies swarming to their sweaty hides.

The railway and dray combination was used to provide more bulky commodities required by the village, too. Freight trains brought in boxcarloads of coal and wood, and lumber and cement. Cars of wood and coal were shunted to the rail line nearest the elevators and were positioned next to storage sheds into which they were unloaded by hand via steel chutes and wheelbarrows on planks.

Boxcars containing items not consigned to the rail-side storage sheds were positioned on the centre of the three rail lines and were unloaded on to the dray for transport to the stores or lumberyard. When there was a shipment of flour to be unloaded, the drayman donned a protective leather garment like an apron but with short trouserlike legs on the bottom, ending just above his knees. After the car had been cleared by the station agent, the tin seal on the boxcar door was broken and the door opened. Inside, the 100-pound cloth bags of flour were stacked in interlocking patterns on both sides of the central door, kept clean by heavy kraft paper lining the floor and sides of the car. These the drayman hefted to his shoulder one at a time and carried out the door and across a plank laid to the waiting dray where they were stacked neatly. All the while the horses stood patiently, untethered, occasionally shifting their weight from one hind leg to the other or shaking their heads and manes to dislodge flies, but always without moving the dray an inch from where it had been positioned for the unloading.

As the load grew, the iron-rimmed wheels of the dray sank into the packed cinders along the tracks, so when the load was completed a tremendous heave by the Clydesdales was needed to get the load moving. It was an awe-inspiring sight to watch the giant horses straining into their collars, their muscles rippling under their glistening hides, as they fought for purchase in the cinders, and the final lurching heave as the heavy load started to move. They were animals of majestic beauty.

The dray then made its slow way to the store warehouse to which the flour had been consigned, and the unloading procedure was repeated, the bags carried in to be stacked in criss-cross fashion while the drayman gradually turned white from the flour that sifted through the bags and pasty streaks of sweat streamed down his face.

Coal was another matter. It came loose, and it would stand four or five feet deep in the boxcars and was held in by planks so the boxcar doors could be closed and opened. At first, a steel chute was placed from the top edge of these planks into the coal shed, and two men, one working from each side, shovelled the coal into the chute. If the coal was of the large-lump variety, the men hoisted the lumps, sometimes sixteen inches or more to a side, into the chute by hand, all done in a constant haze of gritty black dust. As the centre of the car inside the doors was cleared and the level of the coal rose in the track-side bin, a point was reached at which the coal would no longer move down the chute by gravity. The planks, removed from their function as door barriers, were laid from car to bin, and the coal was shovelled into wheelbarrows to be wheeled across the bouncing planks and tilted into the shed. It was exciting for us to be called over by the men to see something they had found in the coal, for example a heavy grey-brown cylinder of stone they told us had once been part of a tree.

In the autumn, the middle of the three lines of tracks would be occupied from end to end, perhaps a third of a mile, by empty boxcars, eventually to be filled with grain from the seven elevators along the south side of the tracks. It was the time of year when we children took the opportunity to indulge in a sport known as "running boxcars" and when the station agent started his annual struggle to try to keep us from breaking our necks.

To run boxcars, we climbed the steel ladder to the top of the endmost car and gained the narrow catwalk along the top. We would run, as hard as we could go, the length of the line of cars, and leap across the openings between them. Why this was so exhilarating I don't know, unless it was because of the height and the slight risk of falling, coupled with the fillip of knowing we were doing something we would get the devil for if caught.

When the boxcars were to be loaded, they were "spotted" by a shunting train on the track, which ran within a few feet of the elevators, three or four to each elevator with the centre doors of one just opposite the elevator's grain spout. The cars were carefully swept out, lined with heavy, six-foot-wide kraft paper above the load line inside the car, different for each type of grain, doors were nailed inside the frames of the sliding doors, and the big, flexible metal spout was positioned to fill one end of the car first. When all was ready, the elevator agent pulled and pushed various levers to select the bin in the elevator from which the grain was to come and start it flowing into the car. Almost immediately the boxcar and the area between it and the elevator filled with fine dust as the grain streamed into the car. Inside the elevator, this dust built up on flat surfaces until it reached its critical angle and flowed off the edges of planks and ledges, the remainder lying in wedge-shaped heaps, as warm and soft as talcum powder to our touch.

When one car was filled, the next had to be moved into position, which meant moving not only the loaded car but also the two or three others to which it might be coupled. This was done by the elevator agent using a levered jack and probably did much more than any lesson we had in school to convince us of the power of the lever. The handbrake on the boxcar was released, the jack was inserted between a wheel and the rail, the elevator man put his weight on the end of the five-foot jack handles, and slowly the boxcars began to move. Once moving they could be kept going with little effort and, indeed, it often was more difficult to get them stopped than to keep them going.

Beyond the easternmost grain elevator was the loading platform, a timber structure thirty or forty feet long, its deck at the same height as a freight car's floor. Here, flat cars carrying farm tractors and combines were unloaded, the machines being driven or towed from the cars to the platform across moveable steel plates, a relatively simple task. But unloading one of the larger boxcars carrying brand-new automobiles (known as automobile cars) was an exciting and somewhat risky business, done by the automobile dealer and hired or volunteer help.

There were usually five automobiles in such a boxcar, three end-to-end on the floor and two above, one in each end, held in place by timbers nailed to the boxcar walls. Because the cars had been loaded at the factory from a ramp at the end of the boxcar, getting them in had been a relatively simple matter, but getting them out was not easy, because they had to be removed through a side door. The first to be removed, the one on the floor in the centre, practically had to be carried out. After the timber bracing blocks had been knocked away, several men would push, pull, bounce and turn it until it could come out the door at an acute angle with fractions of an inch to spare on each side. The second and third, also on the floor, were got out easily after that. The exciting time came when the fourth and fifth cars were removed. We watched with bated breath, fearful that one false move would send an auto crashing to the floor of the boxcar.

First, a car was secured to the cross members of the boxcar ceiling by sets of block and tackle and lifted slightly from its supporting timbers, which then were knocked out by men wielding sledge hammers and nail pullers while others held fast to the block-and-tackle chains. When the timbers had been removed, the car was lowered carefully almost to the floor, the wheels were bolted on, and the car was pushed out the side door in the same manner as the others had been, while we all heaved sighs of great relief.

It was thrilling for us when the men climbed into the glistening new automobiles, stepped on the starters, and the engines throbbed into life. It was an even greater thrill if they were the first of the new models and we were allowed to ride in them to the garage where they were being delivered. We saw the Model T Ford supplanted by the model A in 1928, and the simple four-cylinder engine by the V-8 four years later. We were thrilled by the first dual horns and, most miraculous of all, by built-in car radios. We never dreamed that the trucks we watched the men unload were the antecedents of those that one day would practically eliminate the railway's role in our village.

There was one item that arrived on the thrice-weekly train from the city that was never entrusted to the dray. This was the Royal Mail. For all the years of my childhood, whether in summer under the blazing sun or in the blizzards of winter, every train was met by the man who ran the post office pushing a large flat-bedded steel-wheeled handbarrow. At the train he took custody of the mail sacks from the mail car and trundled them up the street the half block to the post office. Once there, he locked himself in the back room behind the closed wicket and sorted the mail either into individual boxes, of which there were fifty or sixty, or into compartments in wooden racks in his locked sanctum. Parcels too large for the boxes were noted on special cards, which were hand-addressed by the postmaster, one for each parcel, and placed in the appropriate mail boxes. These cards were addressed in pencil, and on return the names were carefully erased and the cards used again, often becoming paper-thin in the process. Not until all of the mail had been sorted would the wicket be opened again and communication with the outside world resumed.

The train that brought the mail arrived usually around 2:00 p.m., and the mail was sorted and the wicket opened by 3:00 or 3:30. In the winter, however, the train frequently was late and, as Christmas approached, the additional mail and parcels extended both the time the train was stopped at each station and the time the postmaster required to do his work. This meant that the mail sorting often wasn't completed until long after the early winter dark. Anyone who had a box could get each item as it was sorted into the box but had to wait to claim parcels. Those who didn't have boxes had to wait until the wicket opened. As the sorting time stretched out, more and more people gathered in the front room of the post office, which was only about ten by fifteen feet in dimension.

The dark gloom of this small space was scarcely tinted by the dim glow of one coal-oil lamp mounted on a wall bracket and backed by a circular tin reflector that was supposed to intensify the light. Soon there would scarcely be room to move as more and more of the villagers and farmers crowded into the little space and the floor became an inch-deep puddle of slush as snow melted from boots and overshoes. All succeeding people who entered had a tougher struggle to get in as they forced the door open against the pressure of bodies already inside, and, once in, they would have just as great a struggle to get the door closed again as ice formed from the slush in an ever-thickening wedge on the door sill. The room would be filled with friendly banter since everyone knew everyone else, and the only complaint about the wait might come from some farmer who had a long drive home with a team and sleigh – especially if the expected letter or parcel did not arrive.

Finally the wicket would click open. Individuals, more or less in the order in which they had entered the building, would worm their way through the press of bodies to the wicket to claim their mail. The closer it was to Christmas, the greater was the number of parcels handed out, as gifts selected from the mail order catalogues arrived, some so big the postmaster would have to open the door between the back and front rooms to hand them out. Anything that was unwrapped or otherwise recognizable brought an admonition to all from the recipient that his Betty or Johnny was not to be told by anyone what had arrived.

Mail came in on Mondays, Wednesdays and Fridays. On the alternate days, the process was reversed and the trains took our mail in the opposite direction, to the city and the world. For some thirty years my mother wrote to her mother in Nebraska every week and took these letters to the post office before 10:00 a.m. on Thursdays. Her weekly journey down the main street was a village institution marked particularly by her attire. She donned an apron every morning as soon as she was dressed, and it was so much a part of her normal attire she seldom thought to remove it before starting for the post office. Indeed, had she not been wearing an apron as she walked down the street on Thursday mornings, I am sure everyone who saw her would have jumped to the conclusion that something was radically wrong in our household.

Once in a while, circumstances dictated that her letter was finished barely in time to make the train but too late to go through the post office. This provided another great thrill for me as a boy. The letter would be given to me with instructions to take it to the train, and I would dash down the length of Main Street as the train was pulling into the station, rush along the platform to the mail car and post the letter in a slot in the side of the car. It is interesting to recall that in those days of moving mail by train and with all of the processing done by hand, my mother's letter would be delivered to her mother's door in a city 1,200 miles away and in another country in four days, as regular as clockwork.

Each Wednesday the mail brought delight to the children in what almost became an institution. This was the day a Chicago newspaper's Sunday edition arrived, containing about twelve pages of coloured "funnies." One family subscribed to this paper, and each Wednesday their living room was the gathering place for many of the village children, who, with great tolerance on the part of the family, were invited in to enjoy the comic pages. Who can forget the wild anticipation with which we awaited the months-long outcome of the race in which Barney Google's horse Sparkplug surmounted unbelievable challenges? Or the fantastic adventures of Flash Gordon and Tim Tyler? Each page of the comics would do a slow circle around the group of children lying or sitting on the floor and chesterfield, each double page being read by at least two children at the same time and the curt question, "Finished?" answered by a silent nod before the sheet was turned over. Some of the longest moments of our lives were those when a pair of faster readers had finished both sides of a double page and waited impatiently for a slower group to finish their section and pass it on. The funnies read, we trooped to the door to reclaim our coats and hats and mitts and overshoes, which magically had become flying suits and rocket belts.

At the time, we thought little of the service the little post office

Mogan's which was my second home.

provided us. It, like so many other things, was merely accepted as part of our daily lives. But how different it was from the anonymous clanking of the mailbox lid today when we receive our mail in solitude with no close friends standing by to share our joys or to sympathize in our defeats and disappointments. Then, even buying a thirty-five-cent postal note or a few stamps was a social occasion, while handing an envelope to the moustached postmaster was an act of personal trust as well as a display of our confidence in the fact that our world was run by and for human beings.

This kind of close personal relationship pervaded all the village institutions. As children we hitched our sleighs behind the minister's cutter or rode his horse bareback when he took it to the town well to be watered. From the lumberyard we begged the shingles and laths from which we made the many toys we manufactured for ourselves. The hardware merchant willingly supplied us with the handful of nails we might need. We thumbed through the medical textbooks in the doctor's library. We traded banter with the train crews, laughed at the conductor's jokes and pleaded with the engineer for rides in the cab of the locomotive. We skated and danced and curled with our teachers. We learned the drayman's curses and the postmaster's quiet patience. No institution in our town was cold or foreboding or impersonal. Each was a part of our home.

My Father's Business

THE ECONOMIC NEEDS of the village and surrounding rural areas were looked after by a small group of businesses occupying the "downtown" portion of the village, lined up along one block of Main Street running north from the railway with offshoots into the next block of Main and diverging on either side of Main along First Avenue. After moving to Saskatchewan from Nebraska in 1913, my father farmed for four years and did contract land-breaking as well, having brought with him one of the first gasoline-powered tractors in the area. In 1917 he moved into the hardware business in the village in partnership with another former American, from Montana.

The business was located in a double building on the southwest corner of Main Street and First Avenue, facing Main; the other half of the building accommodated a general store. After the hardware partnership was dissolved, the building was extended west along First Avenue to accommodate my father's automobile and farm-machinery business and showroom, always known as "the garage" or "gradge." This made the building roughly L-shaped for the time being. As he embarked upon new enterprises, further extensions were added until the building assumed a misshapen U form with a variety of roof structures – flat and tarred over the hardware store and general store and the parts department of the automobile business, single-pitched with a false front over the automobile showroom, gambrel on a southward extension added to accommodate a power plant and workshop, and lean-to inside the U when a section that became a morgue was added. Thus the building evolved over a period of fifteen or sixteen years, from 1917 until the early years of the Great Depression.

The business portion of the garage facing First Avenue was divided into two parts by a single step. On the higher level were a counter fronting the parts department and my father's office, and on the lower level to the west, were the automobile showroom with doors on its south side leading into the electric-lighting plant and the morgue. The floors throughout, except the morgue, were oiled wood, fitted fir flooring on the upper level and six-inch planks on the lower. Across the front of the showroom were plate-glass windows, one that for years had a bolt and washer securing a starred fracture where it had been struck by a child's bike.

In the showroom near the upper level stood a big stove, which provided most of the heat. This had been locally manufactured using the bottom of a standard circular heating stove to which had been added a cylindrical top about four feet high made of boiler plate. On the south wall of the showroom, on either side of the door to the plant, were two giant radiators, made of one-and-a-half-inch galvanized pipe, serving the dual functions of assisting in cooling the engines that drove the dynamos and helping the overgrown stove to heat the showroom and shop. A wide automobile door in the west wall gave access to the showroom from outside. The showroom could hold three cars comfortably with room to spare, but in a pinch five could be squeezed in by much very careful manoeuvring.

More or less out of the way between spring and autumn were an old writing desk and several round-backed captain's chairs. With the first snowfall, these were moved closer to the stove, where they remained for the rest of the winter, providing a site for the card games that seemed to continue endlessly throughout the business-free cold months, played by some men from the village and a few farmers who spent the winter months in town. The usual game was one known as smear, and therein lies a tale.

It involves the very religious mother in one family, who had looked on benignly as the children's grandmother taught them to play a card game she called high, low, Jack and the game. However, the mother learned one day that this was the same game as men in the garage played under the name of smear, sometimes wagering nickels on the outcome. The game was immediately banished from the household.

It was in the showroom, too, that the village men gathered in the early winter to lay plans for flooding the skating and curling rinks, or later to make up the draws for the local bonspiels. During the worst years of the Depression, serious discussion always centred around financing the operation of the rinks for the coming winter. It speaks much for their determination that always a way was found.

Near the heat of the homemade radiators stood two big wooden barrels. These, during the winter, were constantly topped up with clean, new-fallen snow, which, when melted, provided the "distilled" water for batteries in automobiles and for radio A batteries. Once any small amount of sediment had been allowed to settle, this water was treated with great care. No metal was allowed to come into contact with it, and it was dispensed carefully by ceramic pitcher and glass containers while the bottom foot or so was never used. If these barrels were well filled at the end of winter, they provided enough water for this purpose to last most of the summer, and only occasionally was it necessary to import big carboys of mechanically distilled water.

Between the plate-glass windows and the entrance door to the east stood two metal racks, about three feet high. Each contained a dozen bottles for lubricating oil of two different qualities and various viscosities. The bottles for the lower quality were jarlike, with screw-on metal tops equipped with spouts; those for the superior quality were tall, tapered and quart-sized with coloured screw-on caps denoting the viscosity. These bottles were filled from barrels equipped with hand pumps. Filling them and wiping them glistening clean became one of my first useful jobs in the garage. At that time there were no dual-viscosity oils for year-round use, and everybody had to change the oil in their cars to a lighter grade in the winter. To save money in winter, some people drained the heavier, summer oil from the engines and kept it warm in pails in their houses, pouring it back into the cars just before starting them up.

The 1920s were the years when the automobile took over most transportation on the prairies, with economic, social and cultural consequences that have been widely discussed. My father allied himself with the Ford Motor Company, although at that time it wasn't unusual for him to make a deal to sell a Chrysler or Durant or any other make a customer might want. Automobiles sold at an astonishing rate then. In one year during the mid-twenties, operating from a village with a population of no more than 250, my father sold 125 Model T Ford cars and trucks. But the Depression diminished this rate and, to a considerable extent, reversed it by repossession. Many of the Model Ts were converted to horse-drawn Bennett Buggies, many cars were repossessed to be sold at auction by finance companies, and many more were simply left to rust where they stood.

During his early years in business, equipping the newly established farms with essential machinery provided him with much of his custom. For example, a major proportion of the windmills erected in the area to pump water for people, animals and gardens bore the inscription L.E. Jones Co. Ltd., his firm's name, on the inside of the galvanized angle-iron uprights. And hundreds of miles of barbed wire with the tons of staples required to fasten it to fence posts came through the hardware business.

By 1926, the village had assumed the proportions and form that was be more or less its shape until after the Second World War. In that year my father installed a power plant to supply the village with electricity, erected the transmission lines, and wired most of the homes and businesses. It seems almost unbelievable now, but the wooden poles for the power lines were purchased for one dollar each, while the crew that erected them was paid fifty cents per pole, the holes being dug with hand-powered post-hole augers. Unfortunately, Father followed Edison's lead in using 110-volt direct current, which caused many problems later when alternating current became the standard for appliance motors.

Power was fed into the system from two dynamos, each belt driven by a big single-cylinder semi-diesel engine, one considerably larger and more powerful than the other. Power distribution was controlled by two vertical slate switch panels with big copper knife switches, which emitted snapping blue sparks when opened. These panels were set up so that power could be supplied to half the town from each engine when demand was high, or to the whole town from either engine when the load was lighter. Normally, one engine could supply the entire village, but on summer Saturday nights, when all the stores remained open to serve farmers on their weekly shopping trips to town, the movie theatre was operating and most of the houses were lighted, both engines were required.

Operating hours were dictated by the season, the plant starting up just before dusk and normally continuing until 12:15 a.m. Each Monday and Tuesday, electricity was supplied from 8:00 a.m. until noon for washing and ironing. Saturday nights in summer the service was extended until 1:00 a.m. Shutdown was delayed also when social events such as dances were being held. The dances usually lasted until 2:00 a.m., so the power remained on until about 2:30 to give townspeople time to get home and into bed before the lights went out. Needless to say, all households were also equipped with oil lamps for use when the power had gone off and on those occasions, which became more frequent, when the system broke down.

As is the case so often when mechanical systems go awry, the initial cause of the frequent breakdowns was human error. Early in the thirties, the man hired to operate the plant forgot to replenish the lubricating oil in the larger of the two engines with the result that it seized up and the crankshaft broke. Father could not afford a new replacement. After investigating iron works in Saskatoon and Regina who might repair the engine, he made a discouragingly long trip with it by truck to Winnipeg but was disappointed to learn that, because of its large diameter and composition, it could not be welded. The unrepairable crankshaft was abandoned in Winnipeg and the engine was dismantled, never to operate again.

Through the Depression years, Father tried various improvisations to replace the engine, such as using the belt drives on tractors, but these were only marginally successful, resulting in frequent failures when the load was heaviest – much to the despair of the operator of the local movie theatre. In the early forties, financial conditions permitted the installation of a multi-cylinder diesel engine with direct clutch drive to the larger dynamo, ending the breakdowns.

The man whose carelessness had precipitated the problems was discharged and seldom had regular employment subsequently. He became the town's lone avowed communist and railed against capitalist exploiters of the working class at every opportunity – he being the epitome of the working man and my father the representative of greedy capitalism.

He had his house disconnected from the power system and erected a home-manufactured wind charger to supply his requirements for electric light. On the tail of his wind charger he emblazoned a scarlet hammer and sickle for all to see. One night some of the town's young men quietly took the charger down and overpainted the hammer and sickle with a

Union Jack. It was several days before he noticed the change, but when he did he furiously scraped all the paint from the tail, which waggled ever afterward coated only with rust.

Meanwhile, the smaller of the two original engines, capable of carrying a normal load by itself, chugged away contentedly for twenty years until the plant was taken over after the war by the Saskatchewan Power Commission. Through its years of service, various homemade modifications were applied to it, all of local design. Originally, the engine was started by brute force, requiring a very strong man. He would first heat a soft iron ignition plug red hot with a hand-held blowtorch, then, standing on one of the spokes and throwing his body outward, he would turn over the five-foot flywheel.

The first modification was the installation of a blowtorch that was operated by compressed air and that was permanently directed at the plug to eliminate the need to use a hand-held one (this after one exploded in the hands of my elder brother, severely burning his hands and face). A second modification brought compressed air directly into the cylinder, thus doing away with a man having to endure the somewhat risky business of turning the flywheel over with his body weight. Another introduced a small container of fuel controlled by a valve into the fuel line. This permitted the operator to leave the plant before the power was to go off, giving him time to get home and into bed before the lights went out when the engine died for lack of fuel.

Another essential function of the power plant was to recharge the six-volt lead-acid batteries that were used by everybody to power their radios. There were usually ten to fifteen of these on the "battery line" at any one time, since most families had two, one in use on the radio while the other was being recharged.

It was this battery line that taught me a lesson about carelessness one day in my mid-teens. Asked by my father to throw in the battery line, I went to the switchboard and absently closed a knife switch that directed power from the operating engine to batteries recharging. With my back to the row of batteries, I stood waiting for the changing tone of the engine that indicated that the load had gone on the dynamo and that the engine governor had compensated for it. Nothing of the kind happened.

I turned and saw tiny wisps of blue smoke beginning to curl up from the batteries. I realized instantly what had occurred and snatched the switch open. I had switched the battery line to the engine and dynamo that weren't running. This meant that the dozen or so six-volt batteries being charged took on an impossible load. They tried to push their feeble current backwards through the resistors, which reduced the charging current from 110 to six volts, and then to change the big dynamo into an electric motor, which in turn tried to turn over the flywheel of the standing semi-diesel engine. No wonder the batteries had begun to smoke in a split second! And what a sigh of relief I breathed when after checking each battery with an hydrometer I found that, although several had been severely drained, none were defunct! It could have been acutely embarrassing and financially difficult for my father.

It was in relation to this power plant too that I got one of my best-remembered lessons in life, as well as a perception of my father's wisdom. I had reached that age of infinite sagacity that all teenagers are sure they have attained at one time or another and had decided I was going to leave school and get a job. To my surprise, my father assented and even offered me a job at a dollar a day plus my room and board – a princely income for a youth in those Depression years.

The first task he assigned me was to fill the coal bins in our home and in his place of business. This involved taking a truck and a shovel, having the truck weighed on the lumberyard scales, shovelling the truck full of coal from the storage bins beside the railway tracks, having the load weighed, and once more shovelling all of the coal out of the truck into the bins of the house and garage. Before that task was finished (it took a whole day) I was sore of arm and back and had a much better appreciation of how much coal there was in the world! But the master stroke was yet to come.

My assignment for the next day was to go about the town reading the meters to record the consumption of electricity. In blithe ignorance I started my task, whistling happily as I walked up the street. At the first home I entered I was greeted with the question, "Why aren't you in school?" I replied proudly that I was not going to school any more and that I had a job with my father. This precipitated an immediate and stunning lecture on my foolishness. At the next house the process was repeated, and the next, and the next. After a few of these encounters I was not answering so proudly. By the end of the twentieth or so lecture on what an idiot I was, I was beginning to believe it. That evening I had a meeting with my father in which I resigned from his employ, and the next morning I went back to school. The subject never came up between us again, but I am sure he knew what the reaction of the village housewives would be when I announced that I was quitting school.

As my brothers and I grew up into our mid-teens, we were assigned greater responsibilities in our father's business, and each of us, in succession, took our turn at "minding the plant." This involved hours of sitting in the garage, often alone, from just after supper time in the evenings until midnight when the plant was shut down for the night. The steady thudding of the single-cylinder semi-diesel engine, combined with the high-pitched whine of the dynamo, had a mind-deadening effect that led easily to sleep. But if something caused an extra load to be thrown on the generator, the change in pitch of that steady whine had an effect that truly could be described as electric. One snapped to one's senses as if galvanized and waited for the engine to resume its previous pace, indicating that its governor had compensated for the additional load. With experience, one could tell what was going on in the town by the reaction of the engine and dynamo. One relatively large momentary dip on a winter evening was caused by the caretaker at the rink turning on all the lights of the curling and skating rinks, another signified that a movie-theatre projector had started up, and so on.

Behind the engine room in the gambrel-roofed part of the building was an area originally intended to be a garage workshop but which, for most of my childhood, was used only for storage and occasionally for spray painting a second-hand car. The business of mechanical repair of automobiles had moved into a separate building nearby where the work was done by an independent mechanic working for himself and on contract for my father. This storage room was a favourite haunt for me and my friends for two reasons. Firstly, it was a place where we could hammer, saw and build to our heart's content. Here we built our "bugs" – miniature automobiles made of wood, with rope steering lines and wheels from a child's wagon or an abandoned baby buggy. Secondly, it contained a rope-operated "elevator," by means of which we could gain access to the huge attic that ran the length of the building beneath the barnlike roof.

This attic contained a treasure trove of discarded items that today would be worth their weight in gold but that, at the time, were considered to be only outdated car parts of little value. Under layers of dust were stacks of interleaved Model T fenders, nested together with layers of butcher paper in between. There were brass radiator shells, glass panels for the split windshields of the Model Ts, carbide head- and side-lamps, boxes of flanged radiator caps, buggy-type springs, engine parts, and a host of other items over which antique-car buffs of today would drool. They were still there when my father retired, and in 1949 the entire complex burned, taking its treasure trove with it, as well as the general store and hardware.

This back room was used also to store the combined ambulance and hearse, which my father had constructed. Originally, it had been a Graham-Paige sedan of awe-inspiring proportions. Where it had come from I don't know, but it must certainly have been one of the biggest cars ever to come to that part of the country in the early years of the Depression. It stood on wire-spoked wheels almost three feet high with two spare wheels and tires mounted in depressions in the front fenders on either side of the massive hood.

To convert it to a hearse, my father removed all of the interior fittings and replaced them with a single seat for the driver. The floor was decked over above the drive shaft housing and fitted with rollers. The central door post on the right side was cut out and put back again with a hinge-and-bolt arrangement so it could be swung out or removed completely when the side doors were opened. The folding luggage rack was removed and a large hole was cut in the back with an acetylene torch, over which was welded the luggage compartment from a Model T coupe, standing on end so its door opened outward to the rear and adding another eighteen inches or so to the car's overall length. With these modifications, the car was capable of transporting the largest coffin. As a compromise between its two functions – ambulance and hearse – it was painted a matte grey.

This sort of reconstruction was not at all unusual in prairie villages and on farms of the period. Someone always was making something from something else, and it seemed that most of the men in the village and on the surrounding farms had an almost unbelievable ability with things mechanical. This is all the more surprising when one considers that many of the things with which they worked, from electrical generators and diesel engines to automobiles and farm machinery, were unknown to them in their youths. They seemed to take to things mechanical as naturally as it was to walk, and their fertile imaginations produced a plethora of useful items, many of which later became commonplace and sources of wealth to those with more financial acumen.

Some examples were the electrical-power systems fashioned from automobile generators and batteries, powered by the wind and driven by homemade propellers, and also the gadgetry that was applied to the engines of the power plant. Another example was the snowmobile. There were two types: track-driven with skis on the front; or propeller-driven. The latter were powered by salvaged four-cylinder automobile engines and were capable of speeds on snow-covered fields of forty or fifty miles an hour. All were "off the top of the head," completely designed and constructed by their builders right down to their laminated and finely balanced propellers.

My father's attempt in the late 1920s to create a workable snowmobile was only partially successful. He modified an old truck chassis to take skis in place of the front wheels and added a second set of wheels to the rear, connected to the drive wheels by caterpillar-type tracks. He constructed a cab that would seat five or six people. On one memorable occasion our family was invited to a New Year's dinner at the home of farm friends who lived about three miles from the village.

The journey out was accomplished with great success in daylight at eight or ten miles per hour, but the return trip, undertaken long after night had fallen, was a different story. The electrical system failed, making the headlights inoperative. So one of my brothers walked ahead with a lantern, attempting to guide the vehicle across snowy patches in the fields but frequently encountering "dead ends" where there was no snow. The journey was uncomfortably cold and slow. I don't recall any more expeditions in that vehicle, and its final disposition is a mystery to me. The propeller-driven snowmobiles were much more successful.

Another outstanding example of this natural mechanical aptitude was provided by a man who spent most of his time doing carpentry, cabinet-making and tin-smithing, and who always peered at us short-sightedly through thick-lensed glasses begrimed by the detritus of his work. Before the First World War he solved the radial-engine crankshaft problem by what is known now as the planetary-gear system. He designed and built a working model of a radial engine of the type later used universally on aircraft that was far in advance of the rotary engines of the time.

This model was undergoing assessment at the University of Saskatchewan but was lost when the Engineering Building there was destroyed by fire in 1913. For reasons I do not know, he didn't build another model. Thousands of engines of the inferior rotary type were built during the First World War, then someone else solved the problem and tens of thousands of aircraft with radial engines have been built. One can only speculate about his fame and fortune had he been able to market his design. Happily, I can report that years later he designed and successfully marketed a quick connector mechanism for irrigation pipes.

The free and easy access that we, as youngsters, were granted to all places of business in the village was exemplified by my father's garage. Bicycles became our constant companions as soon as we were big enough to ride them, and their maintenance frequently was centred on the garage. It was not unusual to see the concrete sidewalk in front of the establishment littered with the parts of two or three bicycles at a time as we performed our maintenance tasks on them. Everything we needed was at hand – wrenches, pliers, oil cans, gasoline for cleaning parts, inner-tube patches, a compressed-air hose – and I don't believe it ever occurred to my father or his employees that we should pay for anything we used.

Under a counter in the garage there was always an open tin of tire patches for fixing leaks in inner tubes, and no one seemed concerned about who used it. In it were thin rubber sheets and shaped patches of various sizes backed with glazed cloth to keep the adhering side of the patch completely clean, tubes of rubber cement and scrapers to roughen the tube being repaired to ensure a good bond. But best of all was when my father would let us use a "hot patch."

A hot patch consisted of a small metal pan with the rubber patch stuck on the bottom. In the pan was a mixture of a combustible material resembling slow-burning gunpowder. When an inner tube had been suitably prepared, this pan was clamped tightly to it, the edge of the paper cover on the combustible mixture was pried up with a knife point, and the mixture was ignited. The burning process took only a few seconds and, after the pan had been allowed to cool, the clamp was removed and a neat patch was found to have vulcanized itself to the tube. But most memorable was the pungent aroma of the burning mixture. Dense smoke spiralled upward and flattened along the ceiling of the garage during the burning process, and if one got a good whiff it was throat-rasping and choking. But we loved the burnt-powder tang that hung in the air for minutes afterward.

The play of childhood merged almost imperceptibly into the work of the adult world, and we were not far into our teens before we were using the skills we had learned repairing bicycles and building bugs on the more mundane tasks of repairing automobile tires or helping to assemble farm machinery, which was shipped broken down into its component parts. But my first "adult" occupation in connection with my father's business was tending the gasoline pumps.

Farmers, while busy on the land, postponed trips to town until Saturday evening unless their work was being held up by the absence of a spare part. On that evening all of the businesses were open, the poolroom and theatre ran full blast and everyone was busy. While the farmers carried out their business in the garages or blacksmith shop, their wives shopped in the general stores for the week's necessities. Such cars and trucks as had been driven into town were refuelled at the gas pumps – and nearly everything was put on a charge account, to be settled up in the fall when the crops were in. I remember one Saturday night in particular when we had had a very busy time throughout the whole evening. When we closed up shop for the night, my father opened the cash register and there was not a dime in it – just a large stack of charge slips.

We had two gasoline pumps, a single and a double, carrying three grades of gasoline. The pumps themselves stood about eight feet tall and were topped with glass cylinders about three feet high within which were mounted markers graduated in gallons and half-gallons. These cylinders were filled with gasoline by means of hand pumps actuated by levers about three feet long, and the fuel was hosed into automobile tanks by gravity. As the gasoline was put into the car, the level in the glass cylinder fell past the markers to indicate the amount delivered, and before the next customer could be served the cylinder had to be pumped full again.

The cheapest grade of gasoline sold at three gallons for a dollar, so three gallons was the standard order. However, occasionally a customer would ask to have the tank filled, and as I grew more tired late in the evening it was with sinking heart that I would watch the gasoline in the cylinder recede past the eight- and nine-gallon marks; I knew that as soon as the customer left I would have to pump the cylinder full again. As I grew, the task became easier, but for a couple of summers I could work the pump only by grasping the handle with both hands and throwing my body weight from side to side.

The top grade of gasoline was Esso Extra, which sold at forty cents per gallon; the second was Imperial Three Star (the origin of the designation of the star hockey players selected on Saturday-night hockey broadcasts, at that time sponsored by Imperial Oil) at thirty-seven or thirty-eight cents; and the third was a variety that had no name at thirty-five cents per gallon, or three gallons for a dollar. This last variety sometimes was casing-head gasoline, or "skunk gas," only minimally refined and high in sulphur, giving a definite rotten-egg odour to the exhaust of the vehicle burning it.

When not occupied serving gasoline, I gradually worked my way into assisting in the parts department. A long counter at the front of this department was covered for about a third of its length with parts catalogues for various makes and types of farm equipment – "one-ways," combines, binders, seed drills, for example. Farmers needing parts would tell us the make and model of the machine, and we would look for them in the exploded diagrams in the appropriate parts book, then record the part number and telephone it to a warehouse in Saskatoon for shipment to us by train, or by bus when a bus service was established up in the late thirties. Occasionally it would be necessary to order a part from Regina. In that case, the part would be shipped by CPR to a town twelve miles away, our own village being served by the CNR out of Saskatoon. When I began driving (although still not of legal driving age) it was a great adventure for me and one or two of my friends to be allowed to take a car and drive the twenty-four-mile round trip to collect such a part.

One customer at the garage became my *bête noire*. He was an immigrant from Finland who hadn't mastered English. I solved the problem by showing him catalogues until we came to one that matched his machine and he pointed out the part he needed. He seemed to single me out for his orders, even waiting for me to come in from the gas pumps. Perhaps it was the satisfaction we experienced when I succeeded in understanding him that pleased him.

There was one supremely happy moment each Saturday night. As the crowd in town dwindled after midnight, the time would come when it looked as if business was finished. Dad and I would walk down Main Street to the Chinese restaurant to have ham sandwiches and chilled banana cream pie before we returned to the garage to set the automatic shut-off on the electric-lighting plant. Then we walked up Main Street together through the soft, cool summer night to our home.

My father's business was a good example of the way our lives changed between the time we were capable of memory and the time we finished high school. Originally the Model T was its mainstay. The first Model A appeared the year I turned five, its advent proclaimed by a large billboard that my father erected on the west side of Main Street, displaying an almost full-sized reproduction of the new car. When I was approaching nine, the Model B arrived, with the first vague hints of streamlining and available with a V-8 engine. Model changes followed almost annually after that until the war. By 1939, my second brother, who had thrilled to race a Model T around the country at twenty-five or thirty miles per hour, was flying Hawker Hurricanes with the Royal Air Force in England at over 300 miles an hour.

The spare parts that we carried for farm machinery in my early childhood were for share-bottomed ploughs, seed drills, binders and threshing machines, all powered or served by teams of horses; twelve years later they were for one-ways, swathers and combines, tractor-powered or self-propelled without exception.

We could hardly wait each spring to see the first of the new cars as they arrived from the east, wondering what new marvels had been incorporated. First, the enclosed body replaced the folding top and side curtains. Then woven upholstery appeared, along with the red triangle on the back fender of some models that marked the advent of four-wheel brakes. Early in the thirties, streamlining changed the form of cars forever. Hydraulic shock absorbers arrived, as did stabilized steering, and the "turret top" or all-steel body. Radios appeared, and interior heaters began to make winter driving much less risky and uncomfortable. Speeds leaped upward. A car trip to the city, ninety road miles away, was rare before 1928. Three years later, such an undertaking was relatively commonplace, but it still took three to four hours each way, depending on the condition of the roads. By 1935, the trip could be made easily in just over two hours – but still depending on the roads.

The roads were terrible, generally speaking. Only a very few of the main highways in the province were gravelled to give them an all-weather surface, and they were paved only near the major centres. A car travelling over about twenty miles per hour generated great clouds of dust on the gravelled and dirt roads. In dry weather the dirt roads were gradually graded, worn and pounded down to dusty smoothness except for persistent depressions where water would stand after a rain. When it did rain, these roads turned rapidly into greasy ribbons of slick mud that rutted quickly into slippery messes.

One fortunate feature of the cars of those days that has not been surpassed by the modern automobile was their ability to plough through mud. Their high, narrow wheels and relatively more balanced power made them much more manageable under slippery conditions, and it was with derisive smiles that we, riding in a Model A or some car of equivalent vintage, would offer a tow to a fat-tired later model that had slithered into a ditch.

We learned quickly that there were tricks to driving various types of cars. For example, in the old Model T, power was sent from engine to drive shaft by a series of clutch bands. As the car grew older and more tired, the bands that had been used the most became more and more worn until eventually they would slip and were unable to transmit sufficient power to climb a steep hill. The solution was to use a band that wasn't as badly worn and, because this usually was the reverse band, it wasn't unusual to see someone stop their car at the foot of a very steep hill, turn it around, and back up the incline.

And we learned that there were other hazards associated with the Model T. Before the advent of the self-starter, cars were started by cranking. This required retarding the "spark" – in other words, changing the timing to the spark plugs so they fired closer to "top dead centre," which was accomplished by moving a lever on the left side of the steering column upward. This was done while moving a lever on the right side down to feed more gas to the engine. If the spark was advanced too far, there was a distinct risk of a backfire, causing the crank to reverse its direction almost explosively. For this reason we were taught never to wrap a thumb around the crank handle but to keep it on the same side as our fingers. Thus a backfire merely wrenched the crank from the hand instead of breaking or dislocating the thumb. But even this didn't protect you from a severe blow to the back of the arm or wrist when the crank whipped around before you could get your hand out of the way. There was more than one arm or wrist broken when this precaution was ignored.

Because of the high clearance of those vehicles, they were capable of forging their way over rough and soft ground, and roads were not quite as important as they are for today's cars. Thus, a car was often seen meandering across the prairie far from any defined road. Many of these spur-of-the-moment trails became well used and eventually became permanent roads. North of our village, the surveyed road allowance cut across a slough bottom and each spring the road became impassable. By detouring to the prairie grass along the verges of the slough, however, it was possible to make one's way around it and back to the road. Eventually, when this road was improved, the highway followed the trail around the slough and not the true road allowance.

On one occasion as a child, I accompanied my father on visits to several farms where he had business. It was early in the spring and, to save time between two farms, we abandoned the road and drove across the prairie between them, skirting deep puddles, small sloughs and the remaining snowbanks. Eventually we came to a large slough only a few hundred yards from the farm we were attempting to reach but around which we could find no way. However, it was still covered with ice, which my father tested on foot and found to be quite strong. We drove out onto the ice and made it about three-quarters of the way across when suddenly the ice broke and down we went in about two feet of very cold water and mud.

The farmer came to our rescue with a team of horses, and soon the car was towed out, but my father was chilled to the bone after wading in the icy water to fasten the tow chain to the car. Fortunately, after drying out in the farm home and being warmed with strong hot coffee, he suffered no permanent harm.

On another of these off-the-road adventures, my father and I were driving in some hills a few miles south of our town. We came across a group of circles of stones each about ten feet across. These we deduced were stones that had been used by Indians to weight the bottom edges of their teepees and rolled off when the teepees were taken down. On such trips we often came across the foot-deep oval depressions created by wallowing bison.

Such automobile adventures were exciting, but one of my most thrilling, if frightening, vehicular experiences was on a tractor. My father had made a sale of a Ford-Ferguson tractor-cultivator unit but, since he didn't have one immediately available, he made arrangements to get one from another dealer at Outlook, about thirty miles away. I was taken to collect it and drive it back to our town.

All began well. The rubber-tired tractor bounced gaily along the road at about fifteen miles an hour, the sun shone brightly and I settled down to a couple of hours of solitude. However, adventure waited, literally, around the first corner. Here the road made a ninety-degree turn to the west and went down a long straight cut into the valley of the South Saskatchewan River. This cut maintained a steep, straight downhill grade for nearly half a mile to a two-lane bridge across the river, and a similar cut carried the road up the steep high bank on the other side. From the top of the hill, the bridge looked like a toy that had been removed from someone's model railway set.

The idea occurred to me that I should coast the tractor down the hill. Foolishly, I elected to do this by taking it out of gear rather than leaving it in gear and disengaging the clutch. Within a matter of yards the machine had accelerated to a speed I knew would never permit me to get it back in gear. Because the surface of the road was loosely gravelled, I realized quickly that any attempt to use the differential brakes, with the risk of getting more braking on one side than on the other, would probably cause the tractor to flip over. The best thing to do, I decided, was to hang on and pray that no other vehicle would force me to pull over into the looser gravel on the edge of the road.

I don't know what the world's speed record for farm tractors is, but I'm sure I set a mark that may never have been exceeded. The tractor hurtled down the steep slope, gaining momentum with every turn of the wheels, while its big tires caused it to bounce higher and higher with each minor irregularity in the road. I hung on for dear life and prayed that I could hold the front wheels straight, the steering mechanism having been expressly designed for sharp turns at low speeds in ploughed fields, not for road racing.

My only lasting regret is that the tractor had no speedometer. I estimated the speed at between fifty and sixty miles an hour by the time we bounced over the final bump at the lip of the bridge and I settled down, with a tremendous sigh of relief, to coast smoothly along the concrete deck of the bridge. The tractor had gained sufficient speed to coast all the way across the bridge and about a quarter of the way up the hill on the other side, at which point I pulled over to the side of the road, switched off the idling engine and fought for several minutes to get my breathing and pulse rate back to normal. The rest of the journey was uneventful even though I had to cross the deep glacial valley just east of our village. This time I left the tractor in gear and let its governor regulate the speed of the descent down the winding dirt road into the valley.

One aspect of youth at that time was the relative ease with which we slipped into the driver's seat. Although the legal age for driving was sixteen, farm boys were typically broken in on grain trucks and tractors, and most of us had considerable driving experience by the time we were sixteen. I can recall my first driving lessons from my father, when I had to sit on his brief case to see over the dashboard. This was a cooperative effort in which I operated the steering and gear shift while my father worked the clutch, brake and accelerator.

One driving adventure was almost ended by a run-in with the law. On this occasion my father had asked one of my friends and me to pick up a second-hand truck from a dealer at a village more than a hundred miles from our home town. My friend was seventeen and so had a driver's license. I was only fifteen and didn't have a licence, but by this time I was a fairly experienced truck driver anyway. It seemed in those days, however, that when farm youngsters were drafted by their fathers to drive harvest trucks the Mounties turned a blind eye to us. Thus it was decided that my friend would drive us in a car to the pickup point and I would drive the truck back in convoy with him.

En route, we had to travel for many miles on the gravelled main highway between Saskatoon and Regina. Proceeding at forty to fifty miles per hour, we began to overtake another car, which was producing a pall of dust. After eating this dust for several miles we finally decided we should pass the vehicle ahead, and we accomplished this by my friend tramping down hard on the gas and keeping both hands on the wheel to control the car in the slithery gravel while I leaned across and held the horn button down. Through the clouds of dust the car ahead finally came into view, by which time we were doing about seventy miles per hour. Hearing our horn, the driver ahead pulled over to the right, and we flashed past, with time only to take a quick glance at the other vehicle – a glance that revealed its driver as an officer of the RCMP! A backward look told us his vehicle was accelerating behind us, so without further deliberation we decided that our best course of action was to carry on at high speed and deluge him with our dust. This tactic seemed to work, because he was soon out of sight in the rolling grey clouds boiling up from our wheels.

Only a mile or two farther on, however, we began to encounter the dust trail from yet another car, which we were overtaking rapidly and, as we were getting into the thickest of the dust, the road took us past one of the small villages along the highway. My friend took advantage of this to brake sharply and turn into the village at a sedate pace. Seconds later the RCMP vehicle roared past, partially hidden by the dust from the vehicle that had been ahead of us and that he now seemed to be pursuing in our place. After waiting a bit, we proceeded on our way at a more reasonable speed and reached our turnoff point from the highway without encountering the Mountie again.

But the day was far from over. We arrived at our pickup point and got the truck, an aged Model A, shortly after noon and began the trip home, expecting to complete the journey by late afternoon. The truck had other ideas. For an hour or so all went well and we travelled together at thirty to thirty-five miles per hour. Then the truck began to overheat. Soon its radiator was boiling. I turned into a farmyard and was able, after a cooling period, to refill the radiator. This time we were able to proceed for nearly three-quarters of an hour before the same thing happened. The next time the interval shortened to about a half hour.

Fortunately, we were travelling through a hilly area with many sloughs from which we could obtain water for the truck's radiator. But because we were preoccupied with the problem, we missed a turn on the unmarked roads and wound up wandering westward on assorted roads and trails, not knowing quite where were. One of our stops was made at a country school at which we enquired of the young teacher if she knew the distance and direction to the village where we should again intersect the gravel highway. She didn't know, being new to the area. She relayed our enquiry to the children in her classes. None of them knew. But after leaving the school we travelled only a few miles before sighting the elevators of the town about which we had asked. Such was the parochialism of the times!

Our journey continued in stop-and-start fashion as darkness fell until, at a familiar farm about fifteen miles from our village, we gave up, parked the truck in the farmyard, and phoned my father. As it turned out, he and my friend's father had been consulting about the tardiness of our return, and in a short time they arrived. My friend and his father headed home in their car while I, on my father's instruction, took the car we had been using and proceeded home while he nursed the recalcitrant truck the rest of the way to our village, arriving in the wee hours of the morning. The next day the mechanic examined the truck and found that all that was wrong was that the gas line was nearly plugged, the resulting super-lean mixture causing the engine to overheat. Undoing the gas line from the carburettor, he applied the air hose to its end, gave it a few sharp blasts, and the truck ran like a top! I don't know how long it ran before the line plugged up again.

Another of the tasks assigned to me when I became big enough was to bolt steel lugs onto the wheels of new tractors as they arrived from the factory. Because of my lack of weight, to tighten the nuts on the half-inch bolts, I had to put a four-foot piece of pipe on the end of the three-foot socket wrench to do the job. Sometimes a second steel rim was bolted to the outside of the standard wheel with additional lugs to provide better traction. In my memory it seems like only a matter of days later we were mounting rubber tires on tractors and pumping into them several hundred pounds of a water and calcium chloride mixture, which was a rubber-preserving anti-freeze and added weight for traction.

In the late twenties and early thirties, nearly every deal for a car or truck or tractor involved horse trading – literally. My father had a standing arrangement with a farmer who traded in horses. This man bought the horses Dad took in on deals, most of which were loaded into railway cattle cars and shipped to eastern Canada. This meant also that Dad had to be a pretty good judge of horseflesh if he wasn't to lose his profit on the deal by promising too much for the horses and taking a loss when they were sold to the horse trader. After only a few short years of this type of trading there was scarcely a work horse left in the country.

Our childhood association with the garage gave us many interesting bits and pieces of materials that contributed to our amusement and education. Dead storage batteries, smashed to bits with a hammer, yielded quantities of lead that could be melted in a tin can over a small bonfire, skimmed to remove impurities and poured shimmeringly silver into any sort of mould we could find. A few inches of stiff wire held vertically in a can lid with a stick while molten lead was poured around it made a combination desk spike and paper weight, often embossed on the bottom with the label of the can's original contents, such as cocoa or baking powder. Even more exciting was to apply the same process to a bullet mould creating perfectly formed slugs for hand loading into brass cartridge cases as home-made rifle ammunition.

The trash bin at the northwest corner of the garage supplied a veritable treasure trove to delight small boys. Here were deposited the burned-out light bulbs from the town's street lights. These made excellent targets for sling-shot practice or thrown stones and for BB guns and .22 rifles, especially when tossed far out into a slough where they bobbed elusively in the waves. Here, too, we found pieces of heavy-gauge soft copper wire that, with a bit of inner-tube rubber, could be fashioned into miniature sling shots just right for firing chewed pellets of paper in school. Naturally, the loss rate on these by confiscation was high, so each boy made several at a time if there was sufficient raw material available.

One of the most coveted bits of trash was the high-tension ignition coil from Model T automobiles. Each was contained in a well-constructed wooden box with dovetailed corners about three-by-four-by-six inches in size. Inside were coils of hairlike copper wire, hundreds of yards long, wound into cylinders between layers of thin waxed paper; down the centre of each coil was a half-inch bundle of soft iron rods about six inches long, each not quite as thick as a pencil lead.

After one of these had been opened, even walking about the village became something of a hazard because the nearly invisible copper wire was unrolled and strung around street light poles, across gates and doorways and wherever our fancies imagined we could trap some unsuspecting pedestrian. The risk of damaging the coils while removing them from their containers was great, so one of the main fascinations was to see how long a piece of the wire could be unrolled before it broke. One boy held the roll on a stick while another took the end and walked backwards slowly so the wire unrolled as gently as possible. On very rare occasions it was possible to unroll a length of it along the street for a block before it snagged on something or was broken by an unsuspecting passer-by. Afterwards, for days, broken wisps of the gossamer wire could be seen glinting in the sunlight as they streamed in the breeze from posts and hedges.

The bundles of soft iron rods were separated into their individual lengths and provided infinite exercise of the imagination as they were bent and twisted into every conceivable shape to make abstract loops and whorls or representations of more concrete objects, such as spears, arrows, stars or chains.

Nearly always available in the garage were folders advertising automobiles, brilliantly coloured and printed on fine glossy paper. With a couple of these and a shoe box scrounged from one of the general stores, we were able to wile away hours. Profile pictures of cars were cut from the folders and pasted on pieces of shoe box cardboard, which then were trimmed carefully around the pictured cars. A flap of cardboard was stuck on the back to hold the picture upright. No finer toy car existed for pushing around on a smooth linoleum covered floor.

It was early in the Depression when Father, looking for ways to augment his income, decided to go into the mortuary business. He served an apprenticeship with a funeral home in Saskatoon and earned his qualifications. A lean-to extension on the gambrel-roofed building, inside the U of the complex, became a morgue.

My brothers and I learned little of this aspect of his business because he never discussed it with us, but we knew from his facial expression when he had been working in the morgue how deeply affected he was by having to prepare for burial so many of his old friends and acquaintances. At such times we took care not to bother him with our problems. I can recall seeing him emerge from the morgue with tears in his eyes, but these he always attempted to conceal – he was a man of his time in believing in "the stiff upper lip."

The only direct connection his sons had with this part of his business was to make the occasional trip to Saskatoon in a truck to fetch a coffin in its rough-box. We found a certain macabre humour once when my second brother made such a trip. He was caught in a rain storm when returning late at night and slid off the road into a ditch where he spent the night beside a cemetery!

In addition to the many facets of his business in the village, my father continued to farm, and I truly believe he was happiest when driving a tractor to seed grain or at the controls of a combine when harvesting. Even after he had retired from business and moved to the West Coast he returned every spring and fall until his death to be involved in seeding and harvesting. As one of his hired men remarked to me, "He thinks the wheat won't grow unless he watches the seed going into the ground." In fact, his farming became the salvation of his business.

By the late thirties, although the effects of the Depression were beginning to ease, he was deeply in debt to the company that had financed his automobile and farm-machinery transactions. It was an enormous debt for a one-man company in those days – equivalent to more than a million dollars in today's dollars. This occurred because so many of his customers had been unable to meet their payments. In 1941 he asked me to assist him with some work on his ledgers. I learned, to my astonishment, that this particular work involved going through the ledgers, tearing out and discarding page after page, each page representing a debt owed to him that he knew he would never collect. In one afternoon we discarded pages representing approximately $10,000 owed to his business. Many of the debtors had left the area, while others had merely refused to pay. At the same time, we prepared letters to be sent out to those from whom some payment was considered at least a possibility.

By the late thirties, prairie crops were improving, and his farms, which for most of the Depression had been sink holes for money, began to show a profit. Then came the war. Father saw a golden opportunity (if the weather cooperated) and committed his land in large part to the growing of registered flax seed, the war having created a tremendous demand for flax. Fortunately, the weather did cooperate and by 1945 his debts were paid off, largely from the profits of the farms, although the general easing of the money situation also brought in payments of some long-standing debts.

The war, however, closed down the automobile business. After the United States entered the conflict in December 1941, the production of automobiles for civilian use was discontinued as manufacturing plants converted to the production of war material. In addition, gasoline was rationed and products such as tires became unavailable. In early 1942, Father took delivery of the last Ford car he was to get for nearly four years and decided to keep it himself – mostly because it had new tires. The car was a "standard coach," that is, a basic two-door sedan with no extras. Its list price, when sold at my father's garage, was $832!

This car remains in my memory because of an incident that took place at the end of the war. I had made an agreement with my father that when I returned from the Air Force after the war, I would buy the car. When that happy day arrived, Father told me that another young veteran had been offered a job as a travelling salesman if he could get a car, and he asked if I would relinquish my claim to it. I agreed because I intended to return to university and had no real need for it. The car was sold to the young veteran at a used-car price based fairly on its original value – this at a time when second-hand cars were being sold on a sort of black market at wildly inflated prices and their keys for an additional few hundred dollars. Our young friend happily drove the car away and immediately resold it at a huge profit. The memory still rankles.

Because I grew up in such close association with my father's business, the torrent of memories it evokes is limitless. But the other businesses and occupations of the village were just as much a part of all our lives.

Stores and Shops

DURING MY CHILDHOOD our village was served by stores and businesses capable of providing for most of our needs. What they couldn't supply was usually available through mail order from Eaton's or Simpson's catalogues. There were two general stores, a grocery store, a butcher shop, a drug store, three garages, a blacksmith shop, a theatre, which doubled as a concert- and dance-hall, a hotel, a lumber yard, a restaurant, a poolroom-barbershop, a bank branch (which was closed in the early years of the Depression), two combined real-estate and insurance agencies, a hardware store, a shoe and harness repair shop and a livery stable. The numbers of some types of businesses varied from time to time as fires destroyed their buildings, but often they re-opened again in new or different quarters. Thus, what once had been a car dealership became a combined garage and general store while two small buildings, which had housed the now-defunct newspaper and a real-estate office, were joined together to house a grocery store and butcher shop. After the big fire of 1939, the restaurant and poolroom migrated to new buildings directly across the street from their former locations on lots that had been emptied by previous fires.

Only three of the shops on the principal business block of Main Street kept their initial functions and locations throughout my childhood and youth – the drugstore, hardware store and one general store, the last two disappearing in a fire after the Second World War.

Patronage of the various establishments was governed by many factors, ranging from politics to personal antipathies, and from the economics of a better deal to opportunities for barter. Thus, a farm wife might exchange her eggs for her household necessities at one store this week and another the next, depending upon which store needed the eggs. Some villagers shopped almost entirely at one or another of the stores, as did our family, because my father rented its premises to the owner. In turn, the storekeeper bought gasoline for his car and electric power from my father's business, and everything was put on charge accounts. I remember the figure of forty dollars as being the target limit for general-store purchases for our family of six each month, because that was the amount of the rent. If we planned judiciously, our accounts could be balanced with little actual cash changing hands at month's end. But both businesses then had to find ways to satisfy their creditors, that is, the wholesalers who supplied them – not an easy task during the Depression.

Although the survival of one's own business was of primary importance, everyone recognized that the survival of all or most was vital to the community, and various stratagems were employed to ensure this. One was to make agreements about who would sell what. Accordingly, my father and the owner of the hardware store made an agreement defining which competing items one or the other would sell. Father, for example, gave up the sale of a list of hardware items such as dry batteries while the hardware closed its single gasoline pump, which had sold the same brand of regular gasoline as my father's, but it continued to sell the high-test gasoline and kerosene used in cookstoves and lamps, which was dispensed into customers' one- and two-gallon cans from barrels with hand pumps. Such an agreement did not eliminate all competition, as the other garages also sold gasoline and products of both hardware and automobile varieties, but it did tend to equalize the two businesses concerned. Again, mutual business was done on charge accounts settled at the end of each month when rent for the hardware store's premises came due to Father.

The hardware store, fronting on Main Street, was reached via a wood-and-glass-panelled door centred in the front and flanked by plate-glass display windows, their first sections vee-ing out from the doorway, forming a covered entrance. Inside, two long walls, in length about three times the width of the shop, were lined with shelves almost to the ceiling. In certain areas, many of these shelves were divided into compartments to contain a myriad of bulk items – nuts and bolts and screws and washers and nails of various types and sizes, all sold in any quantity desired, and some, such as nails, measured out by weight. Purchases left the store either in the buyers' pockets or in paper bags of graduated sizes and strengths.

Beyond the shelving, a wall with a wide door in the centre divided the store proper from a storage area, while beyond this in turn was a work-shop used by the tinsmith. Cut out of the storage area to the left of the door was a small office, the domain of the hardware-merchant's wife, who did much of the bookkeeping. Her office faced into the store and was separated from it by an L-shaped counter parallel to the wall of the store room and one side wall. The counter supported the cash register and scales. Always on the counter, as in all of the shops, were the pencils and pads of blank sales slips to be made out in duplicate to record the ever-growing charge accounts. Here, too, was a glass display case containing a variety of jackknives and hunting knives with leather sheaths and dollar pocket watches, which we ogled covetously. Early in the thirties there were even a few wristwatches, which we wouldn't wear because we con-sidered them unmanly. Nearby were boxes of ammunition, shot-gun shells of various gauges, mostly twelve, but with a few four-ten and even, occa-sionally, eight-gauge for a farmer who used the recoil of the oversize gun to pull fence-posts! Of immediate interest to us were the cardboard cylin-ders of BB pellets and, when we grew older, boxes of .22 shells, which sold at twenty-five cents for fifty "shorts." The "longs" and "long-rifles" we seldom bought because of their higher cost, and anyway the "shorts" were quite effective for our usual quarry – gophers.

In the opposite corner stood eight-foot-high rolls of linoleum, kegs of nails and other bulky items. Down the centre of the store were display tables of kitchen ware and, in the weeks before Christmas, a variety of toys and games, which we examined admiringly day after day, including everything from steel-bodied toy cars with working headlights powered by a flashlight battery, to sleighs and toboggans. It was cause for fearful panic if one particularly coveted item disappeared from the display just before Christmas with the merchant mysteriously vague about the iden-tity of its purchaser.

In this store, too, the generosity toward children was evident. If, for one of our projects, we required a handful of nails or a few wood screws, they were unstintingly handed out to us with no thought of payment, although the store's owner usually made it clear that they had a monetary value.

One incident in the mid-thirties put the hardware store owner and my father at loggerheads for a time. During one of the crashing hailstorms we suffered frequently, one of the plate-glass windows fronting the store was shattered. Strangely, although the most violent winds during the storm were from the west, the east-facing window collapsed inward onto a display of aluminum cookware with disastrous effect. The hardware merchant insisted that Father reimburse him for the damaged cookware. Father, although he had a new window installed, was not convinced that he should pay for the damaged goods and classified the window breakage as an "act of God." The argument was never resolved, but Father didn't pay for the cookware.

The hardware store was faced, as were the general stores, by competition from the mail-order houses, for a good proportion of the items it carried in stock and, more significantly, for the custom of those who could afford to pay cash, which they had to do when buying from the catalogues. To counter this potentially serious loss of business, the merchant proclaimed to all that he sold as cheaply as one major mail-order house. He kept one of their catalogues on his counter and when anyone made a purchase he ostentatiously looked the item up in the catalogue and billed the customer at the same price – plus a shipping charge. This in spite of the fact that the mail-order houses shipped most items prepaid. However, it did save the purchaser the cost of mailing an order and buying a postal note.

The tinsmithy in the rear of the hardware store was a place of marvel to youngsters. We watched in awe as the tinsmith manufactured things, rolling, bending and cutting sheets of galvanized iron, known as tin, into wonderfully precise shapes and soldering them together. His soldering iron nested on a special rest on top of a blowtorch, its heavy square head wrapped in the roaring flame until he removed it, dipped its tip in flux, and skilfully melted neat rows of lead solder to join pieces together. In this manner, and employing his skill as cabinet maker, he manufactured an oversized four-compartment ice box, which was built into my mother's kitchen to match her cupboards. Nor were we denied the thrill of cutting, bending and twisting scrap pieces of tin into shapes meaningful to us but probably unrecognizable to anyone else. Here two pieces of scrap lumber were easily turned into a weather vane with tin propeller and tail.

Next door to the hardware store, in the same building and with an identical layout, was a general store; the only difference was that the space in the hardware store used for storage and tinsmithing in the general store was a warehouse. Immediately inside the front door, on the left, was a large "stand-up" desk, fronted floor-to-top with varnished tongue-and-groove lumber. In winter, this desk migrated to warmer regions, half-way along the length of the store. Here the storekeeper and his wife did their accounts and paperwork. The wall behind the desk, right to the store-room entrance, was covered with shelving bearing dry goods toward the front of the store and groceries toward the rear. There were bolts of cloth of various kinds and colours, cards of buttons, rings of safety pins, needles, thread, knitting wool and needles, paper patterns for making clothing, crochet hooks and thimbles, women's stockings and underwear. Fronting the shelves were two or three small racks of ready-to-wear women's clothing.

Opposite, for nearly half the length of the store, were floor-to-ceiling shelves of footwear – men's and women's dress shoes, children's shoes, work boots, galoshes and rubbers – while on tables in front of them were rubber boots and stacks of running shoes. This department was thrown into chaos one memorable day when someone parked a car across the street from the side wall of the store and left it without the brake on. The street sloped gently toward the store. The unattended car rolled across the street, gaining speed as it did so, jumped the curb and slammed into the wall. Damage appeared slight, since the car's bumper broke only one six-inch strip of shiplap in the outside wall, but inside, dozens and dozens of boxes of shoes were precipitated from their shelves, shoes, boxes and box lids ejected indiscriminately onto the floor. It was many hours before all of the assorted sizes, widths and styles were matched up again, returned to their proper boxes and re-shelved.

Along this wall, too, several shelves were devoted to men's shirts, dress shirts with three or four of a size in cardboard boxes, and work shirts folded in stacks. Other stacks held men's underwear and socks, overalls and jeans, handkerchiefs and bandannas, straw hats and cardboard imitation pith helmets, work and dress gloves, leather and wool mittens. It was here that the storekeeper measured a man on the rare occasion when one might order a made-to-measure suit, the measurements being sent off to a tailor in the city along with the numbered selection made from cloth samples stacked on the counter. It was by this method I procured a suit before starting university. The suit shocked not only me, but also almost everyone who saw it under certain conditions. It was of a light cord material and an attractive solid blue colour. At least it was blue when seen in daylight or under incandescent lights; in the city, where fluorescent lighting was taking over in many restaurants and other public places, it blazed a brilliant purple! It is worthy of note that it was in the mid-thirties a major advance was made in men's trousers with the advent of the zippered fly.

Where these walls met the end wall that cut off the warehouse was the grocery department, which was behind a squared U of counters, the one forming the bottom of the U being the longest. On the centre of this counter stood a set of scales emblazoned with the slogan Honest Weight, No Springs; at the ends of the counter were bolted holders with cutting edges for rolls of two widths and weights of brown wrapping paper. Beside the scales stood a wire rack containing various sizes of paper bags, graduating downward from large to small. The smallest were known to us as "nickel bags" and the next size larger as "dime bags" because these were the sizes usually used when we bought candy. Adults, too, used these designations, so it was not unusual to have a customer ask for a "dime bag" of raisins or somesuch, regardless of the actual price. On each side of the scales, hanging from screw eyes in the ceiling and fed from conical balls resting on the top shelf behind the counter, dangled cotton strings for tying packages. It was with envy we watched the dexterity of the merchant as he wrapped a parcel and tied it, ending with a knotted bow and breaking the string with no apparent effort by a quick twist around his finger.

At the end of this counter, where it met the side of the U fronting the men's wear, was a tall glass display case holding cigarettes, cigars and tobacco, for both smoking and chewing, with cartons of cigarette papers for those who rolled their own. To smoke "tailor-made" cigarettes during the Depression denoted either a degree of affluence or a wrong-headed sense of values. Cigarettes were sold in slide-out packages, commonly in sizes holding ten or twenty, except that one brand, Turret, could be purchased in a package of five for a nickel. Smoking tobacco came in paper packets lined with tinfoil or larger tins; chewing tobacco was manufactured in rectangular slabs, called plugs, and was displayed in opened tins, ready for individual sale.

Only a small proportion of the men chewed tobacco routinely, but in the winter while curling many used a small piece to prevent dry mouths. Cigars came in boxes made of a soft wood resembling mahogany with hinged lids. These were always sought after as handy containers for everything from children's treasures to a family's collection of charge-account slips. This latter use became embodied in the colloquial language in the phrase "cigar-box accounting." Hundreds of these boxes must have come into the town, but it was always difficult to obtain one, and often the shopkeeper had promised a box to someone before it was half empty.

Opposite, where the other side of the U led to women's wear, was another counter, this one bearing a high, glisteningly enamelled hand-cranked coffee grinder and a cheese cutter capable of holding a whole wheel of cheddar cheese and equipped with a big, broad-bladed knife hinged to the bottom frame holding the circular board upon which the cheese was placed. With this, the storekeeper could cut a wedge of any size, catching the cut slice on a square of waxed paper, or shave off paper-thin translucent slices to be handed to the customer to taste. Bits of cheese broken off during the cutting process were fair game to anyone who might be standing by.

The front of the longest counter was divided into rectangles of about eight by ten inches fronted with framed glass. These could be lifted out, each revealing a shallow box. These were filled to provide displays of navy beans, dried peas, tapioca and coffee beans, or, when not filled with dry food products, coloured advertising signs and panels cut from boxes of breakfast foods and other products were substituted.

Behind the counters, the walls, from about the height of the counter tops upward, were lined with shelves almost to the ceiling, displaying grocery products in cans, jars and cardboard boxes. Below was a series of covered bins containing the bulk products displayed in the counter's glass panels. These were dispensed into paper bags by means of large metal scoops, and we were constantly amazed by the accuracy of the storekeeper's judgement of weights. No matter what the size of the order or the product being sold, the bag, when placed on the scales, seldom differed more than a fraction of an ounce from the quantity desired. If the weight was a little low, more was dribbled into the bag from the scoop; if a bit high, it usually was left in the bag and only the quantity ordered was charged for.

It was common also for people to order bulk groceries by cost rather than weight, thus someone might ask for twenty cents' worth of beans. On the customer's side of the fan-shaped top of the scales, one saw only the red tip of the pointer moving along the arc of marks for pounds and ounces, but on the grocer's side the fan was covered with rows of quarter-inch-high numbers, each row starting with a price figure. Thus, if the product was worth fifteen cents a pound, the grocer watched a wire paralleling the pointer move across the row headed by "15" until it reached "20," thus weighing out twenty cents' worth. This also showed the storekeeper the cost to be charged for any random quantity as, for example, when the customer said, "That's enough." And there were no electronics involved!

Depending on the season, the counter with the cheese cutter often was covered with the six-inch-high wooden boxes of fresh produce and small fruits brought in thrice weekly by train. Housewives made it a point on "train days" to go to the store soon after the dray had made its deliveries in order to get their pick of the limited quantities and varieties of fresh fruits and vegetables ordered in by the merchant. In the winter, the space displayed similar boxes of dried apples and apricots, raisins and dates. The emptied boxes discarded by the merchant supplied youngsters with easily worked boards for a multitude of projects and, when finally past use, made excellent kindling.

In the centre of the U made by the counters, a three-foot-square hot-air register was set into the floor directly above the furnace in the basement, its blast of heat a welcoming greeting to the farmer or his wife who had just made a long, cold trip into town in a sleigh. Snow from their footwear melted in the heat and dripped through the grating to sizzle on the top of the furnace. After completing their purchases, the farmer might sit on the counter of men's wear and his wife might stand over the register, her coat and skirt billowing in the surges of heat, while exchanging gossip with other customers, the storekeeper's wife and the merchant himself, who stood, arms folded, leaning on the bins behind the counter.

Between the front door and this register, down the centre of the store, were tables and racks of various merchandise. At the grocery end there might be stacked boxes of apples in the fall, McIntosh, Delicious, Northern Spy and a yellow variety known as Winter Banana. These were replaced as Christmas neared by small wooden boxes of Japanese oranges and large bags and boxes of different varieties of nuts. The Christmas season, too, brought a particular mixture of hard candies; hard cylindrical ones, red on the outside covering a white interior, down the centre of which ran a green image of a Christmas tree, appearing magically wherever the cylinder might be broken; red-and-white striped peppermint candies, flat in cross section, folded back and forth on themselves in serpentine folds, and hard-shelled spongy candies in many colours shaped like nuts or fruits.

Often one would enter the store to find its owner in consultation with a well-dressed individual whom we might or might not know by name but who was not from our village. This would be one of the travelling salesmen who covered the country regularly, representing the wholesale houses in the city, promoting their products and taking orders for future delivery. During my early childhood, they travelled by train and we got to know many of them because our town had a good hotel. By the time I was sixteen, they travelled almost invariably by automobile but still were attracted to our hotel for their overnight stops.

Across First Avenue from the general store stood the hotel, a three-storey rectangular box shining white with green trim. Before my time, it had included a saloon and a barber shop in the basement that was entered by an outdoor stairway, which, just on the beginning edge of my recollection, was dismantled and paved over with concrete. The hotel was one of the first buildings erected in the town after its birth in 1913, and some of its registers, still extant, are almost a nominal roll of the land-seeking immigrants to the area, whose home addresses were given as exotically named towns in England, Scotland, Finland, Russia, or towns in eastern Canada and the United States.

Because the village did not have running water or a sewage system at that time (nor did it have for more than thirty years), each room in the hotel was equipped with a commode, upon which were a big china washbasin and matching water pitcher and, inside, a receptacle into which the basin could be emptied. Neatly coiled and hanging from a firmly embedded hook under one window in each room was a soft cotton rope of almost an inch in diameter. This was the emergency fire escape. Toilet facilities were provided off one end of the corridors on the two upper floors, emptying directly into a tank wagon, which was backed into position inside the building and removed for emptying by the dray horses.

The kitchen was huge, to accommodate an immense wood-and-coal-burning cookstove, the cooking surface of which was nearly ten feet long. When preparing meals and baking in hot weather, the kitchen temperature must have been unbearable, but bear it the wives of the hotel owners did for many years. Facing the stove was a long island counter with shelving above, open to both sides, bearing a vast collection of pots, pans, assorted knives and sharpening steels and stacks of dishes. In one corner of the big room stood a table and several chairs where the hotel owner's family took their meals, joined by me at lunch time when I was still in school and my parents were away, but only if there were no other customers.

The hotel's saloon had a short life, having been closed down by Saskatchewan's prohibition act of 1915, but its long hardwood bar stood in an outbuilding for many years before disappearing finally from my ken. A men-only beer parlour was opened in the hotel in 1935. It was also allowed to sell beer to be taken out. This provided us as children with one of our most important sources of income because it bought back for one cent each the empty bottles we collected.

The public attitudes toward drinking anything alcoholic after twenty dry years were ambivalent, ranging from loudly vocal opposition on the part of most wives and mothers to much less audible, but nevertheless majority, support by the men. The attitude taken at home by the wife was evident in the mode of entry to the beer parlour of the husband. One walked boldly in the door opening off Main Street in full view of the entire village. Another went in more discreetly through the hotel lobby entrance on First Avenue as if to buy a pack of cigarettes at the desk. Still another, hoping not to be seen, made his way through the high wooden fence surrounding the back of the establishment and entered via a back door. And there were some men who never set foot in the place.

The hotel owner was an avid supporter of the village hockey teams. The rotunda of the hotel became the gathering place to listen to the Saturday-night hockey broadcasts on the radio, particularly during the playoffs when pools were drawn up and, when completely sold, deposited on the registration desk. A friend and I, still in our junior teens, for one final game contributed twenty-five cents each to buy one ticket on a pool that was to pay the holder of the winning score fifty dollars. Our ticket was the winner – until one more goal was scored with only seconds to play! A more direct contribution to hockey was made by the owner after he had gone into the trucking business. His stake truck, covered over with canvas and with him at the wheel, transported midget to senior hockey teams to games in other towns up to thirty miles away, often through snowstorms and sometimes returning late at night in downright blizzards with the team members pushing the truck through the deeper snowdrifts.

Another offshoot of the hotel business was keeping the town supplied with ice for the icebox refrigerators in most homes. Ice was cut and trucked more than twenty miles from the South Saskatchewan River and stored, buried in sawdust, in an outbuilding behind the hotel that had once been a stable. The sawdust insulated the ice sufficiently so that the stock lasted for the whole summer. It is remarkable that, although the river always looked like a muddy stream, the ice was perfectly clear, and no harm came to any of us from using it to chill lemonade or popping slivers of it into our mouths when we watched the two- to three-foot blocks being cut into icebox-sized pieces.

The iceboxes gave the village children another daily chore, that of emptying the pans beneath them that caught the water from the melting ice. Forgetfulness here brought scoldings from our mothers while we mopped up the overflowing water from kitchen floors.

Obtaining water was a difficult problem for the hotel. By the nature of its business, it probably was the largest consumer of water in the town, so keeping it supplied by hand-carried pails was a never-ending task. At one time, the owner decided to bore his own well, which would have permitted a great improvement in the hotel's facilities. Prospects looked good since the hotel was on a direct line between two existing wells – the town well, which had an almost inexhaustible supply of water at a depth of about sixty feet, and a private well at a home little more than a block to the west. Due to some vagary in the underground pre-glacial landscape above which the hotel now stood, only salt water was produced by the hole that was drilled to a depth of several hundred feet.

The hotel was staffed mostly by the families of its owners, of which there were two in my memory. The husband did the manual chores and bookkeeping, and his wife cooked, laundered and often acted as chambermaid. The sons of the second owner, still youngsters, swept and mopped, frequently scrubbing the spotless unpainted white hardwood floor of the kitchen. Occasionally a daughter of one of the area's farm families was hired to assist the wife, depending upon the briskness of business, the financial situation and the availability of such a person. In the winter, the hotel owner and his sons, as all of the businessmen of the town did for their premises, cleared the snow from the sidewalks in front of the hotel. A major winter chore was the constant manual stoking of the coal-fired boiler that heated the establishment.

The second owner's wife became almost the sole caterer to one aspect of the town's social life. Dances were held in the theatre on the opposite side of the street from the hotel, the music starting between 9:00 and 10:00 p.m. and carrying on until 2:00 a.m. with a break at midnight for lunch. Home-made basket lunches were always accompanied by coffee made by the hotel-owner's wife in a copper boiler on the stove in her kitchen. At midnight, two men carried the big boiler across the street to the theatre, placed it on the hot-air register in the centre of the dance floor, and coffee was served from it in big enamelware pitchers. There was always a certain amount of spillage, which fell on top of the furnace below the register and cooked there, filling the building with the odour of roasting coffee.

Another contribution by the hotel-owner's wife to the lives of children was in the matter of "shinplasters," which were twenty-five-cent paper banknotes that, even in my childhood, were becoming rare. This woman, however, always seemed to have a supply of them, and so, when a child had a birthday party, it was quite usual for one or two of the gifts to consist of a decorated envelope containing one of these, obtained by the donor from her supply. It seems strange that she was so willing to part with them until one thinks of the closed-circuit nature of the village's cash flow. Undoubtedly, it was only a day or two after the party before she had the same shinplasters back, obtained from the stores where the recipients had spent them.

Shinplasters were not the only oddity in the money system of the time. There were both "big" and "little" nickels, the former being the same size as the current five-cent piece and the latter smaller and thinner than the current dime. A variation on the big nickel was minted during the War, when it was made of a type of bronze metal and included the slogan "We Win When We Work Willingly" embossed in Morse code inside the rim. There were also "big" and "little" pennies, the smaller like today's and the "big" penny about the same diameter as our current dollar coin but thinner and frequently carrying the likeness of Queen Victoria or King Edward VII. It was after the establishment of the Bank of Canada in 1935 that banknotes assumed their present size, superseding larger notes, which became known, before they disappeared altogether, as "horse blankets."

Directly across the street from the hotel was a building that at one time housed the community's weekly newspaper, *The Enterprise*. It must have been one of the first casualties of the Depression, because it went out of business when I was so young that I barely remember its clattering machinery and fonts of type. During its existence it printed commercial bills and letterhead stationery for the town's merchants, much still in use long after the shop itself ceased to function. The premises, empty for some time, later became a grocery store and butcher shop, and then a general store.

West of the hotel on First Avenue was the lumberyard. Within a wooden fence of vertical pickets six or seven feet high were stacks of lumber of various sizes and types of wood, of flat bundles of cedar shingles and round bundles of laths, arranged along both sides of a rectangular roadway inside the enclosure. In one corner was a three-walled, two-storey shed, open on the side facing into the yard, giving some protection from the weather to types of milled lumber laid across stringers, the front of the second storey consisting of a catwalk accessed by stairs at one end. To small boys, this structure was like a huge jungle gym, and we frequently disported ourselves there, usually to be chased out by the lumber merchant.

The fence was interrupted at the southeast corner by the office building, which also housed a warehouse for the storage of materials to be kept dry – paper bags of cement, plaster and water-mixed paint known as calcimine. In the south wall of the office was a double window, overlooking the platform of weigh scales edging on the street atop a small rise, and inside which were the bars and sliding weights of the scales. Here were weighed the vehicles and their loads of coal brought from the lumberyard's bins by the railway tracks. The scales had been installed when horse-drawn wagons were the principal movers of freight and the platform was barely large enough for even the early trucks.

The lumberyard's scrap provided raw materials for many of our youthful projects. Broken laths could be made into rubber-band pistols and broken boards into rifles, while straight-grained tapered cedar shingles made perfect arrowlike darts, naturally weighted at the thicker sharp end, and slung with terrific force by a string tied to a stick, its knotted end fitting into a notch in the dart.

Farther west on First Avenue was the telephone exchange, housed in a building that also provided living quarters for the telephone operator. The switchboard was manually operated, in the early days by a single woman, and later by the members of a family. The number of telephones in the town was such that no telephone number had more than two digits. For that matter, few people used telephone numbers. After alerting the operator with a whirl of the crank on the side of their telephone set, they merely asked to be connected to a particular person or store. Village homes had private lines but farms were on party lines, each farm with its distinctive "ring" of long and short bursts of sound from the bells, which were created either by the operator with a handcrank or by others on the same party line with the cranks on their own phones.

Duty hours for the operator were limited, usually from seven in the morning until seven at night, but sometimes in an emergency the operator could be roused in the middle of the night by persistent ringing. But it better have been a real emergency! If the operator was engaged in a household chore or answering a call of nature, it might be necessary to delay your call for a few minutes and then try again. And there was no service on Sunday.

The town's first blacksmith shop, a tin-walled building, stood on the south side of First Avenue west of my father's establishment, but later another was built, a half block east of Main Street, again on the south side of First Avenue, opposite the livery barn. There were several blacksmiths during my growing-up years, but for most of my youth the shop was operated by one man and his son. The original shop became a storage shed for some of my father's machinery and, being unheated, provided refrigeration for truckloads of frozen whitefish that my father imported for sale from northern Saskatchewan occasionally during the winter months.

The double door of the new blacksmith shop faced north, and this, combined with the brilliance of the prairie sun and the soot-grimed windows, made it difficult to see into the building from outside. After crossing the threshold it would be moments before we could perceive what was going on in the place even though the gloom might be needled by the blue pinpoint of flame from a welding torch or streaked by a brilliant pinwheel of orange-red sparks from one of the several grindstones.

When one's eyes became accustomed to the gloom one saw immediately to the left a large forge, a big anvil with an array of assorted hammers and tongs, and a large steel container of water for quenching glowing metal. These all faced a large clear area just inside the doors into which could be brought large pieces of machinery to be worked on or horses to be shod. Again on the left, along the wall and suspended from the rafters, ran a long shaft carrying wheels of various sizes from which drive belts powered the blower for the forge, a trip hammer, a drill press and an assortment of grindstones, emery wheels and buffers. Toward the back of the building stood another forge, not often used, and around the south and west walls ran a continuous workbench constructed of two-inch planking and above which was ranged a collection of nearly every type of tool imaginable.

A normal-sized door opened to the south, and through it, in a slanting block rigidly defined by smoke and dust, the sunlight glowed, its brilliance just as blinding as had been the gloom on entry. The floor was earth, packed hard except for a film of fine talcumlike dust that whirled in the more heavily trafficked areas and accumulated in soft billows in out-of-the-way places.

In a small alcovelike lean-to against the east wall stood a one-cylinder engine, which had a belt that provided power to the shaft driving the implements. Beside it, a large spike driven into a wall stud held its starting crank, while on its top, just above the steaming water in its cooling jacket, a clear glass cylinder about the size of a coffee mug jiggled its content of lubricating oil in a constant frenzy of pattern and colour.

If the shop were busy, we children stayed out of the way, hanging on to the fringes of male conversation as the blacksmith went about his work. I have never been able to overcome the feeling of awe that came to me when I watched a piece of glowing iron or steel transformed by a few deft hammer blows into an object of definite shape and purpose. The skill of these country artisans was a thing of wonder. With a few rough measurements and only the eye to guide them (it's pretty difficult to lay a tape or rule along a piece of red hot metal) they made in just a few minutes parts for machinery that seemed always to fit with only slight adjustment or none at all.

The shoeing of horses was an impressive spectacle. Most of the time we could watch, but if the horse to be shod happened to be particularly skittish, terrified by the gloom and strange sounds of the shop, we were told to make ourselves scarce in terms brooking no argument.

Early each winter the giant Clydesdales of the dray team were brought in to be re-shod; the shoes were huge and had half-inch spikes on the bottoms for purchase on ice and hard-packed snow. Even though we knew it was so, we could hardly believe that the process of paring, clipping, filing and nailing of the horses' hooves was painless for them, and we expected at any moment to see the blacksmith flying through the door, propelled by a powerful kick from one of the horse's hind feet. But it was with deceptive ease that the horseshoes were removed from the forge, bent to the proper shape, the hooves trimmed and the new shoes nailed on with the protruding ends of the nails neatly clipped off and filed down. Then the horses were led back across the street to the livery stable, stumbling slightly on the door ledges because of the unaccustomed height of the spiked shoes.

We adapted horseshoe nails to our own uses. Bright shiny new ones, their rectangular heads faceted like jewels, were bent into finger rings. More lethally, we used them to make darts. Each dart was made from a horseshoe nail, sharpened to a needlelike point on an emery wheel, a cork of about one inch in diameter and a chicken feather. The nail was pushed through the cork until its head was embedded and its point exited through the smaller end of the cork. The feather's quill end was set into the cork so the feather stuck out in the opposite direction from the nail's point, forming the tail of the dart. The natural curve of the chicken feather imparted a spin to the dart when thrown, adding to its accuracy.

If the shop were not busy we were permitted to heat bits of waste metal in the forge and pound them on the anvil into weird and wonderful shapes. If the shop's engine wasn't running, the forge blower was cranked by hand, and we marvelled at the speed with which a pile of cool and barely smoking cinders and a piece of iron could be blown to a white heat. On the anvil, each blow of the hammer on the softened iron produced a satisfying "thunk" and clang as the malleable metal changed shape and black scales of partially oxidized iron danced off the ringing anvil to the dirt floor. Then with a bubbling hiss the metal would be thrust into the container of water to cool.

Another privilege was to be allowed to don an extra pair of the dark-glassed goggles used for welding. Without the goggles, one saw only a glare of white-hot metal, the blue tip of the welding flame fanning out into orange and yellow, and the shower of sparks that flew off occasionally with a startling "pop"! With the goggles, one could see the metal flow like luminous water, guided into neat ripples of cooling metal by the blacksmith's skilled manipulation of the tip of the flame.

Even more impressive was the spectacle of the smith cutting a piece of metal with a cutting torch. The torch had a special tip where oxygen and acetylene flowed through small holes, converging to a point. We watched in shivery anticipation as the smith, his goggles on his forehead, adjusted the flame and splayed it on the metal to be cut, heating it. Then his goggles came down over his eyes and he bent to the task as we stood, mouths agape, watching the flame slice effortlessly through a half-inch plate of steel while the molten metal danced in the flame and fell to the earth floor beneath in smoking blobs.

Behind the blacksmith shop there would accumulate a collection of wagon wheels of varying sizes. This presaged an event of double interest to us. The first was pecuniary because we could sell old rubber tires to the blacksmith at five cents for a small car tire and ten cents for a bigger truck tire. These the smith used as fuel when the time came to put new steel rims on all of the wagon wheels. The second was more mundane – we just liked to watch the actual business of putting on the new rims. Even though we never knew ahead of time exactly when this was to occur, we were informed by a towering column of oily black smoke soaring skywards from behind the blacksmith shop, visible for miles. Whatever we were doing, we gave it up and hastened to the scene.

The fire was built in a circular area about ten feet in diameter. On the fire were placed the new steel rims. Nearby was a wooden platform of heavy planking, octagonal in outline, about a foot high and about eight feet in diameter with a hole in the centre to accommodate the hub of a wagon wheel laid upon it. To one side were placed several pails of water, and a shallow trench with a curved bottom was filled with water. When the rims had been heated sufficiently, the smith and a helper selected one of the correct size and carried it with three-foot tongs, sizzling and smoking with blobs of melted rubber, to the wheel. Being expanded by the heat, the rim would almost fit around the wheel, but not quite, and hammers were used to drive it on.

Licking flames appeared where the hot metal contacted the wooden wheel, quenched immediately by squirts of water from a pump oil can, enough to put out the flames but not enough to cool the steel too soon. When the rim had been properly seated, the wheel was up-ended and revolved several times in the water-filled trench amid great clouds of steam. The cooling rim contracted around the wheel, gripping it with such a pressure only the most exceptional accident could dislodge it.

One after another the rims and wheels were mated until all were done and the smith and his helpers, faces streaked with greasy soot and shirts black with sweat, seated themselves on the edge of the platform, peeled off their heavy leather gloves and began to pack their pipes or roll cigarettes while we, sad that the show was over, examined carefully the fit of the new rims and then, two or three at a time, wandered off.

When we were small, our wanderings might take us to the livery stable across the street from the blacksmith shop and up into its hay-filled loft. The boards of the loft floor were worn velvety smooth by the hundreds of tons of hay moved across them through the years; they were positively caressing to bare feet. Sunlight on the long roof and slashing through the gloom in golden bars warmed air and hay to a temperature that invited small boys to divest themselves of clothing and race about in unhampered freedom, running, climbing and plunging in the mountains of piled hay with only the occasional prickle from dried stems to remind us that we were, after all, still mortal. Sometimes, at that tender and sexless age, we were joined by our female friends and we romped together in uninhibited and innocent joy. But the thud of hooves or the jangle of harness below would shatter the idyll and, like Adam and Eve, we became conscious of our nakedness and with guilty speed slipped into our clothing in preparation for our expulsion from the lofty Eden.

Inside the south-facing main entrance of the stable was a large, plank-floored room that provided parking for six or eight cutters or buggies, out of the weather. Along one side of this area were an office and a harness room. By the time we had reached our teens, the livery business had fallen off to a point where the office was abandoned. It became one of our more usual hangouts and a place for us to play smear or hearts or poker for hard, oval peppermints, which became our gambling currency and a bagful of which we could purchase for a nickel.

Beyond the big room was the stable proper, two long rows of stalls down either side of the barn, with a passageway off to the east leading into a lean-to that was used for various purposes, either as overflow space for the main stable or, later, to house a few cows and occasionally a bull with a ring in its nose. In the floor of the loft above, square holes were cut over each manger, through which hay could be pushed for the horses stabled below.

When some special event was taking place in the winter, the main door of the stable would be surrounded by two or three dozen horse-drawn vehicles in most motley array. There were smart, shiny black one-horse cutters with scarlet runners and offset shafts, and bigger cutters drawn by two horses, all piled with wool blankets or buffalo robes, often over charcoal-fuelled foot warmers. There were little cubelike structures made of shiplap on a single set of bobsled runners and with a stub of three-inch pipe protruding through the roof to carry away the smoke from a miniature stove screwed to the floor. There were wagon-box bobsleds piled a third full of straw for comfort and warmth. Except for the cutters and bobsleds, nearly all were homemade, their shapes, sizes and construction the products of the ingenuity of their builders and functions of the size of family they were built to carry.

When they arrived at the stables, the teams were unhitched from the vehicles and led the few yards to the watering trough at the town well. They stuck their mouths through holes chopped in the ice on the surface and noisily sucked up the freezing water. Then they were led into the barn, great plumes of vapour steaming from their nostrils, and spirals of steam wisping off their glossy coats, to clump into stalls, lower their heads over hay in the mangers and wait with unbelievable patience until it was time to start the long journey home through the crackling, frosty night.

In summer the livery stable got less business because teams from the farms could stay outside and would be lined up along the hitching rail running south behind the blacksmith shop and along the backs of the west-facing businesses fronting on Main Street. The hitching rail consisted of a solid wood fence at least forty feet long and about seven feet high. Along each side and four feet or so from it stood a row of wooden posts, bored near their tops to support a continuous rod of two-inch pipe. To this rod the horses were tied still harnessed, except for the occasional saddle pony, to as motley an array of wheeled vehicles as the sleighs they had drawn in winter. Among the buggies and wagons, there stood always a few examples of that symbol of the Depression, the Bennett buggy.

The Bennett buggy was named, much to his chagrin, after R.B. Bennett, who had the misfortune to be Conservative Prime Minister of Canada from 1930 until 1935, during the worst years of the Depression. Few prairie people could have told you what the initials "R.B." stood for. In spite of the fact that he later retired to England and became a viscount, to prairie people he always had been and always will be just "R.B." Bennett.

There probably couldn't be a more fitting symbol of the Depression than the Bennett buggy. Originally it had been an automobile, most often a Model T Ford, and it is difficult to say whether the buggy evolved or the car devolved. At first it was nothing more than the automobile fitted with a tongue and whiffletrees so that a team of horses could be hitched to it for economical motive power. As time went on and it began to seem that the Depression would never end, various segments and parts were removed and those remaining re-arranged until little was left but the chassis with its rubber-tired wheels. With engine, transmission and radiator removed, the front seat might migrate forward until it was between the front wheels, or the cowling, windshield and front seat might move forward as a unit. Some form of box was built on the chassis to make a general utility vehicle. Whatever form each might take, all were called Bennett buggies. From the standpoint of the horses, their greatest advantage was that they pulled much more easily than wagons with steel-rimmed wheels – that is, until the tires wore out.

Nor were the left-over parts all discarded. Automobile seats became sofas or seats on farm wagons. Generators became wind electrics, propeller-driven to generate power for primitive six-volt farm lighting systems. Worn tires were sliced in two longitudinally to make circular watering troughs for poultry. Engine blocks and other steel parts that hadn't rusted away disappeared in the scrap drives of the Second World War.

Near the centre of the west side of the "downtown" block of Main Street the first butcher shop had stood, and it was destroyed by fire when I was only five or six. Its owner's name remained, however, neatly embossed in the concrete of the sidewalk, where its door had been when the town installed concrete sidewalks in the downtown area in 1929. Only the name remained when the family left town after the fire. The business was continued in a grocery store in the former print shop before moving to a location directly opposite its first site, in a building formerly occupied by a Red & White store, which had succumbed to the Depression. My only memories of the first butcher shop are of its sawdust-covered floor and the squat wooden barrel of dill pickles in front of its counter.

My memories of the butcher shop in its third location are better. A counter crossed the building from one side to the other, bearing a set of glistening white scales and topped for part of its length by a glassed enclosure. Here were displayed a few string-tied cuts of fresh beef or pork and boxes of prepared meat products – sausages, bologna, wieners, smoked hams, sometimes smoked herring.

Most cuts of meat were prepared while the customer waited, cut to order from sides of pork or quarters of beef on a massive square wooden chopping block centred in the space behind the counter, standing on fat wooden legs in the sawdust covering that part of the floor. Near it stood a box into which discarded bones were tossed, always available to some boy for his dog. On a rod high on the rear wall were sharp meat hooks from which the various portions of quartered animals were hung before being butchered. To one side, on a separate short counter, was a hand-cranked meat slicer on which sides of bacon or rolls of bologna were sliced however the customer wished, the first slice always shown to the customer for inspection and approval.

In what had been the grocery storeroom at the rear of the building a big ice-cooled room had been built, into which all of the meat products were moved when the shop closed. In winter, the shop was heated only to a barely tolerable temperature, and the butcher always wore a heavy wool cardigan under his white apron.

Outside, on a vacant part of the lot behind the shop, a high tripod of poles was erected when the butcher brought a whole carcass into town to be butchered, although this often was done at the farm where the animal had been bought. Our presence was barely tolerated when this was taking place, because restless children stirred up too much dust for the butcher's liking. If we stood quietly, however, we were allowed to view much of the process.

The butcher in his white apron sharpened his knives with a rhythmic "scritch, scritch, scritch" on the unguarded sharpening steel, the razor-sharp blades seeming to miss the fingers in which he held the steel by a hair's breadth. Then with knives and saws it took him only minutes to quarter a beef and carry the quarters into the shop to hang on the big hooks in the cool room to age before being butchered into roasts and steaks.

There were two poolrooms during my growing-up years, one succeeding the other as a result of fire. The first stood on the east side of Main Street in the middle of the business block, and the second stood on the west side almost directly opposite the former location, approximately where the first butcher shop had stood. When we were small, our presence was tolerated in the barber shop, and we might be permitted to enter the poolroom proper for long enough to buy a chocolate bar or a bottle of pop. If we stayed too long we were told to "vamoose" in no uncertain, but usually colourful, terms. The age for legal admission was eighteen, but by the time we were fifteen or sixteen our presence, and our money, were welcomed.

We began by playing eight ball or Boston on the smaller tables with bigger pockets and balls, then graduated to the larger tables for snooker and "pea pool," a gambling game. The charge for any game played on the snooker tables was ten cents, while those on the smaller tables were five cents each.

On Saturday nights in summer when the farmers came to town, there was a continuous game of pea pool in progress throughout the evening on one of the large snooker tables. The personnel among the five or six players changed as some losers dropped out, their cues taken by others, while the winners played on. The game was a form of Boston, the numbered balls having to be pocketed in order from one to fifteen. Before the break, each player was given, unseen by the others, a "pea." The pea was a half-inch red ball with one flat face bearing a number from one to fifteen. They were shaken in a leather container shaped like a bottle, and one was rolled across the table to each player. As the game progressed, if a player pocketed a ball with the number corresponding to that held by another, the latter was "killed" and paid the shooter a nickel. If, during the play, a shooter pocketed the ball with his own pea number on it, the game ended and each player owed the shooter a dime. The winner paid for the use of the table. There were one or two in their teens among us who became very adept at pool playing and made a considerable amount of their spending money from the Saturday-night games of pea pool.

The second poolroom also included a barbershop, operated by the poolroom's new owner. It shared the front of the building with an area containing a counter and shelves from which chocolate bars, cigarettes, tobacco, soft drinks and ice cream were sold. Occasionally a woman might come into this area of the business, but in the main, except for the wife of the poolroom's owner, who often tended the counter, it was a male preserve. No woman other than the owner's wife ever entered the poolroom proper, and a farm wife looking for her husband would ask one of the available boys to go in and inform him that she had finished her shopping and was ready to go home.

The confectionery part of the poolroom was in competition with the drugstore three doors south on the same side of the street. For most of my childhood and youth, the drugstore had a soda fountain, and the front half of the shop held round tables with chairs, both of the typical "soda fountain" style of the era, legs and chair backs of twisted, curled and lacquered quarter-inch steel rod, the round chair seats and table tops of veneered wood. The soda fountain stood along the south wall of the east-facing store, its marble top about eight feet long and head-high to a six- or seven-year-old, with the soda water spigots in its centre.

Beneath its top, on the druggist's side, was a row of hand-press pumps, each dispensing flavouring syrup for sodas; glass containers with shiny, square metal lids, slotted to hold the handles of long spoons, contained thick mixtures of chocolate and marshmallow or chopped nuts for making sundaes. Below these were the ice-cooled containers of ice cream and soda water set into a counter with hinged lids. A glass of syrup-flavoured soda water sold for five cents as did an ice cream cone; sundaes were ten or fifteen cents depending on the size of the scoop of ice cream used, a soda with a five-cent scoop of ice cream was a dime, while that marvel of marvels, a banana split, was far out of our reach most of the time at twenty-five cents. Bottled soft drinks also were a nickel. One brand of ginger ale sold for ten cents a glass, purchased almost exclusively and ostentatiously by only one of the town's businessmen. On reflection, the druggist's family must have eaten a lot of overripe bananas; he seemed to have fresh bananas available always to satisfy a very small market.

Next to the soda fountain was a glass display case containing what we called one-cent candies. There was a great variety of these – ranging from strips of paper to which perhaps a dozen or so sweet pill-sized blobs of sugary candy were stuck, to licorice in the shapes of bent-stem pipes, cigars with simulated fires of tiny red beads of candy on one end, and plugs with a red tin disc in the centre just like a plug of real chewing tobacco. They sold for one cent each, and it could occupy a considerable amount of the druggist's time waiting for a child with two or three pennies to make up its mind about which of the assortment was wanted.

Along the east wall, just inside the offset front door, was a magazine rack on which were displayed two or three copies of twenty or thirty different magazines, glossy women's magazines and men's magazines such as *Esquire* and *Popular Mechanics*, and many "pulp" magazines – westerns or "cowboy" tales, love stories, and my favourites – magazines full of tales of flying, such as *Flying Aces, G-8 and His Battle Aces* and *War Birds*. Most of these sold for fifteen or twenty cents each, while the more authoritative non-fiction ones like *Popular Aviation* were astronomically priced at twenty-five cents and up.

There was a way around the high prices for the non-fiction magazines. The supply was not guaranteed, but having some was better than having none. When the new issues of magazines came in, the druggist returned for credit the colourful front covers from the back issues and placed the stripped magazines in a couple of piles on a counter just inside the front door. These he sold for five cents each. It was with great trepidation that I eyed the magazine rack each time I was in the store, fearful that a particularly coveted aviation magazine had been sold at full price. I probably had the biggest collection of coverless aviation magazines in the province.

Shelves around the walls of the store carried patent medicines and cosmetics, cigarettes and cigars, pipes and tobacco, while another room, at the rear, with a half-door, held the prescription pharmaceuticals. On the outside of the north-facing window of this room the druggist had mounted maximum and minimum thermometers, each with a little bar of some material in its glass tube that remained at the highest and lowest temperatures reached since the thermometers had been reset. This the druggist did daily. These, in particularly hot or cold weather, brought almost all villagers into the store to discover how hot or cold it had been the day or night before or to get an accurate reading of the present temperature.

There were two druggists in succession during my childhood. The first left the town when I was only six or seven years old. The druggist who took the shop over remained for all the years of my youth with his wife and a daughter. The family had living quarters in the rear of the drugstore and for a time boarded one of the school teachers. This led to an incident that I still recall vividly.

A friend and I were wandering after dark one winter's day, and our course took us between the drugstore and the shoemaker's shop, which was to the north. As we passed about six feet from a lighted window, we were startled to see a naked young woman in the school teacher's room, apparently in the process of dressing after bathing. It was the first time either of us had seen a mature woman in such a state of dishabille and, as we were fully illuminated in the light shining from the window, we fled in some haste. Not even in the most risqué of magazines of the time had we ever seen anything quite so revealing!

The drugstore was the source of an item that we fancied greatly as children if we found one but that always disappeared mysteriously if we took one home. These were little aluminum boxes, circular in shape and about two inches in diameter, with an embossed legend on the lid that read, Three Merry Widows – Alice, Mabel, Becky. It was only when we were older that we learned the reason for their vanishing. The boxes had originally contained condoms, an item even the mention of which was taboo at that time.

This taboo was so strong that several years later, when we were in high school, a friend and I were unable to figure out a way to obtain some of the forbidden item. We had set up a hydrogen-generating apparatus in my mother's kitchen, using zinc from demolished B batteries and sulphuric acid from the drugstore. The hydrogen was led into an old soccer-ball bladder then squeezed into toy balloons. Some rose shakily, others not at all, because the balloons were too heavy. We knew enough about them to know that the lighter condoms would have made the ideal balloons to send off with our names and addresses attached, but we never could muster the courage to try to purchase them.

This manufacture of hydrogen had another consequence, of which I still have a souvenir. While waiting for hydrogen to fill the bladder, my friend was idly shaking the bottle of oily concentrated sulphuric acid. A small droplet oozed from under the bottle cap and flew into my right eye.

Fortunately, I had the presence of mind to stick my head under the kitchen pump while my friend pumped the handle vigorously, flooding my eye with water. But ever since, even though my eyesight was good enough to become a pilot during the war, when I look at a straight line or a line of type with that eye alone, the line has a little kink in the middle of it. On an eye-testing chart I could read all the letters required but the one upon which I was concentrating my right eye appeared always to be a half inch above the others in the same line.

Another item that a friend and I purchased from the drugstore, usually by pooling our resources because it was relatively expensive, was a package of cough-suppressant tablets containing licorice, linseed and what I recall as being a chloroform compound of some sort. We treated them as candy as they had a very appealling hot, sweet flavour. Consumption of this "treat" came to a sudden end when we were discovered eating them by my friend's father, the doctor, who forbade the practice because of the possible harmful effect of the chemical content upon children.

The druggist daily carried out an operation that we considered a little odd, especially in winter. Soon after rising in the morning he opened the doors and windows of both the shop and the living quarters, flooding the place with sub-zero air for perhaps ten minutes. From my perspective now, I believe it was a very wise thing, because the shop probably was impregnated with the combined odours of the previous day's business, from tobacco smoke to prescription chemicals. One can only wonder why he didn't do it in the evening after his business closed. I can remember overhearing the boarding teacher telling someone that she kept her bedroom door firmly closed while this procedure was going on.

A few yards up the street, north of the drugstore, the shoemaker had his combined shop and living quarters, a small two-room building. In the front was his shop, perhaps eight by twelve feet in dimensions, which seemed always to be cluttered with a varied collection of boots, shoes, pieces of harness, rolls of leather, sometimes a saddle, and any other leather items brought to him for repair. In the rear of the building, the second room, only slightly larger, contained his living quarters.

The shoemaker worked at a table under the front windows facing the street, the table covered by an assortment of tools, objects being repaired, bottles of black and brown leather-colouring liquids holding ball-like daubers with wire handles, harness buckles and bells, boxes of shoe laces and a compartmented tray holding various sizes of nails and rivets. Behind him was his foot-powered sewing machine, which we watched with fascination as it tick-tacked around a new half sole being put on a shoe, the stitches regularly spaced in a groove he had cut neatly in the bottom of the leather following the contour of the sole's edge. The job was finished by a bit of trimming of the quarter-inch-thick leather with a razor-sharp handleless knife, a few nails driven in across the instep by his oddly shaped hammer and clipped off inside the shoe, and by a daubing of colour matching the shoe around the edges.

The shoemaker was essential to a fashion in footwear that was prevalent among youthful swains when the Depression began to lose its grip on the country. This was for the installation of "clickers" on shoes. These were truncated arcs of steel that were set into the back edges of the shoes' leather heels and that made a very satisfyingly loud "clack" every time the heel struck the floor or pavement. For rubber-heeled shoes he also sold a similar article, with short spikes incorporated into it that could be hammered into the rubber. The result, on rubber-heeled shoes, insofar as the sound effect was concerned, was only marginally satisfactory, producing more of a weak "ping" than the solid clack of the steel-and-leather combination. Also, the spikes had a way of working their way out of the rubber, usually at an inconvenient time, such as in the middle of a tender moment on the dance floor.

The shoemaker's job was essential during the Depression when it was necessary to make do with anything repairable rather than spend precious cash to buy new items. Shoes and work boots often were re-heeled and re-soled more than once, a new strap revitalized a purse, and a twenty-five-cent repair might save having to spend several dollars to purchase a new piece of harness. It was not a throw-away economy. The waning of the Depression had the opposite effect on this business than it did on most. People began to buy new shoes and leather goods rather than continue to make do with repaired articles, and the declining numbers of work horses almost eliminated the need for harness repairs.

At the foot of Main Street, where Railroad Avenue crossed its T, stood the railway station, an essential contributor to the town's well-being in those days but, sadly, now gone. Its single building comprised the passenger facilities, a combined ticket, freight, express and telegraph office, a freight shed and living quarters for the agent-telegrapher and his family.

Originally the outside of the building had been finished with wood siding, but later it was re-covered with white-painted stucco, the name of the town painted in large black letters on each end under the eaves.

On the side of the building facing the tracks was a bay window allowing the agent to see along the tracks in both directions. Above this was a hand-operated semaphore with red and green lenses set in it to front an oil lamp so that the red shone when the semaphore arm was up and the green shone when it was down. On the wall beside the bay window was the train board, a black chalkboard, on which the scheduled arrival times of passenger trains had been entered and which never altered during my childhood and youth. Beside these were rectangles in which the agent chalked the expected actual arrival times, obtained by telegraph from other stations along the line. In good weather, trains arrived on time to the minute but in bad winter weather they frequently were late, sub-zero winds often making it difficult for the engines to keep up steam pressure and the drifting snow in cuts along the valley slowing its progress. On one memorable occasion, after I had left the town, a train engine was completely buried in snow in one of these cuts, attested to by photographs I was shown.

The passenger facilities consisted of a small waiting room equipped with a pot-bellied stove with an umbrella-like top and a long curved-backed bench. The room was decorated with large reproductions of steamships, the liners affiliated with the railway. It was a matter of wonder to us that the station agent, through his telegraph, could arrange, and make out the tickets for, voyages on these, which docked at ports more than 1,000 miles away in either direction. A grilled opening above a narrow counter gave the public access to the agent to buy tickets, arrange for freight or express shipments to be obtained or dispatched, and to send and receive telegrams. It was for one of these purposes that I had one of my most nerve-wracking experiences at about age seven.

My father had a boxcar loaded with new automobiles on the track at the loading platform for which the charges had to be paid before it could be unsealed. At the time he was too busy to attend to this personally so I was sent to the bank with a cheque for over $1,000, which I was to cash and then deliver the money to the station agent. The railway accepted cash only. The one block from bank to station never seemed so long. I was positive a Billy the Kid or a John Dillinger lurked in every doorway and vacant space I passed. I wrapped my hand securely around the roll of bills in my pocket, and I am sure the outer bill was well soaked with nervous perspiration before I reached the station. I rushed back to my father's office to assure him the mission had been completed successfully without loss or theft. It was a good many years before I had such a sum in my hands again.

In the station agent's office there stood a large iron safe, a big cupboard in which he kept his files and documents, and in the bay window a low counter upon which his telegraph key clattered, amplified by a Prince Albert pipe-tobacco tin secured to the instrument. He used the type of key known as a bug, with side to side action rather than up and down. Pressed one way it sent a swift series of clicks or telegraph-code "dots" while the "dashes" were formed by a quick pressure the other way. We were always impressed by the way he could seem to be occupied by something else when he was interpreting the meaning of a message issuing from the clattering bar.

To the right of the grilled window was a slotted wooden rack holding tickets, some preprinted for various destinations and others blank, to be filled in by the agent for less often requested destinations. To the left were stacked the large books from which he determined the charges for the various services provided by the railway. On a hook beside the bay window area hung several long wooden sticks with foot-wide loops on their ends. These were used to pass messages to the crews of trains not scheduled to stop in the town. Telegraphed train orders were written out, attached to one of these and taken out by the agent, who stood at the edge of the platform holding the stick so one of the engine crew could hook it with his arm, retrieve the message and drop the stick back on the platform.

The telegraph was the prime instrument for swift long-distance communication, particularly internationally. Undersea cables criss-crossed both the Atlantic and Pacific. Sadly, with the onset of the war, the types of telegrams and cables the agent had to deliver to his friends and acquaintances too often contained the phrases "missing as a result of . . . ," or "killed in action," or "wounded in action," or "died on active service." Strangely, in the case of our own family, one of these messages also showed the close-knit web of small-town life all over the North American West.

My brother, a pilot in the Royal Air Force, was reported "missing in action" after air operations on 28 May 1940, during the British evacuation of Dunkirk. Through some error in Britain, the notification cable was addressed to my father's birthplace, Wymore, Nebraska, rather than to our hometown in Saskatchewan. The receiving telegraph agent in Nebraska knew that some members of a family there had relatives in Canada. He contacted one of my uncles, who recognized my father's and brother's names, gave him the correct address, and the message was relayed to our agent, this nearly thirty years after my father had emigrated to Canada. One wonders what would happen to such a misaddressed message today.

But back to our local station. A door led from the office to the waiting room on one side, and directly opposite it, on the other side of the room, another gave access to the freight shed, a large room with a few shelves along one wall for smaller items but otherwise providing floor storage for boxes, barrels, and other large pieces of freight and express. Except when a train was due, the express wagon also was kept here to be pulled out on to the platform through a wide door when needed. Opposite this door was another similar one, later sealed, up to which a dray could be backed. Railway security people of today would be shocked at the casualness with which these operations were conducted. The word *security* was unknown in this context. Although the shed doors were always locked at night, they were seldom even closed during the day when the weather was good, and the thought of theft was almost non-existent — *almost*, because there had been a theft back in the pre-prohibition era.

I know this only by hearsay, but I often heard it talked about when I was a youngster. One of the town's reprobates had carefully taken note of the position of a wooden barrel of whisky, which had arrived but had not yet been delivered. Late at night, equipped with a brace and bit and a bucket, he crawled under the shed, computed the position of the barrel by counting the flooring planks, and bored a hole through the floor of the shed and the bottom of the barrel, catching a good portion of the leaking whisky in his bucket. Some time after this incident, the open space under the freight shed was skirted down to the ground.

A third door on the inner wall of the office led to the living quarters. These consisted, on the ground floor, of a combined living-dining room and a modestly sized kitchen with a large wood-and-coal burning cookstove, which also supplied the heat for the living quarters, and a small back porch, which was used also as a pantry. A narrow stairway with a right-angled turn a few steps from its bottom led from the living room to the upstairs, where there were three bedrooms and a fourth smaller room, a sort of utility room in summer doubling as an indoor facility with a chemical toilet in winter.

Upstairs heating was achieved via grillwork-covered floor openings admitting warm air from the downstairs stoves via convection. There was no running water, and potable water was obtained by the bucket from the town well, but water for other purposes was delivered from the trains into large barrel-like galvanized tanks with hinged lids. The station's coal supply also was delivered as needed by train. The station had no electric power until after the war. Lights, both signal and interior, were kerosene fuelled, and all nighttime activities around the trains and station were accompanied by the swaying shadows cast by hand-carried coal-oil lanterns.

One agent operated the station throughout my childhood and early youth. After I had begun university, another agent took over, whose daughter I met on a blind date on New Year's Eve, 1941, while visiting home-town friends. She was spending her first Christmas holiday in our town, being occupied with the study of music in Saskatoon. We were married in 1946 when I had returned to University after serving in the RCAF during the last three years of the war; she had spent the same period becoming a registered nurse.

By the beginning of the Second World War, trucks, buses and private automobiles had begun to whittle away at the railway's business. Now, its only function is the transportation of grain from the town's elevators, and only these freight trains use the tracks. But what we, who were children during the railway's heyday, miss most are the great chugging steam engines that powered the trains. I am sure that children lying in bed there today don't derive nearly the stimulation to their imaginations from the monotonous muttering rumble of a diesel engine as we obtained from the clanking, chugging, snorting, bell-ringing monsters whose whistles even had individual character imparted to them by each engineer.

Another symbol of the changing times grew up along the railway tracks during our childhood and youth. These were the tank farms that supplied the fuel for the increasingly mechanized farming industry and motor vehicles. At first there was one of these, with two vertical tanks about twelve feet in diameter and twenty-five or thirty feet high. These two became four, and a second installation grew up as well with six of the big tanks in two rows of three, close enough together so that we could jump from the top of one to another after climbing the vertical ladders to their tops. Above the top of each ladder was a frame of pipe to provide a safety barrier for those getting on or off the ladders, and these became a major feature of our games of follow the leader, a game in which each follower had to do whatever the leader did or be branded faint-hearted. One or two of the more daring leaders defied the rest of us to hang from our knees from this frame. It took some time, but eventually I think we all managed it.

At first, the fuel supplies were pumped into these tanks from tank cars on the tracks but, again, by the beginning of the war, some of them were being supplied by tank trucks. These installations were operated often by young men only a few years older than ourselves, and we visited these to watch barrels being filled for delivery to farms. Empty barrels were rolled on to scales to be filled by weight, as products such as gasoline and distillate expanded and contracted with changes in temperature. Old labels on the barrel tops were painted over with a whitewash type of paint, and new labels indicating the contents were stencilled on in black before the barrels were loaded on to trucks for delivery to the farms along with pails of grease and five-gallon cans of lubricating oil.

All of these businesses were open to us from our early childhood on and this free-and-easy access allowed us to learn innumerable things that were useful to us in our later lives no matter where they were lived. It has been said that a city boy can never learn everything a country boy knows, and in our small village we were all truly country children.

Sports

EAST OF THE BLACKSMITH SHOP and on the south side of First Avenue stood the rink. Actually, there were two rinks, sharing a common waiting room – a two-sheet curling rink and an open-air skating rink. The building housing the curling rink and waiting room ran east and west with the waiting room at the west end, entered via a door on the north side. Directly opposite this door, another on the south side opened to the skating ice. Each door had an automatic closer consisting of a piece of clothesline rope running over a pulley and weighted with some heavy object such as a piece of pipe or an old gear wheel. On cold still winter nights, the squealing run of the rope through the pulley and the slam of the door could be heard throughout half the village.

The building was constructed of shiplap on two-by-four studding, unfinished inside. Immediately inside the north door, to the right, was an enclosure about eight feet square divided in two by a north-south partition. One half, against the building's west wall, served as a coal bin and the other as a lockup for hockey equipment and as a box office for hockey games. On the centre line of the waiting room close to the west wall stood a large stove, round and pot-bellied. It was topped with a curving, umbrella-like circle of cast iron nearly four feet in diameter upon which we laid our soggy mittens to dry or, because of childish forgetfulness, to scorch.

The east wall of the waiting room had a door in its centre leading to a walkway between two sheets of curling ice. On either side of the door, window frames, on their sides, had been set into the wall to permit spectators to watch the curling in comparative warmth. A double tier of benches with a foot rest for the upper tier had been constructed in front of each set of windows to accommodate spectators. There was a constant campaign by adults to try to keep children from walking on the benches with skates on or using them as footrests while lacing skates, both practices having a tendency to reduce the surfaces of the benches to slivers.

In addition to the walkway running the length of the curling ice sheets, there was a cross walk at either end. At the waiting-room end, a double layer of boxes with hinged and hasped fronts had been constructed to hold curling rocks, each pair owned by one of the local men. The hasps had been intended to lock the rocks away, but if this had been done no one else would have been able to curl; I don't recall any of the rocks having been locked up. Because rocks were bought and owned by individuals, they were not necessarily matched, and, during a game the rocks belonging to each team could not be identified by the colour of the handles. Therefore, nearly all skips carried, threaded on their broom handles, coloured tassels made of bits of knitting wool and mounted on elastics. Before a game, one of these was slipped over the handle of each rock belonging to a team to identify it. This gave an additional advantage to the spectators; even when the rocks were in the house at the far end of the rink it usually was possible to see which team's stone was lying "shot."

The interior of the curling rink was unfinished. Day-time illumination was supplied by windows, which were merely holes about three feet square cut through the shiplap and covered with sheets of white muslin held in place by strips of lath. Through these, when a storm was blowing, a fine powder of ice crystals drifted into the rink, hung shimmering in the air for a moment and then settled on the ice, making the footing extremely treacherous. Wherever a nail head was exposed or a nail point had come through the boards of the shingled roof, a pearl of frost formed and grew through the winter, glittering in the reflected light from the two strings of light bulbs running the length of the rink over the sheets of curling ice. Above each sheet of ice at the home end were strung two wires on which square wooden blocks cut from two-by-two were threaded. One set was used to keep track of the ends played while the other, divided in the centre, showed the cumulative scores for each team. It was the duty of the people playing third on each rink to use their broom handles to slide the blocks along the wires, showing the scores and the ends played.

The temperature inside was just the same as the temperature outside and, for most of the winter, this frequently was well below zero Fahrenheit. When dressing for curling under these circumstances, fashion was the last consideration. In the coldest weather, skips often were infuriated by having to send someone into the waiting room to find a curler whose turn it was to throw his rocks, but who had taken refuge by the glowing stove to the complete neglect of sweeping duties.

The winter life of the village centred on the rink. Most of the men and many of the women curled, and the children skated. Young people began to curl on adult teams in their senior high-school years, starting as leads, but all youngsters tried their hands at the game on almost any occasion when they were in the rink and the curling ice was not being used by adults. And sometimes we would organize a pick-up high-school bonspiel.

The team I curled with consisted of three boys and a girl, the skip being a grade-twelve student, and the lead being a girl from the same junior class as me. Because no one was permitted to curl on Sunday, the whole bonspiel had to be played off on one Saturday. Although the day began disastrously for our rink, it ended almost too well. We lost our first game, which was at eight o'clock in the morning. As a result, we did not curl in the second draw at 10:00 a.m. but began again at noon and, winning every game, curled every two-hour draw subsequently until midnight. We sustained our energy with chocolate bars and candy brought to us by fathers who followed the event with interest, undoubtedly looking for candidates for future rinks of their own.

By the time we had begun the last game, our lead had given in to fatigue and I was reduced in strength to the point where I had to revert to my first method of curling - putting both feet in the hacks and pushing the rock with both hands, following it down the ice on my belly. The third and I threw three rocks each, but sweeping, except for what our skip did, was out of the question. When the last game finally was over, we had won every game except the first, had taken the prizes for two events and also the high-score prize for the entire bonspiel. After the last rock had been thrown, my father carried me home!

When we curled, there was intense competition in the selection of rocks. Many had not been sharpened since the day they had been purchased, while some owned by the more avid curlers were shipped to the city periodically for sharpening. The dull rocks slid much more easily, and for some youngsters such as I, who didn't weigh as much as a pair of rocks, throwing a sharp stone the length of the ice was almost an impossibility. My father kept his rocks very sharp and so, although I could have laid some proprietary claim to them, I seldom used them. Instead, I sought out those belonging to the Sunday-school superintendent, which were dull and slid easily. Before the days of matched sets of rocks, whenever my father curled in a bonspiel in Saskatoon he took his own rocks with him.

The biggest event of the winter for everyone in the village, excepting Christmas only, was the annual adult bonspiel. For the week the bonspiel was in progress it seemed that everybody moved into the rink. We youngsters could scarcely wait for the school day to end so we could dash to the scene. Indeed, if we weren't caught, we would slip out of the school at recess and race to the rink for a moment's glance at the draw sheets to see how our parents and favourites were doing. Nor was it unusual to have our schedules of classes rearranged on short notice while one or another of the teachers hurried to the rink to curl in draws scheduled during school hours.

From the time school was out until bedtime we never left the rink. Each day one of the women's organizations – the Ladies Aid or the Homemakers' or the Hospital Aid Society – served suppers in the rink to a major proportion of the population of the town and surrounding countryside. And what feasts! Hot dogs, baked beans, scalloped potatoes, homemade bread and buns, every imaginable variety of pie, tea and coffee, all served steaming hot from the kerosene stoves put into the rink for the occasion. And how children could gorge themselves when a menu item such as hot dogs was just five cents!

How everyone managed to get into the waiting room is a mystery, but it seemed that everyone was there at once. Adults sat on the skaters' benches and those overlooking the curling ice, while children sat on the footrail of the upper tier of benches, lost in a mass of adult legs and bodies. Youngsters wearing skates clumped in from the skating ice to the hazard of everyone's toes and fought their way through the crowd to the stove to get warm. Coats festooned the walls, hanging from nails driven into the studding, mittens sizzled on the stove top, and a thick haze of cigarette and pipe smoke, cooking steam and kerosene fumes billowed and surged above our heads. What a glorious event!

There was a steady roar of conversation, pierced by a woman's laughter or some child's high-pitched shout. Then one of the curling games would reach a critical juncture and the noise would dwindle. Men and boys, coats open and hands in pockets, filed out the door to line the walkways along the ice, the better to see the climax of the game. Inside the waiting room, others polished mist from the viewing windows to see the action better, and many of the women serving supper abandoned their posts and, wiping their hands on their aprons, elbowed their way into the crush along the windows to watch the last exciting shot.

As the rock came down the ice there would be a hush, broken only by some voice saying softly, "He's wide!" and another, "No. He's on it." Then a single voice roared from the ice, "Sweep! Sweep! Come on, sweep!" Whether the shot was made or missed, there were cheers from some and sighs from others, and a stomping, buzzing crush as spectators and curlers together crowded through the door into the warm waiting room while one of the men, pebbling can slung over his shoulder, bucked the stream to get out the door to start getting the ice ready for the next game. Three or four of the older boys already would be half-way down the rink cleaning the ice by pushing a timber wrapped in woolly sheepskins.

The adult bonspiel took place in February as a rule and it seemed that always there would be a day or two when the weather became very mild, causing considerable concern about the condition of the ice. This happened with such regularity that a thaw in the late days of winter came to be called a "bonspiel thaw." If it occurred while a bonspiel was in progress, unless the ice became completely unplayable, curling continued often to the point where only the strongest curlers could heave a rock the length of the ice. In those circumstances a call for draw weight often meant, "Throw it as hard as you can!" while in front of the house there would be an impenetrable clutter of rocks that had just made it over the hog line.

There is, in my memory, an association of individuals with particular places. In the case of the rink, I always think of a farmer who lived only a mile or two from town and who spent many winter days and evenings there curling, watching others curl and, most of all, talking. He gesticulated freely while holding forth, his pipe in one hand and a match in the other. He carried an inexhaustible supply of large, strike-anywhere, kitchen matches. It was the matches that fascinated us.

While talking, he packed his pipe with tobacco, interrupting the process frequently to use his hands to lend emphasis to some particular point, waving his pipe and tobacco pouch in wide arcs while the skirts of his long overcoat swirled and flapped around his legs. It seemed invariably that the climax of the point he was making approached just as his pipe was ready to light. Out came a match to pop into flame on contact with the hot stove. His flow of words continued. The match dwindled in length. With a wide gesture related to some emphatic statement, the match was hurled away just before the flame reached his fingers. Another appeared as if by magic. It, too, was lighted as the tale went on. This one might almost reach the bowl of the pipe before being flung away. The process was repeated while we watched, entranced.

Another match might even yield one or two thin puffs of smoke between bursts of words before fear of interruption caused him to remove the pipe from his mouth and throw that match away. By the time the discourse was finished, many matches later and with the pipe still unlit, the junior members of his audience were reduced to a state of giggling helplessness. Because his discourses were always on a topic of the greatest seriousness to him and directed principally to the adults present, he never connected our laughter to his actions but attributed it to our political or economic imbecility and lack of serious attention to the force and lucidity of his argument. With a shrug of disgust he would walk over to the windows overlooking the curling ice – and light his pipe.

Another great crush occurred in the waiting room when there was a hockey game because it was the only warm area available for teams and spectators alike. The local players arrived at the rink with all of their gear on except their skates, padded shins showing incongruously beneath overcoats, and hockey-gloved hands grasping hockey sticks from which, over their shoulders, dangled their skates. Visiting teams arrived either similarly attired or changed just up the street in the office of the livery stable, although one or two players, less bashful than the others, might strip to their longjohns in a corner of the waiting room behind a screen of opened coats while giggling girls turned their backs on the spectacle.

The hockey of the time, even in small villages such as ours, was of good quality, with the emphasis on skating, stick handling and shooting accuracy. Body checking was allowed but "boarding" was not, that is, no body checking was permitted within four or five feet of the boards. Fisticuffs were very rare. But one thing puzzled us greatly as children – how was it that our home-grown team, which we were sure had the best players in the country, could be defeated so often?

The mode of arrival of visiting teams varied with the years, their locations and their affluence. Some, from villages on the same rail line, might arrive by train, the time of the game having been set to dovetail with the passenger or mixed train schedules. Some from nearby communities arrived by bobsled or, later, by stake trucks covered with canvas. When these last two methods were used, the players usually entered the waiting room trailing wisps of the hay or straw put into the sled and truck boxes to help keep them warm and to provide some comfort.

The hockey rink was surrounded by a wooden fence about twelve feet high except on the side formed by the curling rink and waiting room. Parallel to the long side of this fence and about eight feet inside it was another fence about five feet high. This formed the boards of the hockey ice, and the space between the two fences was used to hold snow shovelled and scraped from the ice surface. A similar five-foot fence ran along the side of the curling rink about four feet from it. This space was meant to hold spectators, but it, too, usually was filled with snow, and often the spectators' feet atop the packed snow were higher than the top of the fence.

There was only one temperature during hockey games – very cold. At the end of each period there was a rush of spectators and players for the warmth of the waiting room. This led to some interesting situations when two players from opposing teams who had developed a rather intense dislike for one another during the play happened to hit the waiting room door at about the same time with perhaps a female spectator or two in between. The education of the women in profanity, not to mention unlikely genealogies, was advanced rapidly. But there were certainly some females who needed little instruction even if their knowledge was seldom used in polite society. I recall the shock several of us experienced as teenagers when, during a hockey game, a player near us was hit in the crotch by a puck, his jock producing a resounding metallic sound. "My God!" exclaimed a young woman standing close by, "He's got brass balls!" Never before had my young friends and I heard a woman even hint at a reference to such portions of the male anatomy.

As children, we had very little in the way of proper hockey equipment except skates, hockey sticks and a scarred puck salvaged from the throw-aways of the senior team. We played hockey in the same clothing in which we did everything else, merely removing the outer layers as the activity intensified and our bodies warmed. Skates did the circuit of the town as they were outgrown by one child and acquired by another.

This was the time of the advent of "tube" skates, and the first of these were looked upon with more than a little suspicion as probably not coming even close to the Automobile Ds, which we considered to be the ultimate. But soon our favour swung the other way, and we all clamoured for the tubes and derided the old-fashioned straight blades. A few of the young men and women sported long-bladed racing skates, but these really were not suitable for the limited area of a skating rink, although they were excellent for long stretches of ice when a big slough froze over.

My first pair of skates bore some appellation such as North Star. The blades were so wide that they would stand by themselves on a smooth surface. The boots soon assumed a sort of cockeyed stance in attempting to adapt themselves to my unsteady ankles. Ice skating, in spite of the favourable environment, just was not one of my strong points and, although I tried desperately to emulate the hockey skills of my older brothers and friends, it was soon apparent that my role where hockey was concerned should be that of an interested onlooker. When we had juvenile hockey teams I did my utmost, but having found that my most effective play was to fall on the ice in front of an oncoming attacker, and learning very quickly how painful that could be, I retired my stick for good.

As was the case with many of our sports, we learned that if we were to enjoy ourselves, we had to work too. Often when the rink was being prepared in early winter, if we were not in school we assisted with the flooding to make the ice. Midway on the south side of the rink, between the fences, was a small unheated shack enclosing a well and pump engine. This served double duty during hockey games as a players' bench and penalty box. By means of a series of pipes and hoses hooked to the pump, it was possible to spread water over most of the rink surface – except when the well went dry, as it did during the Dirty Thirties. Then the team of dray horses and one or two teams from nearby farms were hitched to big tank wagons to bring load after load of water from the town well. Although much of this could be spread with hoses by gravity, pails were used to fill low spots and gaps along the boards and in corners. Our mothers, who often were sorely tried to keep us at our chore of bringing two or three pails of water a day home for household use, must have wondered how we had the energy to cart dozens of them around the rink.

When the ice had been made, keeping it clear of snow was a constant struggle. Saturday morning was set aside as a time for younger boys to play hockey, and it seemed we seldom arrived at the rink without finding the surface of the ice streaked with drifts and the corners piled deep with snow, which had swirled in during the night. But with a dozen or so of us scraping and shovelling with all our might, it usually didn't take long to have it all cleared off.

Evenings were reserved for mixed public skating. The ice was dimly illuminated by a half dozen bulbs on wires strung across the rink from one side to the other, adequate for social skating but not bright enough for hockey. Keen young boys who arrived at the rink first would start a game of pom-pom-pullaway (the icy version of the game we played on foot in the school basement) but soon girls and parents and older brothers and sisters arrived, and our reckless, dash-about game was forbidden. Then the scratchy record player started up and, to the strains of "The Skaters Waltz" and other popular tunes of the day, the big counter-clockwise wheel of skaters started up, to continue for the rest of the evening. One result of this constant circling to the left was that many of us had to work really hard to learn to turn to the right with ease. As we advanced into our teens we began to skate in pairs with our female classmates and some-times with our female school teachers or the nurses from the hospital. We began by skating hand in hand and later with our arms linked. Before too long we were skating with both arms behind our backs, the girl's left hand in the boy's left and her right in his right, taking long strides in time with the music. Small children might play tag in the relatively clear space in the centre of the circle or hug the safety of the boards, while solo adult skaters wove in and out among the others, often practising pirouettes and other intricate manoeuvres. I don't recall anyone having had true figure skates.

The character of the ice changed with the temperature, and as the weather got colder, the ice became harder and harder. When the ice was in this condition, a skater wheeling with one toe cocked to dig the heel of a blade into the ice carved a great slash in the surface while the ice chips flew and tinkled like broken crystal. As the ice's temperature dropped to the point when it ceased expanding and began to contract, there might suddenly be a loud report as a large crack appeared zig-zagging across the ice surface, creating a hazard for the skater who might be paying more attention to his or her companion than to the ice.

To skate on such hard ice, one needed sharp skates, so it seemed we were constantly after our fathers for money to have our skates sharpened. One father attempted to economize by doing the job himself. Imagine the son's chagrin, and the merciless ribbing he took from the rest of us, when it was discovered that after sharpening the skates, his father had carefully rounded the edges of the blades so they would slide better!

What seemed to be the smoothest ice one ever skated on was that in the curling rink in the spring when it had just started to thaw and was covered by a thin film of water. The smoothness with which our skate blades slipped along through the water with scarcely a sound was almost eerie after their noisy ringing on the hard ice outside all winter long. This was the time and place for a form of shinny, played on the melting curling ice with old hockey sticks and a rubber ball. To the normal hazards of such a free-style game were added the risks of a fall into the meltwater covering the ice or being caught in a shower of spray as someone took a wild swipe at the ball. When we had gone home, soaked and shivering, and had been properly told off by our mothers, the skating season was definitely over.

Because, up until the mid-thirties most automobiles were put away for the winter, the scant traffic on the streets consisted almost entirely of horse-drawn vehicles. These usually kept Main Street well packed down and turned it into a playground for youngsters running and sliding in slick bobsled tracks, experimenting with sails on sleds and toboggans and, most often, impromptu hockey between two or three youngsters in galoshes with broken hockey sticks and a frozen horse bun for a puck. Often one or more of the village dogs took part in these games, chasing the "puck" and soon rendering it unusable. However, there was a plentiful supply.

In the dying days of winter there was one more sport in which we were able to indulge. This was tin-can curling. In the early spring a sudden thaw filled some of the small shallow sloughs around the town with water, which the last cold snap of winter froze into smooth sheets of ice. This was the signal for us to start rounding up the best tin cans we could find. Jam and coffee cans were good, but best were the big cans in which the shops received chewing and pipe tobacco. From all of these we manufactured our curling "rocks." Each was filled about three-quarters full of water, the lids were jammed into them on a forty-five-degree angle to make handles, and they were set out on back steps overnight to freeze solid.

As the water froze, its expansion beneath the layer that formed first across the top caused the bottom of the can to bulge outward in a smooth curve extending beneath the rim of the can and creating a surface upon which it would slide easily. Off we went to the slough carrying these, any old stubs of broom we could find, and a piece of board through which nails had been driven at suitable intervals to inscribe circles on the ice. Hog lines and Ts were scratched into the ice too, and hacks chipped out. We used the same rules as regular curlers did, hampered only by the fact that our rocks would not draw. A certain amount of care had to be exercised when making a take-out. If the rock was thrown too hard, the collision with its target could shatter the ice in both. Loud and vociferous were the recriminations if a favourite rock was dealt such a blow, even though, anticipating such an event, we had each equipped ourselves with several.

One day when we arrived, the ice on the pond would feel rubbery, the ice in the tin cans would have loosened from the sides and our short curling season was over. One by one the "rocks" melted themselves through the ice, the dark colours of the cans heated by the sun. In the summer in the slough grass, a welter of rusted tin cans and a scattering of old broom handles was all that remained of our curling rink.

In the first very warm days of spring or early summer, before its earth floor had completely dried after the melting of its burden of ice, the curling rink was delightfully cool, and the damp, smooth-packed earth floor caressed our bare feet. Here it was our custom to play a form of cricket using apple-box boards for wickets and a piece of board or perhaps an old baseball bat as a substitute for a cricket bat. The rubber ball when soundly hit ricocheted among the posts and walls of the narrow building like a bullet. The only accepted way to make an "out" was to hit the running batter with the ball, thrown as hard as possible. An out could sting quite smartly, but retaliation was possible when the thrower came to bat. As summer progressed, the curling rink became warmer and warmer inside, being completely enclosed and having a black shingled roof. Soon its temperature soared above that of the air outside and we abandoned it for cooler precincts, not to enter it again until the next winter.

A summer event comparable to the winter bonspiel as a major occasion for the whole village was the annual sports day. Ours usually was held in July, and the principal sports were men's baseball and women's softball. This meant most of the surrounding villages had to be consulted to set a date, because each would have its own sports day and all would have their teams playing in each others' events.

The day before the scheduled date, most of the young men of the village, and a good proportion of its businessmen, busied themselves getting the sports grounds at the north end of Main Street into shape. This involved raking the grounds with teams of horses or tractors, repairing chicken-wire backstops, perhaps making new bases for the ball diamonds out of gunny sacks and sand, and laying foul and base lines with a sort of wheelbarrow, the four-inch-wide cogwheel of which clawed white lime from its box as it was pushed along the ground.

Many worked at constructing temporary booths, two large ones and three or four smaller ones. The large ones were intended for a food outlet and for a bingo game, while the smaller ones were for various games of chance. No one seemed to worry about anti-gambling laws. The booths were constructed of lumber borrowed from the lumberyard and so the sizes of the booths were determined by the standard lengths of lumber. All were assembled without the nails having been driven completely home so they could be taken down easily. Booths were roofed over with borrowed tarpaulins and decorated with branches of willow and poplar brought from the grove surrounding the pond at the abandoned stone house.

Prizes for the various games of chance were imported from the city, ranging from celluloid kewpie dolls on slender bamboo canes and ceramic dogs and cats to more valuable items such as kitchenware and dishes. On the single occasion when I won a sports-day bingo, I took as my prize a hand-tooled leather belt with silver buckle and tip, which my father cut down to my waist size and which, years later when I had long outgrown it, graced the waist of my wife's slacks.

All of this work on a hot July day offered young entrepreneurs a method of making some money to be spent the following day. We bought a dozen or so lemons on credit from the Red & White store and began making lemonade. Some mother's kitchen became the manufacturing establishment as well as the supply source for necessary items such as sugar, glasses and a large chunk of ice from her icebox. On a child's wagon we carefully towed a pail full of lemonade, a pail of water to rinse glasses and a number of tumblers to the sports grounds and its practically guaranteed market of thirsty men. When the supply sold out we paid the merchant for the lemons and divided the profits among the two or three of us who had undertaken the enterprise.

One of these preparatory days is memorable because of the near disaster with which it ended. As finishing touches were being applied to everything in the evening, a huge cumulus cloud appeared in the west and seemed to be tracking toward us. As it came closer, its top towered into bright cirrus-appearing streaks and a dark skirt of rain could be seen beneath it. Then the ominous calm before the storm stilled everything, and we all dashed for cover. The storm struck. Gales of wind streaked rain and hail across the sports grounds while lightning flashed and thunder roared. It was all over in a few minutes and, as the storm moved off to the east, everyone dashed to the sports grounds to survey a disastrous scene. White lines were washed away, booths wrecked, tarpaulins torn, branches scattered over a wide area downwind of the sports field, many coming to rest in the hail-wrecked garden bordering the eastern side of the grounds. As darkness fell, most made their way home except for a few who had immediately begun to plan for the morrow.

The next morning, the day of the event, the village men turned out early and began the necessary reconstruction. The July sun shone bright and hot, rapidly drying the ground and evaporating the remaining water from puddles, most of which had sunk quickly into the dry prairie earth. With everyone working at top speed, the booths were rebuilt, the ball diamonds repaired and the sports day began shortly after noon as scheduled. But the treasurer had to hope there would be a good turnout, because the lumberyard had to be paid for a large quantity of damaged lumber.

Admission was charged at a barrier erected across the north end of Main Street, staffed by volunteers equipped with a metal cash box on a trestle table and a supply of small white tags on strings, the kind usually used in the shops as price tags. These were issued to each person who paid admission and were tied to a buttonhole on a shirt or often to the small button on the top of a baseball cap. Although there were two or three other lanes and streets opening into the grounds, no one ever used them to avoid paying admission, and no one ever suspected that it might be done. It just wasn't done. The principal use of the tag was to gain re-admission to the grounds if one left to go to the Chinese restaurant or the beer parlour, the only two businesses that remained open in the afternoon of sports day.

Many of the spectators made it a point to arrive at the admission gate as early as possible so they could park their cars facing the ball diamonds, and about twenty feet from the foul lines. There they remained all day providing comfortable seating for their owners, their friends and families. If the day was hot, as it usually was, car doors were left open and towels or articles of clothing were hung in the windows facing the sun. Often the cars were left empty between games as the occupants patronized the food booth or games of chance or walked over to watch a game at the softball diamond, and no one concerned themselves about the possibility of theft. However, a cracked windshield from a foul ball was not uncommon. When a game was in progress, a good play was applauded by a cacophony of car horns, ranging in sound and volume from the relatively meek "kay-oo-gah!" of older cars to the twin-horned blare of newer models.

Baseball teams were composed almost entirely of local men, those in their late teens and early twenties, and some who were well into middle age. Occasionally an exceptionally good pitcher or hitter from some re-mote place would be given a job by a village businessman to make his services available to play for that town's team, a practice that, for winter, provided some hockey players as well.

We youngsters spent most of our time in the vicinity of the baseball diamond with occasional diversions to the booths or to the softball games. There were two reasons for this, one of which was pecuniary. Firstly, we enjoyed watching the baseball and, secondly, there was a chance to make some money. Visiting baseball teams supplied their own equipment, but the baseballs were provided by the organizers of the event. The man in charge of the baseballs paid us a dime for each foul ball we retrieved and returned from the garden to the east, from behind the backstop or from behind a row of cars. The competition was fierce, but occasionally a ball would land close enough so that even the slowest of us could beat the others to it. Such a windfall was immediately expended at one of the booths, perhaps by taking a chance at the ring toss or by purchasing a hot dog, a soft drink or a cob of corn liberally smeared with butter from one of several pound blocks ranged along the food booth's counter. But the resentment was bitter if a ball that landed close to the row of cars was tossed back into the diamond by a spectator before one of us could get it.

Altogether, sports day was one of continuous excitement and enjoyment. As we grew into our middle teens, it allowed us to widen our circle of friends and acquaintances as we got to know our peers from other villages who had come to the event, and we to theirs. As we boys matured, and especially after we had reached the age at which we could get our driver's licenses, the widening circle of female friends led to dreams of romance and future dates for dances, movies and even more entrancing pastimes. As the Depression loosened its grip, our range was expanded considerably and social events such as dances were within reach at distances of ten, twenty or even thirty miles.

Often sports days ended with a dance in the evening in the local theatre, beginning after the last baseball game was played as the sun was setting. It was not unusual to see male dancers still in baseball uniforms (although not all teams had them) and female softball players dancing in slacks, which, in my younger years, were looked at as not being quite proper for women. There usually were a few overly boisterous males who had spent more of the day in the pub than watching the games, and we boys did our usual late-evening search for empty beer bottles.

Other than once or twice when the sports days were preceded by decorated bicycle parades, children took no active part. We had no organized baseball or softball after the school year ended, although we all played in school at recess and noon hours, often with a teacher acting as umpire. In those circumstances a game might go on for several days, but it meant also that the players had no proper coaching. We learned to swing a bat properly or pitch by watching our seniors and by picking up tips in conversation with them. My older brother was ambidextrous and learned to pitch with either hand. This caused frequent consternation and argument after he had graduated to senior competition and would pitch one or two balls to a batter with one hand and the next with the other. In the summer we played pickup games of the "scrub" variety. The days of Little League Baseball were yet to come, at least in our part of the world.

We were introduced to one other sport in the mid-thirties. Several of the businessmen and our doctor arranged to have two tennis courts laid out on vacant lots on the south side of Second Avenue across the street from the school. The courts were of packed and rolled clay and sand surrounded by a high chicken-wire fence and were outlined with white tapes held down by large staples. Soon, many teenagers were also involved in the sport, mostly on a very casual basis. However, we learned the basics of the game and spent many happy hours playing.

The courts were oriented north-south. Because all of the maintenance of the courts was done by the players, a pattern emerged in which the court on the west side was kept in excellent condition by the senior players. We younger ones, as a result, preferred to play on that court, but it was accepted as being their territory if the men wished to play, and we moved to the eastern one. This was slightly lower than the other, and after rain it got wetter and stayed wet longer. It was not long, therefore, until the eastern court began to deteriorate, and within three or four years it displayed a considerable quantity of dandelions and its tapes began to disintegrate. As there were seldom more than four senior players who would play doubles, the second court was allowed to disintegrate almost completely. This state of affairs was abetted by the beginning of the Second World War, which put the quietus to many small-town sporting activities as it drained the villages of most of their active young sportsmen, either by enlistment in the armed forces or by moving to the variety of jobs that suddenly became available in cities far from our village.

Farms

ALTHOUGH I AND MOST of my peers were village children, many of our friends and schoolmates lived on the surrounding farms. We loved to visit with our country friends, and the expeditions we made to nearby farms to watch the work in progress provided valuable experience.

Spring seeding was done while we were still in school. In my childhood days, when farming was still being done in large measure with horses, seeding was notable for the absence from school of many boys from the senior grades who were needed to assist their fathers. On Saturdays we could walk to nearby farms and watch the plodding teams of six or eight horses making their way, at what today seems like a snail's pace, up and down the fields pulling disc plows or seed drills, each accompanied by its flock of wheeling Franklin's gulls feasting on the insects and seeds the machines turned up. Often, too, they were accompanied by clouds of grasshoppers hatching out of the sun-warmed soil. On Sundays the fields were quiet as men and horses rested.

By the late 1930s, the teams and drills were mostly gone, replaced by tractors and one-ways, which roared across the fields at a much faster pace in clouds of dust – but each still with its flocks of gulls and grasshoppers. Now, too, farmers began to work on Sundays – only a few at first but more and more as time went on – as they hastened to take advantage of whatever moisture the winter snows had added to the soil. Unfortunately, during the driest years, there often had been little snow in the winter.

Some farmers began planting long lines of caragana and evergreen trees at intervals in their fields to act as snow catchers during the winters. The caragana seemed to do well, but many of the evergreens succumbed to the vagaries of prairie weather. Most farmyards had a rectangle of assorted varieties of trees and bushes around them – caragana, Manitoba maple, poplar and evergreens. Trees in these shelter belts seemed to do reasonably well, probably because bushes such as the caragana collected enough snow in the winter to sustain the less hardy types. There were some farms, however, that had no growth around them, and their buildings stood starkly on the prairie like apple boxes scattered on a football field.

A farm task that fell to me as a small boy was poisoning gophers. Along the east side of my father's half-section ran a road allowance that was really only a trail through the prairie grass. It was riddled with gopher holes. There were several hundred along its mile length, and each seemed to harbour at least one family of those wheat-field raiders. In an attempt to eliminate them, I was sent out with a pail of poisoned wheat and a flat stick to deposit a blob of the mixture at the entrance to each hole. The bait had a cloyingly sweet smell, which I suppose was intended to entice the gophers but which, when inhaled in quantity on a calm hot day, was nauseating to a small boy. Although it never made me physically ill, there are similar sweet odours that I cannot tolerate to this day.

My father had no farm animals, the half-section being used solely for the production of grain. At the north end was a fenced yard containing a well with a hand pump and a four-stall barn with a single pitched roof and no loft. This was used, before the days of tractors, to house temporarily up to eight horses when the land was being worked. A circular trail developed in the grass around the pump, which became, when my father was not present, a race track. The racing vehicles, driven by my two older brothers, were a Model T truck and a Fordson tractor with lugged steel wheels. The tractor usually won because of its much smaller turning circle. Even though the truck was speedier, its radius of turn widened as it went faster, so the distance it travelled around the circle became greater and greater.

My acquaintance with farm animals was partially the result of my friendship with a schoolmate who lived about four miles from town and
Herby Way

who often invited me to spend weekends with him. Sadly, our friendship is just a memory, because he was killed flying in the Royal Canadian Air Force during the Second World War.

His father kept pigs, chickens, geese, a half dozen Percheron work horses and several cows. When visiting, I participated in my friend's farm chores, forking hay from the loft into mangers, feeding "slop" to the pigs, scattering grain for the fowl and, after many unsuccessful attempts, finally managing to learn to milk cows with all the attendant satisfactions and risks. I remember one cow in particular. She seemed bent on doing whatever she could to hinder my learning. If she wasn't switching her tail in my face, she was moving her hindquarters so as to push me off the upturned pail I was using as a stool. Then she would refuse to let her milk down. I think she knew I was an ignorant village boy because, when I became more adept at milking, her frustrating antics ceased. It was very satisfying to hear the hiss of milk streaming into a pail in alternating fine jets. And on a cold winter day it was comforting to lay one's cheek against her warm flank. It was a long time before farms were equipped with milking machines.

One incident taught me that one can overstep the bounds of generosity. The farmyard where it occurred lay a mile to the east of my father's and was operated by a couple with whom I spent many happy vacation days as a small boy. They were always very generous to me so I thought nothing of helping myself to some nearly ripe plums growing in their garden. In fact, I picked them all, reaping a couple of pailfuls, which I took home. Needless to say, my mother and father were horrified. I was given the corporal punishment a child thief deserved, and my father paid the farmer for my loot. By dint of adding a great deal of sugar, my mother was able to convert most of the unripe plums to jelly. My conscience chided me severely every time the jelly was served and I contemplated Mother's carefully labelled jars proclaiming accusingly, "Herb's Plums"! Happily, my Taylor relationship with the farm couple was resumed as if nothing had happened.

Harvest time was the most exciting period for children. When I was very young, just at the beginning of the Depression, my friends and I would make our way to the grain elevators where, before the sun was at heat height in the sky, there were line-ups of teams with wagons and even a few early-model trucks waiting to deliver their loads of grain, their drivers gathering in small groups to discuss the harvest while they waited. The groups dissolved from time to time as the men returned to lead their teams forward, reassembling to wait while each wagon at the head of the line was unloaded.

The conversations were always of the crops. "What has your wheat been grading?" "What is it weighing to the bushel?" "How many bushels to the acre are you getting?" "How high is the dockage?" Even in the worst years, most of the conversation was good humoured, with jokes traded at one anothers' expense.

"Did you hear about so-and-so here pitching his mackinaw into the threshing machine with some sheaves and charging up the straw stack to find it? He said there were some papers in the pocket he wanted!"

There was general laughter among the men while the object of their amusement sheep-facedly squirmed in embarrassment.

Or, the tale of a farmer who was renowned for always looking at the dark side of things. When another observed that the crop he had on one piece of land was the best in the country, his rejoinder was, "Yes, but it's awfully hard on the land."

We children listened to the banter, learning about people. We petted the horses, examined the trucks, and if a farmer didn't object, climbed into his wagon and buried ourselves in the grain. Sitting on the side of a wagon we picked weed seeds, chaff and bits of grasshopper from handfuls of wheat, which we then chewed into gluten gum. By the time we had a satisfactory quantity of gum, our stomachs were uncomfortably full.

Eventually the wagon we were on would be driven up the steep slope into the elevator, stopping with its front wheels on the hoist, and we would be told to get off while the wagon and load were weighed. Occasionally an elevator man would let us stay on and we thrilled with excitement as his hand went to the air valve controlling the hoist. If the team of horses was skittish, the farmer stood at their heads holding their bridles while air rushed noisily through the pipes and the hoist began to raise the front of the wagon, two planks on its edges angling up to hold the wagon wheels.

The farmer lifted the slide at the back of the wagon and the grain began to flow out and through the grating in the elevator floor to the pit below. As the angle of the wagon increased, we clung to the sides while the wheat slid out from around our legs and the wagon tongue moved upward between the horses until its point of attachment to the wagon was higher than their rumps. When the wagon was practically emptied, we could help the elevator man by sweeping the remaining wheat from the corners of the wagon box before the hoist was lowered with a hissing of released air and the empty wagon was weighed.

During the unloading, the elevator operator caught a brass cylindrical measure full of wheat, which was weighed to determine its weight per bushel, thus giving the lie to the tables on the backs of our school scribblers which stated flatly that wheat weighed sixty pounds to the bushel. The kernels of grain were examined for size, condition and colour, perhaps bitten to assess their hardness, and the sample was shaken through a series of screens in circular shiny brass mountings to determine the dockage charged against the load because of weed seeds, pieces of grasshopper and other foreign matter. We watched with awe as the elevator man quickly calculated the value of the load, handling with obvious ease the decimals and fractions we struggled with in school. His calculations and completion of the grain ticket for the farmer were done with an indelible pencil producing greyish figures which turned magically to a brilliant purple whenever they ran across a drop of sweat or when he moistened the tip with his tongue.

After pocketing his grain ticket, the farmer climbed on to the wagon via one of the front wheels and slapped the horses' backs with the reins, starting them down the steep ramp out the other side of the elevator, the weight of the wagon pushing them to a trot as they neared the bottom. He might keep them at a trot for a short distance, harness jangling, before they slowed to a walk for the long journey back to the threshing rig. Sometimes much of the hauling to the elevators was delayed until after the harvest by storing the grain in granaries on the farm. Before mechanical loaders took over the greater part of the work of filling the granaries, we did it ourselves, with big scoop shovels, and it meant days of toil.

In the very early thirties, much of the grain was harvested by horse-drawn binders, which cut the wheat and bound it into sheaves. Crews of men followed the binders, of which there often were three or four working behind one another, gathering the sheaves and piling them into stooks. These contained up to twelve or fourteen sheaves, depending on the density of the crop, leaning against one another with the heads of the grain uppermost and one or two laid crosswise on top to hold the stook together and to shed rain. When I was seven or eight years old, the sheaves usually were pitifully small, and even a child could build stooks with them, but in a field with a heavy stand of grain the sheaves were too big for a child to handle. Fields ready for threshing lay silent, with rows of stooks standing sentinel over the stubble like soldiers on a parade ground.

Often we visited threshing rigs on farms close enough to town so we could walk home after riding to the farm in an empty grain wagon or truck. We were fascinated by the great threshing machines, some still powered by steam tractors, although the internal combustion engine was by then taking over. A few farmers owned their own rigs, but many took their turns at hiring the threshing outfits that followed the harvest from south to north as the crops ripened. When setting up, the steam tractor huffed and puffed its way across a field, towing the threshing machine to its desired location. Unhitched from the machine, the tractor chugged its way around until it faced the intake end and then jockeyed back and forth to align its big belt wheel with the one on the threshing machine.

The heavy rubber-and-fibre belt was unrolled and looped over the tractor's and threshing machine's belt wheels with a half twist in it. The tractor reversed to draw the belt to the proper tautness, and its operator pulled a lever to start the belt singing between the two machines, then set the throttle to the proper speed, the ball governor atop the boiler whirling. If all was accomplished handily, the tractor driver might give a couple of toots with the steam whistle in celebration before checking his firebox and throwing in another shovelful of coal. Close by stood a wagon the tractor had towed behind the separator, as the threshing machine frequently was called. This was loaded with barrels of water for the boiler and a supply of coal to replenish the bins built into the tractor.

If the farmer had been waiting for the threshing rig, as soon as it was set up, loads of sheaves would be waiting to be threshed, loaded by hand and pitchfork on big wagons we called hay ricks. These drew up beside the threshing machine and the sheaves were tossed on to a moving slatted canvas belt that carried them into the machine. The machine shook and rattled and banged as its various claws, beaters and screens separated the grain from straw and chaff. On one side the grain fell from a spout into a waiting wagon with a grain box while at the end of the separator opposite the tractor a big moveable pipe, twelve or fourteen inches in diameter and ten or twelve feet long, spouted the straw, chaff and bits of broken binder twine into a pile that soon became a straw stack, the pipe being moved as needed to shape the stack and allow for the vagaries of the wind.

As soon as a rick was unloaded, its driver started it off across the fields to load it again with sheaves, leading the horses from stook to stook. It took several hay ricks to keep a constant supply of sheaves at the threshing machine. Occasionally we accompanied the ricks and might even throw a couple of sheaves on, but soon the load would be so high that only a man with a pitchfork could put the sheaves on top. One thing that discouraged us from handling the sheaves was that during much of the early thirties a goodly portion of each sheaf consisted of Russian thistle, which ripened with the grain and filled each sheaf with thousands of sharp barbs. We soon learned, too, not to go into the stubble without shoes and our socks pulled up over the bottoms of folded trouser legs, as there often was more thistle than grain straws, cut off at the same height by the binders.

It was this method of farming that brought the hundreds of "hoboes" to the prairies during the Depression. There was a great demand for men to stook the grain, to load and pitch sheaves, to shovel grain, to drive the wagons and look after the horses as well as to assist with other farm tasks such as milking, which had to be done, harvest or not. In a few short years, as motor-powered machinery became available, the threshing crews practically disappeared. A farmer with one other man, possibly a son, could swath and/or combine a crop that previously had required a crew of a dozen or so to harvest, while the grain wagons were replaced by a single truck often operated by a farmer's wife, son or daughter.

The harvest crews had to be fed, and this placed a tremendous burden on the farm wives, who had to prepare three, or sometimes four, meals a day for any number of hungry harvest hands. Eggs, bacon, porridge, bread, beef, beans, potatoes, onions, cabbage, carrots and on and on, all were prepared by the farmer's wife with possibly the assistance of a "hired girl," a daughter, or another farm wife or two if the harvesting was being done by farmers cooperatively. My mother came to the Saskatchewan grain belt in 1913 at the age of twenty with a year-old son, to face as one of her first tasks feeding a crew harvesting flax that had been left standing from the year before. When she had moved from Nebraska, she had brought with her a few dozen jars of wild-grape jelly, some of which she served at one of the first meals she prepared for the crew, expecting that some of the men might want to put a bit on their bread. Instead she found they were spooning it in great quantities into bowls and eating it with cream. That was the only time she served it.

One product of the threshing-machine harvest that children loved was the straw stack. It was a natural playground to be climbed, jumped down, tunnelled into, sometimes with two or three levels to be somersaulted down. The penalty was prickly chaff and thistle, which got into our hair, our clothing and our skins. This we ignored until time to go home, when suddenly we would find it very irritating, often to the point where we had to strip and shake the offending material out of our clothes and try to brush it off our sweaty skins, performing this task on the side of the stack opposite any nearby farm home.

Another valued use of the straw stack for young people was to supply the fuel for a wiener roast. A group of us, ranging in ages from early to mid-teens, would get permission for such an outing from a farmer who had a stack that he intended to burn. We equipped ourselves with wieners, buns, perhaps some soft drinks or lemonade, and those very-hard-to-find-on-the-prairies items, long sticks sharpened to slender points. Some used sturdier sticks to which they had bound toasting forks. As nearly all of the sticks available had once been lumber, they were dry and very flammable. More than one youngster trembled in anticipation of punishment when he failed to notice the string binding his mother's toasting fork to the stick had burned through, dropping the fork into the fire.

The wiener roast started with a relatively small fire of straw on the downwind side of the stack. After we had eaten our wiener, handfuls of straw were ignited and deposited around the perimeter of the big straw stack. In moments flames swept up the outside layers of loose, well aerated straw with a swooshing roar, leaping forty or fifty feet into the air. Then, when the outside layer had been burned off, the fire died down to a low, pulsating glow of lurid red, whipped occasionally to white incandescence by a gust of wind while a pillar of lovely, blue-white pungent smoke ascended over all.

At night it was a spectacular sight. Seen from the village, the countryside sometimes was dotted with these ruby-red pinpoints of flame for as far as the eye could see, while fires in burning stubble drew lines across the fields as though the children of giants were playing tick-tack-toe. The advent of the combine eliminated straw stacks, and, as the value of straw as a binder for the soil came to be recognized, fewer and fewer farmers burned stubble, ploughing it into the soil instead.

By the time I was in my mid-teens my father was using a combine with a crew consisting of one of my brothers on the tractor and himself at the control of the combine, which raised and lowered the cutting blade and table to suit the height of the grain being harvested. If the crop had been swathed, the same control adjusted the height of the pickup, while Father also kept a sharp eye out for rocks, which could easily be picked up with the swath and which invariably caused damage to the internal workings of the combine. I completed the crew as truck driver in a Ford one-ton truck with sides built up so it could hold sixty or more bushels of wheat, a load well over its designed capacity.

This extra weight provided some thrilling moments as, for example, when I had to drive over a railway crossing that was just steep enough so that its pitch, combined with the weight of the load, caused the front wheels to leave the road for an appreciable distance. I have to admit that sometimes I wondered if they were ever going to come back down, but a touch of brake did the trick.

As another result of driving that truck I claim a certain distinction. It isn't everyone who can boast of having had a collision with another truck in the middle of half a square mile of perfectly flat land in broad daylight. It happened this way.

Because the crop was not heavy that year, there was always a waiting period after I returned from the elevator before the hopper on the combine filled with grain. I had nosed the truck up against a wagon containing oil drums to take advantage of the small amount of shade they produced and was reading a book to help pass the time. After a few minutes I looked up to see my father waving from the top of the combine, indicating that I should bring the truck. I started the engine, shifted into reverse and started to back away from the wagon. There was an immediate crunch. Just as I had started to back up, a friend, who was driving for another farmer and who had decided to pass the time of day, parked his truck behind and slightly to the right of mine, completely invisible to me as the upward extension of the grain box covered the back window of the cab and there was no right-side mirror.

For a moment I sat stunned, completely unable to imagine what I had hit in the middle of that supposedly empty field. Fortunately, my truck had barely begun to move, so there was little damage, the tailgate of my truck bending down the front foot or so of the fender of his. The incident demonstrated the advantage of the utilitarian design of trucks of that period compared to the splashier models of today. Because the fender was almost flat and projected well in front of the radiator, a good tug on it by both of us restored it to its original position. The damage was repaired and we returned to our duties. The entire incident hadn't taken more than five minutes but, ever since, I have been cautious about backing up in any vehicle.

Breakdowns of harvest machinery were relatively frequent, and every farmer was, and still is, his own mechanic. The knowledge each had of his machinery was intimate and often profanely expressed. There was little money for fine tools, and those that came with the machinery were of a quality that could hardly qualify as high-grade tool steel, so skinned knuckles and bruised fingers were common. I remember in particular an incident involving my second brother, who detested farm work and had a temper that could flare wildly.

We were replacing broken slats on the canvas for the table of a combine. This canvas, like an endless belt, carried the cut grain from the cutting blades into the machine. The canvas was fastened to the slats with soft copper rivets put in by hand and rivetted with a hammer. As the small backing plates behind the end to be flattened had to be held for the first one or two blows of the hammer, the risk to fingers was great.

My brother swung the hammer at a rivet and hit his thumb. His temper flashed past the boiling point and, before I knew what had happened, the hammer was hurtling through the air to strike the end wall of the barn with a resounding crash. The three-quarter-inch board that it struck, some fifteen feet away, was split diagonally for a length of four or five feet. I retrieved the hammer and stayed quietly out of the way until his temper had subsided and we continued to work. Nearly forty years later I visited the same barn and, even though it had been moved twice in the interim to two other farms, the quarter-inch-deep indentation made by the hammer head was still clearly visible, as was the weathered split in the board. Of such things are memories made, and I can still picture the scene in my mind's eye, although its main actor has rested in a military cemetery in Belgium for more than fifty years. DALE

As well as having to contend with machinery repairs, farmers had to preserve the health of their animals. A veterinarian was available in a village twelve miles from ours who cared for animals over a wide area, including our family dogs. But one case defied his abilities, and recalling it still sends shudders down my spine.

A sick horse was brought to town and a young man was hired to tend it. The horse went down and beat its head on the ground for two or three days, then it was turned to its other side as it had worn the hair and most of the flesh off the side of its face. Finally, the animal was put out of its misery. No one knew the nature of the illness since there had never been another case like it. I believe now that it was sleeping sickness, equine encephalitis. Perhaps its rarity then was due to the dryness of the prairies and the few mosquitoes around to spread the disease.

A horse of happier memory was Dolly, who pulled the buggy delivering milk to the village. She belonged to a family with several branches farming around the village who took turns providing a home for an orphaned boy with whom I had a sort of Tom Sawyer-Huck Finn relationship. The business was small: one conventional buggy carrying a couple of milk crates in the diminutive hinge-lidded box behind the seat and sometimes one or two more on the floor was able to cope with the daily milk deliveries for the whole village.

The dairy was located about two and one-half miles by road east of the village, its buildings nestling in the bottom of the great glacial valley a few hundred yards from a great wedge-shaped fill that carried the railway tracks across an intersecting coulee. Through the bottom of this fill ran a great concrete culvert big enough for a small boy to run through with head bowed. It had been constructed when an original railway trestle bridging the coulee was replaced with fill. On a hot summer day this culvert was one of the coolest places in the country, and a gentle breeze seemed to drift through it constantly. A stone's throw from the culvert a spring of icy-cold and crystal-clear water rose into a shallow wooden casing with a sandy bottom. Each day some member of the dairying family drove a horse with a barrel on a stone boat to the spring. The barrel full of cold water was taken to the milk house to cool the milk and cream before it started its journey into town. When the milking and separating had been done, the milk cooled and bottled by hand, the crates were loaded into the buggy, the horse harnessed and hitched up, and away we would go.

The road along the edge of the valley ran through uncultivated prairie, full of stones and gravel, and its twin ruts had cut through whatever thin topsoil there had been until they found a base of stones and rocks across which the buggy bumped and rattled. Because of this constant jiggling it was not unusual on reaching its destination to find a tiny disc of yellow butter floating on the cream at the top of each bottle of milk.

The process of homogenization was not yet common, so by the time the buggy had reached town each quart bottle of milk had separated itself into a bottom layer of white milk topped by three or four inches of yellow cream. The consistency of both milk and cream depended to a certain extent on the feed the cows had been eating, as well as the breed of cow. In the spring when the cattle were put out to fresh pasture, separated cream in quarter- or half-pint bottles often was so thick it wouldn't run out of an up-ended bottle and had to be removed in heaping teaspoonfuls. In frigid winter weather the milk bottles often arrived with their caps an inch above their tops on a frozen column of rich, and delicious, cream.

I would occasionally ride my bicycle to the farm to join my friend as he delivered the milk. The horse had covered the route into and around the town so often that it was entirely unnecessary to guide her. Once she was under way, the reins were looped around the whip handle in its socket, seldom to be touched again until the delivery was finished. I think she often was walking in her sleep, but when she neared a complete halt a shouted "Gee-up, Dolly!" would induce a slight quickening in her pace. The whip was used only to flick idly at flies on her rump.

As she ambled along through the shimmering sunlight, we discussed all those things of great moment to young boys, or perhaps jumped off the buggy to throw a stone at a particularly saucy gopher, or watched the grasshoppers whirring and clattering from in front of the horse's hooves. Another time, we made clumsy and sweat-smeared attempts to roll cigarettes with tobacco and papers snitched from my friend's uncle, or choked and sputtered over the mouth-searing smoke from salvaged cigarette tobacco packed into a clay pipe designed originally for blowing bubbles. Again, one or the other of us might make a solo excursion from the buggy on the bicycle on which I had ridden out to the farm, or attempt to keep the bicycle upright while riding along at the barely measurable pace of the buggy.

When the valley road straightened toward the village it was about a mile and a half away. Slowly we would pass the mile post on the railway and then the whistle post for a crossing a half mile from town. When we reached the village, we carried full and empty bottles to and from doorsteps, while the horse, without stopping, towed the buggy along the familiar route. Finally the chore was done, and we parked the horse and buggy at the hitching rail and departed in search of other adventures.

More likely than not, these adventures involved our bicycles, and the boy from the dairy had one that stands out starkly in my memory. It had the tallest frame of any bicycle I have ever seen, and it is a good thing he had longer legs than most or he would have been completely unable to manage it. Even worse, it had wooden wheel rims, which through long use, constant exposure to weather and uneven slackening of the spokes had developed some terrifying shapes. It was only with the finest adjustment that the wheels could be made to turn without the tires rubbing on some part of the frame or forks. To top it all off, it seemed its entire existence was an unending sequence of flat tires and broken chains. My most enduring impression of this machine is a picture of it standing inverted on its handle bars and seat on a roadside while we applied another to the almost continuous series of existing patches that comprised the inner tubes. When the tires did consent to hold air, the predilection of its chain for jumping the sprockets when power was applied to the pedals, coupled with the height of its frame, caused many of us to suffer at one time or another that most painful bruising known to the human male.

One other item I encountered in association with this boy was that most fascinating object for nearly all young males, the pistol. This particular one was, I am sure, the biggest handgun made. It was a .455 Webley revolver used by British army officers of the First World War because of its tremendous stopping power. Its owner, the boy's uncle, told us that if a man were hit only in the arm with it, it would knock him down. We were allowed to look at it, very occasionally to touch it and, once in a blue moon, to hold it. It was huge, heavy, steely blue and ugly - in short, to a boy, utterly beautiful. Then one day, unbelievably, we were allowed to be present when it was taken outside, loaded and fired. Even more unbelievably, we were allowed to fire it once each!

When my turn came, I was aquiver with a combination of excitement and fear, but I would rather have died than miss the opportunity. I took the revolver in my hand, while everyone else stood well to the rear, and tried to aim at a fence post. Alas, my hand was too small and too weak. I could neither hold it steady nor pull the trigger. I tried again, this time with both hands around the butt and both forefingers around the trigger. Suddenly, there was a roar, the pistol leaped upwards in my hands and I stood in dazed delight while the blood trickled down my forehead from where the hammer had struck me when I was unable to restrain the recoil. And wonder of wonders, a round black hole had appeared dead centre in the fence post! It was a sobering revelation, however, when we went to examine the post and found that, although there was only a small hole in the front where the heavy bullet had entered, the back half of the six-inch post was almost completely missing and lay scattered on the ground in shattered splinters. I have fired many different types and calibres of pistols since, but all were as toys compared to that terrible weapon.

Entertainment

ONE SOMETIMES LONGS for the days before television and urbanization when, in a village such as ours, everyone knew everyone else and everyone took part in almost everything. Probably the best example of this was our village's community club, established during the deepest years of the Depression.

It began almost spontaneously in 1935 or '36 when I was eleven or twelve years old. With no money and no commercial entertainment other than the radio, people had to make their own entertainment. My two brothers and two of their friends formed a small dance combo and got permission to stage dances in the school. The combo consisted of violin, played by the son of the local blacksmith, banjo-ukulele played by my younger brother, bull fiddle played by my elder brother, and piano and mouth organ played by the son of the pool-hall owner.

The dances were held in the largest classroom of the school, the desks pushed to the sides of the room and light provided by a couple of Aladdin-type kerosene mantle lamps. There was no charge for admission and women brought sandwich lunches to be shared by all at the midnight intermission.

The music was lively but strictly extemporaneous and largely unrehearsed. What it may have lacked in quality was made up for in enthusiasm and vivacity, with certain peculiarities built in. For example, the piano player was self-taught from a course obtained by mail. For some unknown reason he had got things reversed, so he played the melody with his left hand and the accompanying chords in his right. The effect, although unusual, was not unpleasant. All the music was played by ear, and the only additional entertainment was provided by the orchestra members in the form of solo performances and vocal numbers. Comedy had a place as well, as when my elder brother fitted his bull fiddle with an extra "string," cut from an inner tube, in which he was able to get hilariously entangled without missing a beat or committing a flaw in harmony or rhythm.

These dances were so well attended and appreciated that they provided the seed for what became the very successful Community Club. Most of the town's businessmen backed the venture in one way or another, by donating materials or assistance in various forms. My father, for example, did not charge for electrical power used to stage the entertainments. The village had a more accomplished dance orchestra as well, which played for dances in villages within a radius of fifty or sixty miles, and when the Community Club was formed, this orchestra took over and the venue was moved to the local theatre–dance hall. It was agreed, because these activities provided their principal sources of income, that only the theatre owner and dance orchestra would be paid. Everything else required was provided free. Backdrops for plays were painted by volunteers on huge sheets of kraft paper, normally used to line grain boxcars, donated by the elevator operators. Furnishings for sets came from the homes of the players; it seemed that, no matter how exotic the need, some home was able to fill it from family heirlooms brought when the owners arrived as immigrants.

Season tickets were sold to individuals and families of the community at a very low cost, and admission was charged at the door for those who didn't hold season tickets. These fees were calculated to pay for the theatre rental and the orchestra. Door sales were made also to those from other communities who became more and more numerous as the success of the enterprise became known, eventually making the venture slightly profitable.

Entertainments were staged at intervals throughout the winter season, and the format that developed included a show of some sort lasting about two hours, followed by a dance that lasted until 2:00 a.m. with a lunch intermission at midnight. All of the shows were locally produced with local talent, and it was amazing to discover just how much talent was available. Almost everyone participated in one way or another to stage plays, concerts, and vaudeville, minstrel and variety shows.

Memories of performances flood to mind. A farmer with a beautiful tenor voice sang songs such as "Wagon Wheels" and "Makushla"; the doctor gave us "The Big Bass Viol" and "Asleep in the Deep" in his fine bass voice; two teen-aged sisters with sweet voices sang duets of praise such as "Whispering Hope" while their older sister, a superior mezzo-soprano, sang and also performed piano solos. Sisters from a local farm sang duets and solos of popular songs accompanied on the piano by their mother, who played by ear and often led us to believe her left hand didn't know what her right hand was doing – the melody line always was fine but the accompanying harmony often went astray. The daughter of the husband and wife who were the backbone of the dance orchestra sang solos and tap danced to "The Sidewalks of New York" and, at one performance, she and I sang a Scottish duet, me complete with kilt and plaidie. And I will remember always the beautiful contralto rendition of "Trees" by the nurse/midwife who died, much mourned, not long after.

Various and constantly changing combinations of men and women performed duets, quartets, many of the latter in the barbershop tradition, and choruses. Choral singing became so popular that a choral instructor was brought from Saskatoon periodically one winter to train a mixed chorus, arriving by train in the afternoon, staying overnight with a village family and returning to Saskatoon the next morning. Our doctor took four boys, including his son and me, and coached us for two or three years in quartet singing. As my voice had not yet changed, I sang first tenor in songs such as "The Rose of Tralee" and "Jeannie with the Light Brown Hair," while his son, whose voice had changed, sang bass. This was a wonderful experience and happily, years later, I was to meet the doctor again and was able to thank him for making my life so much fuller.

Plays were staged under the direction of several people including the doctor's wife, who also wrote for a female chorus satirical lyrics that poked fun at most of the prominent citizens of the town, including her husband, and which brought the house down because everyone in the audience knew the targets and their foibles. Happily, her victims had the same sense of humour.

There were instrumental performances – violin, piano, marimba, trumpet, saxophone, trombone, banjo, guitar, autoharp, often performed by persons who astonished us with their musical ability. The fact that first performances were contributed by those with fewer inhibitions seemed to encourage those who were shy to reveal their talents.

Men from the village and surrounding farms staged black-face minstrel shows complete with Mr. Interlocutor, Mr. Bones, end men and chorus equipped with tambourines and banjo. Music for these ran much in the mode of Stephen Foster's "Camptown Races," "Old Folks at Home," and "Someone's in the Kitchen with Dinah" interspersed with more demanding solo numbers such as "Old Man River." My father sang tenor in these performances and Mother accompanied on the piano for vocal practices in our home as a result of which I, by listening in, learned a great many songs.

My star performance was as a ventriloquist's dummy, the "ventriloquist" being the husband of the dance orchestra couple. I played the part of a floppy boneless dummy, and, because of my small size, I could be tossed about easily by my partner. I played the part so successfully that after the performance no one would believe I had been the dummy, so my starring effort brought me little renown.

One performance was memorable for more than one reason. This was a comic staging of *Uncle Tom's Cabin* with an all-male cast. Little Eva was played by a village businessman with a fine tenor voice who stood at least six-foot-two and was very slender. At the point where Little Eva goes to heaven, "she" was progressing upwards by means of block and tackle when a late-arriving couple entered the theatre and announced loudly that Little Eva's house was on fire. There was an immediate exodus as the players dashed for the fire hall – leaving Little Eva dangling. Because I was among those who dashed out, I don't know how or when Little Eva finally got down. It is likely he was able to reach the chains of the block and tackle and lower himself.

This was one occasion when the fire engines were able to prove their worth. The fire was localized around the chimney of the tall, two-storey house, and by means of ladder, axe and hose, two or three men were able to reach the roof peak and extinguish the blaze in only a few minutes with relatively little damage to the house.

The weather was cold enough so that some of the water froze on the roof. One of the volunteer fire fighters called down pleading for someone to get some mattresses to spread where he would land on the frozen ground if he slid off the roof! The mattresses were not provided, but several burly men stood by with a large blanket in which they could catch him if he fell. Happily, he didn't. Unfortunately, there is no photographic record of what was certainly the most unusually costumed volunteer fire department in history. The stage performance was not resumed, but the dance went ahead as usual.

These dances were a source of immense pleasure to us as teenagers. The women of the village were happy to teach us to waltz, foxtrot, two-step, and polka. I remember in particular one small woman who taught me to waltz and with whom I made a point of waltzing at least once every dance until she suddenly "got religion" and ceased to attend. After learning the basics, it was not long before we were adding our own embellishments in the form of jitterbugging. Twice at each dance, once before intermission and once after, square dances were called in which many took part, forming four or five squares. Although it was fashionable among youngsters to deride them, I suspect our derision was the result of our ignorance of their intricacies, because after we had learned some of them we took part with just as much enjoyment as others, swinging our partners off their feet and banging our steel-edged heels in time with the music. And before the war brought Community Club activities to an end, and almost as a declaration of patriotism, we danced the Lambeth walk, a group dance imported from cockney London, so grievously bombed during the German blitz of 1940–41.

The increasing popularity of the Community Club's programs and dances brought in more and more attendees from surrounding communities. This led to a confrontation between the younger set and the individual who was president of the club one season. Because of crowding, he decreed that no one under age sixteen would be allowed to dance. We youngsters were devastated, shocked and enraged at the prohibition because we felt it was *our* club. Beyond this, it split up some couples. I, for example, was just under sixteen while my favourite partner was just over that age. In a matter of minutes several of us had got together, rounded up paper and pencils and launched a petition. It probably wasn't more than a half hour before we had the signatures of almost every member of the club in support of our right to dance. To his credit, the president accepted our petition gracefully and repealed his decree on the spot. The dance floor was crowded but no one cared.

Again, lunches at intermission were provided by the women, usually just for their own families, but occasionally a lunch auction was held. The women always were forewarned of this and so the lunches were packed in gaily decorated boxes and baskets. The purchaser of one of these was entitled to have lunch with the lady who had prepared the box. There was some collusion involved in this; the male member of a couple "going steady" usually was informed of the type of decoration his lady friend had applied to her lunch container so he could be sure of being the highest bidder for it. And there were occasions when a swain was forced by joking companions, aware of the collusion, to bid almost to the limit of his meagre resources. The bids usually started at a nickel or dime and went up in five-cent increments, most topping at around twenty-five cents. It was evidence of true devotion if a bidder could be forced up to fifty cents or even a dollar! At the time, twenty-five cents would buy a ham sandwich with pickle on the side, a coffee and an ice cream cone at the local restaurant, while a dollar would buy a three-course dinner – for two.

One of the happiest factors in this sort of fun was that everyone took part in it, not just the young people. Our elders, too, played the game, and there was much laughter if one of our fathers inadvertently bought the lunch of some teenage girl, or of some woman whom the whole village was aware was not on the best of terms with the purchaser. I like to think that probably some animosities were abandoned as a result.

On one occasion an attempt at collusion between my girlfriend and me went awry. I don't know even now who did it, but someone switched the names on two of the baskets. As a result, I found I had bought the privilege of having lunch with my girlfriend's older sister. It worked out all right in the end, as her boyfriend, also tipped off, had bought *my* girlfriend's basket thinking it was her sister's. We all lunched together.

Community Club activities continued for the first year or two of the war, when I and most of my peers were approaching the age at which military service became a serious consideration and many of the young men of the village already had enlisted in one or the other of the services. One thing that has always puzzled me is the number of prairie boys who enlisted in the navy – boys who had never seen the sea and certainly had no idea of how tough life could be in a North Atlantic gale on a corvette.

Perhaps it was the appeal of the unknown.

By this time, too, our increased mobility had widened our horizons where potential female partners was concerned. There was a dance barn about twenty-five miles from our village where we became regular attendees. This gave us a focus for escorting girls from nearby villages and from even farther afield, sometimes to the point almost of absurdity. On one occasion a friend and I drove ninety miles to Saskatoon to pick up dates who were university acquaintances, drove sixty-five miles back to the dance barn, twenty-five miles to our hometown for lunch intermission at our local restaurant, back to the dance barn, returned the girls to their homes in Saskatoon and drove home again, making a total for the expedition of more than 360 miles. The car used was my friend's father's, and I never heard what he thought of the havoc the adventure had played with his gasoline ration.

There was another attempt made to provide entertainment, this one on a more commercial basis. A farmer who lived only a short distance from town converted the loft of his barn into a dance hall with floor-level lunch service at one end and a raised orchestra platform at the other, some eight or ten feet above the floor level. The dance floor itself was beautiful, fine hardwood mounted on rubber tires laid flat on their sides to give it springiness. It was far and away the finest dance hall for many miles around but, unfortunately, its operation was not a great success, principally because nearly everyone was of the opinion that admission prices were too high.

On one occasion its owner hired one of the finest dance bands in Canada, Vancouver-based Mart Kenny and His Western Gentlemen and advertised the event widely. Again, however, the prices were considered to be too high – as I recall, something like five dollars per person. People stayed away in droves. Some, who might have attended, turned back when they discovered that they were not allowed even to drive into the farmyard parking lot without buying tickets to the dance at the farm gate. But there was one curious incident connected with the event.

One of the inhabitants of the village was a bachelor, somewhat beyond middle age and of irascible temper, who lived among us for many years in a small one-room cottage on Railroad Avenue. As far as I can remember, he never had any employment, nor sought any. In spite of that, however, he seemed to have sufficient funds to live on.

We speculated that he was one of those English outcasts known as "remittance men," men of well-to-do families in Britain who, in effect, were paid to stay out of the British Isles. Whether he was a remittance man or not I do not know, but if he had ever had an upper-class English accent, it had vanished with time. Because he had several fingers missing it is possible that he was a veteran of the First World War with a disability pension. He always maintained a large garden, and the only time I saw the inside of his abode was when, as a junior teenager, I was selling seeds on behalf of a company that offered attractive "prizes" to child sales-persons.

He attended the dance. I believe it was the only time he had ever attended any social function in the village, including the Community Club. Not only did he attend but, according to the few witnesses who were present, he arrived attired in white tie, top hat and tails! Needless to say, this added greatly to the mystery surrounding his origins.

There were other forms of entertainment as well. One couple or another occasionally would hold a bridge party in their home, inviting close friends. This meant much to-ing and fro-ing for teenagers of the families involved, carrying card tables and straight-backed chairs from neighbours' homes to the house where the party was to take place. This, too, was the time when contract bridge was taking over from auction bridge and I recall my mother, for days before attending such a party, perusing *Goren on Bridge*. Her greatest fear was that she would make a mistake while partnering the doctor, who was the village's acknowledged expert at the game and who did not hesitate to chide a partner who caused him to lose a contract.

Partners were changed after each rubber and prizes were awarded to the man and woman who had the highest score at the end of the evening's play, usually a fine china tea cup and saucer for the woman, and for the man a small gift, perhaps a tie or a "flat fifty" of cigarettes, the flat metal boxes of which were another item coveted by youngsters. For the two with the lowest scores, "booby prizes" were awarded, always of a humorous nature. For children of the household, banished to bed long before the party ended, there were always eagerly anticipated goodies of left-over candies, cakes and delicate sandwiches to be relished the next day.

In my very early childhood, up until the Depression's grip put a halt to it, one of the biggest events in the village every summer was the arrival of the Chautauqua troupe. Again, this was an affair arranged by the town's businessmen, who acted as guarantors.

Almost as entertaining as the subsequent performances was the erection of the troupe's enormous tent, which, unlike a circus tent, had its seating arranged as in a theatre rather than in a circle, facing a large stage at one end. To children, brawny men, stripped to sweat-soaked undershirts, looked like giants as they drove into the ground stakes almost as big as fence posts, each with a steel band around its top to prevent the wood from splitting. Three or four men drove each one, rhythmically swinging heavy mallets, their blows striking each stake so rapidly that the post seemed scarcely to hesitate during its downward movement into the ground, the process aided considerably by the comparative stonelessness of the prairie soil. Local teams of horses were recruited to help the men raise the huge main poles along the centre of the tent and to haul the heavy canvas into position. It seemed the tent top was barely off the ground before men were scurrying under it erecting stage and benches and the smaller poles around its periphery. The whole process was awe inspiring to us. Childhood memory can be deceptive, but my recollection is that the tent would seat in the order of 200 people.

Chautauqua began with a costume parade for the village's youngsters with prizes awarded for the most original costumes. The parade looped around one side of the town, went up the three blocks of Main Street and concluded at the site of the Chautauqua tent, at the north end of Main.

The performances staged by the Chautauqua organization were of top quality. They always included music, both instrumental and vocal, but the main features always were lectures by world travellers and savants on a variety of topics, and they were always interesting. My greatest recollection of a Chautauqua performance is of a lecture by a traveller to the islands of the Pacific, illustrated by objects obtained in his travels – giant sharks' jaws with triangular razor-sharp teeth in serried rows, large fan corals, sponges, sea horses and stuffed fish of many varieties.

I remember a male quartet, memorable for most of us children because it was our first encounter with Blacks. And there was something of a sensation created when some of the village's older girls dated the members of the quartet while they stayed in our village. Many of our parents who had immigrated from the United States were aghast at this crossing of what to them was an impenetrable colour barrier. This, even though the dates involved little beyond ice cream and soft drinks at the local restaurant.

While we were still in our mid-teens, another travelling show came to our village, this one a family affair with mother, father, sons and daughters as the performers. They showed a selection of trained small animals – monkeys, dogs and a parrot or cockatoo. The incident that made the event memorable occurred shortly after they arrived and had their paraphernalia scattered in the vicinity of the back door of the theatre.

A group of us teenagers, perhaps a half dozen each of boys and girls, left school together and made our way to the site where we examined the tied dogs and then circled to the front of a cage, backed against some boxes, containing a three-foot-tall male monkey, who faced us, sitting on its haunches, masturbating enthusiastically. The faces among the group of teen-aged girls registered every reaction from wide-eyed shock through blushing embarrassment to giggling amusement and blank incomprehension, but all left the scene hastily. As the group hurried away we could tell that one of the girls who had been amused was laughingly explaining to the non-comprehenders the meaning of what they had witnessed, thereby probably initiating their sex education. I remember almost nothing of the company's performance, it being far overshadowed by the monkey's extemporaneous act.

During the winter I was in grade eleven, a farm boy whose home was too far away to allow daily attendance at school moved to town to take his grade twelve. He resided in a small shack mounted on skids, which had been built on the farm and towed into the village. He went home on weekends and gave the keys to his shack to a friend and me so we could use it. This led to a deception plan for us. He would tell his parents he was spending Saturday night at my home and I would tell my parents I was spending it at his. We then spent the night at the shack, singing until 2:00 or 3:00 a.m. Once in a while a third boy, also a singer, would join us, but as the bed would accommodate only two, he would depart as late as fear of parental discipline would allow.

We sang anything and everything, working out our own harmonies, accompanied at times by me playing a ukulele that I had acquired from my second brother. Our choice of songs was universal – cowboy, country, popular, concert – ranging from "The Strawberry Roan" through "Old Faithful" to "Sunny Side of the Street" and "The Road to Mandalay." I still recall the lyrics and melodies of hundreds of songs, very few of which are heard now, but when one is played on the radio I sing along and recall a time when two teenaged boys were as happy as youngsters can possibly be.

Another impetus was given to our musical education when the woman who played piano for the dance band and who also gave piano lessons undertook to coach a boys' chorus in which nearly all the boys of the village took part. It lasted through two winters and contributed greatly to our group and individual repertoires. Most of the music was secular and what I suppose could be described as traditional. We used a songbook entitled *Canada Sings* and warbled our way through such melodies as "Tramp, Tramp, Tramp, the Boys are Marching" (with suitably Canadianized lyrics), "Jack Was Every Inch a Sailor" and "The Old Oaken Bucket." Practices were held weekly in the director's home, an apartment above what had been the bank. One of the unmusical chores that must have fallen to her was cleaning up the staircase after a dozen or so snow-covered boys had made their way up it. And, by the way, no money changed hands except for our purchase of the songbooks. There is no way of expressing the depth of gratitude we owe to people such as she who added so much of value to our lives.

Spring brought the farmers back to town on Saturday nights, and this meant also the annual re-opening of the movie theatre, which had served as variety theatre and dance hall for the Community Club during the winter. The bill changed weekly, proclaimed by a billboard on Main Street, and the movies were screened on Thursday evenings to attract the townspeople and Saturday nights for the farm families and occasional customers from other nearby villages. There were two showings each night, although often on Thursdays there would be no audience after the first showing and the movie would not be re-run.

The theatre was far from comfortable. Seating was provided on wooden benches with backs, long ones one behind the other down the centre of the hall and shorter ones on each side, providing two aisles. The floor was not sloped and doubled as a dance floor with the benches removed and arranged along the walls and stacked at one end on either side of the entrance door. We never seemed to notice the hardness of the benches, however, even when, in the case of a particularly good movie, we endured them for four hours or so at a stretch to see the move twice. The building was unheated except on movie nights, when the furnace was lit two or three hours before the performance; in spring and fall we occasionally sat through a movie with our coats or jackets on, because the furnace was not lit if the outside temperature was even close to normal room temperature. Admission, when I first began to attend as a child, was fifteen cents, but by the time I reached high school it had escalated to twenty cents.

The first movies were silent movies and were operated by the brothers of a local family. Musical background was provided by a hand-cranked Victrola phonograph at the back of the hall. The villagers must have sat through the strains of "Ramona" and "Look for the Silver Lining" hundreds of times. At times a piano player was hired, located to one side in front of the stage and screen. For a time, in her high-school days, my sister played for the movies.

Some time in the early thirties the theatre was taken over by a young couple who installed the equipment for "talkies." The husband operated the movie projectors while the wife looked after the box office, and the young man who looked after the church was hired as ticket taker. One of my peers had what we considered to be the plum of all part-time jobs. He was hired to rewind the reels of film after they had been removed from the projectors, so he not only got to see all of the movies for nothing but he also got paid a dollar a night! How we envied him. But all efforts by any of us to replace him came to naught.

My second brother also gathered a plum. After they took over the theatre, the new owners held a contest to rename it. My brother's suggestion, "The Gaiety," won and he was awarded a year of free movies.

The husband of the husband-and-wife team worked for my father for many years, except of course on Thursday and Saturday nights during the summer. Partly because of this association, on Saturday nights when business had slowed for me at my father's establishment, the wife would permit me to enter the theatre for the second showing without charge — provided that I had paid admission on the previous Thursday night. This often permitted me to see twice movies that I had particularly enjoyed, most often musicals with Ginger Rogers and Fred Astaire or Jeanette MacDonald and Nelson Eddie or Deanna Durbin.

The range of movies shown was wide, although most were of the B category. As I understood it, the distribution company with which the theatre dealt set certain ratios of films to be made available, that is, in order to obtain a top-quality film, the operator had to agree to take a certain number of titles of a lower grade. There were many westerns starring big-name cowboy actors of the time – Tom Mix, Hoot Gibson. Handsome swimming champion Johnny Weissmuller played Tarzan, and the cartoon was coming into its own with Betty Boop, Popeye the Sailor and Mickey Mouse.

We enjoyed singing along with shorts made by popular bands, the lyrics shown on the screen a line at a time with a bouncing ball indicating how the lyrics fit the melodies. And then there were the serials, one episode of perhaps ten minutes' duration being shown each week and which were sure-fire draws for the children. Each episode ended just as the hero or heroine was about to be attacked by a crocodile or ravaged by the bad guys. Only by attending the following week could we learn how the hero escaped death or the heroine a fate worse than death.

A great feature of movies of the time was the newsreel, which gave us pictures of world events, albeit belatedly. We saw Hitler fulminating to his adulating Germans and Chamberlain arriving in London waving a piece of paper and declaring that he had arranged "peace for our time" – less than 11 months before the Second World War began. One newsreel carried particular import for our family. In it, we were startled to see my second brother with his squadron mates being visited by Canadian High Commissioner to Britain Vincent Massey. The occasion was an informal visit to 242 Squadron, the first all-Canadian fighter squadron of the Royal Air Force in the Second World War. The theatre operator snipped a half-dozen frames from the film, which my father and mother were able to have copied and enlarged, thereby providing them with the last photos of their son before he was killed in action near Dunkirk on 28 May 1940 while flying a Hawker Hurricane fighter.

One Christmas season, as a lure to the town's businesses, the business owners financed a week of movies, free to all comers. There were two films, shown twice each on alternate evenings. One, scarcely on a Christmas theme, was *Ace of Aces*, starring Richard Dix. It was based on the exploits of American First World War flying ace Captain Eddie Rickenbacker. Most of my friends and I, intrigued by airplanes, sat through it at least a half dozen times. The other, if memory serves me correctly, was a musical starring Deanna Durbin.

The *bête noire* of the movie theatre was the sometimes undependable village electrical power supply. Saturday night was the busiest of the week for everyone and so the demand for power was at its highest then. After the demise of the larger of the two original semi-diesel engines, the make-shift substitutes were not always dependable, nor were they even capable of carrying the load. As the load increased, the voltage dropped with disastrous consequences for the sound and image of the movie.

The theatre operator being on intimate terms with the power plant, it was not unusual on a Saturday night to see him abandon his projection booth, dash the two-thirds of a block to my father's place of business, storm through to the power plant and make adjustments to the carburet-tor or governor of the engine providing power to the side of town where the theatre was located. If no remedy could be found by such action, various knife switches on the control panels were pulled, switching off the power to areas of the village that he considered non-essential, depriving some residences of power until the movie was over. Or he might turn off the street lights, which really were unnecessary on a balmy summer night when every shop streamed light from its windows into the street and every resident was capable of finding his or her way around the entire village blindfolded.

Summer family outings often involved packing picnic lunches, bathing suits and towels into the family car and driving the thirty miles or so to Outlook, on the Saskatchewan River. Here, there were a swimming pool and picnic tables on the east bank of the river in a grove of huge trees, which, years later, were identified as being the oldest elm trees in the province.

When the family was prepared for a long drive on a holiday weekend and cars had become faster, they might drive the almost 200 miles to Watrous, where there was a swimming pool filled with odoriferous mineral water so buoyant that one could not sink in it. There was little else to attract people to the site except a few catering establishments and a summer hotel. There were few trees, the picnic area being situated on the bald prairie. These latter outings were usually done in convoy with two or three or more other families. It was an enjoyable adventure even though it meant spending twelve hours or more in the car for the round trip. This was less than ten years after most had first retired their buggies and a ten-mile return trip from farm to town was an all-day adventure.

So, we were not socially deprived. In fact, life was much more social for everyone in those days than it is today, when people spend most evenings watching television and often do not even know their neighbours except casually. I would return to that life without hesitation, fiscal depression notwithstanding. Unfortunately, it no longer exists, so I can return to it only in memory.

Boys and Girls Together

MOST OF THE CHILDREN of the village grew up together from infancy to adulthood. The difference between the sexes was of little moment to us. We shared our games and our pleasures, playing scrub softball or run-sheep-run or auntie-aye-over or tag without discrimination or favouritism. Indeed, some of the girls were just as skilled at playing ball, just as fast runners, as many of the boys in the same age group. We sat intermingled in the movies, read the funny papers in mixed groups and shared our candies with all.

That is not to say that we didn't know there were differences between the sexes. The boys had the knowledge gained from experience with animals as did most farm girls, but some of the village girls were much less knowledgeable, as was evidenced when a discussion turned to getting puppies or the particular lineage of a mongrel dog. Some, even in their junior teens, had no idea of the roles of the sexes and particularly that of the male animal in procreation.

We learned about the differences between the sexes in our play as well. One warm summer day at age four or five a girl playmate and I were romping among the timber pillars supporting the loading platform at the railroad tracks. In the course of our play we divested ourselves of our clothing and gambolled about naked, revelling in the sun and breeze on our bare skins. Uninhibitedly, my playmate announced that she could pee standing up like a boy, and proceeded to demonstrate.

This girl and I seemed to have a knack for getting into trouble in our pre-school years, as when we stole my mother's sugar bowl and hid it in my brothers' tent. The object was to have it available when we raided the rhubarb patch. Once while my mother was doing the laundry in the basement, my friend generously gave me a shampoo on the kitchen floor – with bluing! This girl's mother was a gentle, soft-spoken woman who used to say she believed every child had a guardian angel. My mother's comment was, "Oh, yes. And for her children I am it."

One of our favourite childhood pastimes was playing on the school swings. The swings were suspended from large wooden crossbeams atop twelve-foot poles and were of three-quarter-inch rope with seats of two-by-ten plank sections. For boys, one of the objectives was to pump a swing up to the point where at the top of its upward arc, the ropes were horizontal, or even slightly higher, and we could see over the crossbeam. At this point the ropes would slacken and we started the downward swing with a jolt. Then we sat down and "coasted" until at the end of a decreased forward arc we let go and flew through the air to land on our feet eight or ten feet from our point of departure.

The girls shared our play on the swings. They went solo, the bolder ones emulating the high swings and leaping landings of the boys, but, as there were only four swings, they often doubled up either with other girls or with the boys. In the latter case it was usual for the girl to be seated on the swing with the boy standing facing her, one foot on either side. They pumped the swing cooperatively, he by leaning backwards to the full length of his arms and pressing down hard on the seat with his feet when moving forward, while she leaned back to arm's length and extended her legs while moving forward in her turn. One of the objectives of a boy in this dual configuration was to pump the swing up to that point where it was jolted by the ropes slackening at the top of the arc, in hopes of eliciting a startled scream from his companion.

Sometimes both would stand on the swing seat facing one another for maximum power in both directions while at others the girl would take the standing position. Some tucked their light cotton skirts into the elastic of their bloomer legs, but others deemed this unnecessary, believing, quite correctly, that their bloomers gave them adequate coverage.

In the dual mode of swinging, after the highest arc of the swing had

[handwritten marginal note: Betty Lou Blakley]

been gained and enjoyed, it was common for the child standing to sit down on the thighs of the seated youngster while the swing either coasted to a near halt or was kept in motion by the two alternately leaning back to arm's length with legs outstretched. Dual boy-girl swinging came to an end as we began to mature. I don't recall this prohibition ever being discussed between the sexes; the practice just ended by mutual unspoken agreement.

As we passed through the stages of puberty, we boys were beset by all of the accompanying tribulations – and benefits. Our voices cracked and changed, some of us suffered acne in various degrees, and I grew almost eight inches in two years to nearly five-foot-ten and was no longer Squirt or Runt.

One curse I had to put up with in my early teens was sties. A local woman visiting my mother saw me when I had several at once and suggested I swallow twelve lead shot in a glass of milk. I did so, and not only did my sties clear up, I have never had another. Years later a doctor suggested that, because our bodies require a minute amount of arsenic, that which was used in chilling the shot had provided me with the needed chemical.

As maturation advanced, most boys grew bigger than the girls of their own ages, and the girls changed shape, making the way they walked or ran distinctively different. The free-and-easy camaraderie of childhood gave way to a certain shyness and uncertainly in one anothers' company, and physical contact became taboo, with accidental intimate contacts resulting in embarrassment and confusion. Many childhood friendships remained strong but with a difference, extending even to the way we spoke to one another.

As we boys advanced in age, we developed an interest in the mysteries of the female body that the moral standards of the day gave us little opportunity to observe except in one or two photographic magazines that sometimes carried photos of nude women – all suitably censored with the "naughty" areas air-brushed over.

It has always seemed strange to me that this being so, when we went swimming as a group, many of the girls wore mother-approved flannel bathing suits that covered them more than adequately from neck to mid-thigh. But these, when wet, clung to them like second skins, revealing the most intimate details of their maturing bodies, front and back – from neck to mid-thigh. If a girl at that time had appeared in one of today's bikini swimsuits, her mother (or the police) would have spirited her away wrapped in a blanket.

This female modesty applied even when we went dancing. Jitterbugging was becoming popular, the girl being twirled vigorously by her partner, but seldom were her mid-calf skirts swirled higher than her knees. If a bold boy spun his partner swiftly enough to expose her bare thigh above her stocking tops, he risked getting his face slapped.

As time went on, boys and girls began to pair up for local social occasions such as dances and the movies, and when we obtained driver's licenses we began pairing up with teens from other villages and farms as well. Soon we were into "necking" and, probably, most of us into intimacies a little more serious. In this, the boys almost always were the initiators, but girls cooperated with apparent enjoyment. But for most of us, that is as far as it went. Undoubtedly there were some who "went all the way," but the code of the day reserved sexual intercourse for marriage, and I am sure that the majority of us as teenagers adhered to that code, proved by the fact that among my many childhood acquaintances there were no teenage pregnancies.

The strength of the code can be illustrated by an experience of my own. I and a girl with whom I had had a long relationship felt the urges that young and healthy bodies, plus affection and shared intimacies, can generate. We had a serious discussion in which we promised one another that if the war was still going on when we turned eighteen, making me eligible for military service, we would surrender to those urges. The war went on, and I turned eighteen and joined the air force. Before I departed for my first posting, we dated once again, and over sundaes in the local restaurant we released each other from our promises, and we parted good friends.

And there my tale of growing up in a Canadian prairie village during the 1920s and '30s ends. We were children no longer.

Epilogue

MY CLOSE ASSOCIATION with Dinsmore ended when I joined the RCAF in 1942 after second year at the University of Saskatchewan. After a tour as a pilot in Bomber Command and my release from the air force – before the war ended – I returned to Dinsmore, but for only a few days before joining a geological exploration party in the northern Manitoba bush. There was little attraction for me in the village because most of my friends were still serving in the armed forces.

My visits to the town became fewer and fewer after I returned to university in the autumn of 1945. The visits I did make were mostly in company with the lovely young woman who later became my wife, her father being the CNR railway agent in the town at that time. After our marriage in Saskatoon we moved to Vancouver where I completed university and my wife nursed at Vancouver General Hospital. I graduated with a B.A. in geology and joined the staff of the *Vancouver Sun* as a reporter. We then moved to Edmonton where my most shocking post-war contact with Dinsmore occurred.

I was working on the rewrite and copy-edit desk at the *Edmonton Bulletin*. One day in 1949 I was standing by the Canadian Press teletype when its bell rang, indicating that a "flash" was about to come over the wire. The teletype, letter by letter, clattered this message: "Today a fire in the town of Dinsmore, Saskatchewan, levelled a former automobile dealership, a general store and a hardware store as well as an adjoining building which once housed the town's electric power plant."

I turned to my newsroom companions and, numb with shock, said, "There go my father's buildings!" Even though he was now living in Vancouver, those buildings, and the village as a whole, were close to my father's heart, representing almost the totality of his active business life. For years after that, he returned every spring and fall to Dinsmore to supervise the sowing and harvesting of crops on his land, which was close to the town. His friends joked that he thought the crops wouldn't grow unless he was watching them, but I know it was because of a heart-strings attachment to the town and his friends and acquaintances of more than thirty years.

An at least minor bonanza perished in the fire as well. It had been my father's practice, when stocks of automobile parts became outdated, to move them to an upstairs attic in the rear of the building complex. Today's antique car buffs would pay a fortune for them now. There were new matte-black Model T fenders, nested together with butcher paper between, brass-mounted radiator shells with cores and caps, carbide side-lamps and headlights from days before cars had electrical systems, and scores of other parts for Model Ts and Model As among which we as youngsters had played, once even appropriating a carbide side-lamp as a light for a tent.

With the demise of the railway as the principal conveyance for freight and passengers, many of the surrounding villages slowly withered away, some disappearing entirely without even an elevator remaining to show where they once had been. Some, still shown as dots on road maps, are listed in the 1991 census as "Population: Nil." But Dinsmore grew and, in the main, prospered. Its population increased until in 1991 it reached 374. (In 1921 it was 171; in 1931, 256; in 1941, 215, the decline probably mostly due to enlistments in the Second World War armed forces.) The greatest risk now to local businesses is the ease with which people can reach shops and department stores for major shopping in Saskatoon, now little more than an hour away by automobile on paved roads.

Many of Dinsmore's newer residents are retired farmers and their wives from the surrounding district, and some are their sons and daughters, active farmers who choose to live in the town. Modern automobiles and roads make commuting to and from their farms only a matter of minutes, a far cry from eighty years ago when their fathers and mothers pioneered in the area, and a round trip to and from town by horse-drawn wagon or sleigh could consume the better part of a day.

With many, their homes came as well. Houses were moved from farms into the town, including the one my mother and father had built in 1913 on immigrating to Canada. The town's area has at least doubled, with new streets laid out on what once had been open prairie to the east and on the former soccer field. To the south an airstrip was laid out. The school that I had attended to senior matriculation was demolished and a new composite school built. An enclosed skating rink and new curling rink, the Memorial Arena, went up where before there had been the baseball diamond of the sports days of my childhood. Upstairs in the skating rink, a large room was given over to the Canadian Legion branch, where its four walls held a row of pictures of those who had served in the First and Second World Wars, too many of whom had not returned from far-distant battlefields, while some had returned with terrible scars, both physical and mental.

The principal business block of Main Street changed its appearance so much that I, had I not known where I was, might have had difficulty recognizing it as Dinsmore. New shops had gone up where the general store and hardware in my father's buildings had been. The only buildings that I recognized on my last visit were the bank, the former drugstore, and the building that had housed the Chinese restaurant, which was constructed after the big fire of 1939 destroyed its predecessor. It now is a Co-op store, and a restaurant occupies a new building on the opposite side of the street.

In the next block north, the hotel, one of the first buildings constructed in 1913, still stands. The boyhood friend who had owned and operated it after taking it over from his father now is retired. In this block, many of the buildings of my youth still stand, although their functions have changed; in the newly added basement of the former movie theatre, the town's senior citizens gather daily to chat or play cribbage. In my youth there were no "senior citizens"; the seniors were the business people who were busy building and running the town.

For several years after my mother and father retired to the West Coast, our family was represented in the town by my sister and her husband until his untimely death from a heart attack. My sister, Kathern, stayed on as a teacher in the composite school for twelve years before remarrying and moving to Victoria, B.C. The sole descendant of my mother and father still in the area is my sister's daughter.

My wife and I visited Dinsmore occasionally while my sister was still there, but our visits have become less and less frequent since Kathern remarried and left. Sadly, the last time I was there, I walked the length of Main Street both ways and didn't meet a single person whom I recognized or who recognized me. But the town will always have a special place in our hearts.